MIRACLES
in the Midst of
WAR

ENDORSEMENTS

Paula O'Keefe is a friend and a powerful, faithful, passionate woman of God. It is a great privilege to know her. She lives out Jesus' call to lay down her life for the sake of love as she serves in war-torn Chechnya. Paula is an overcomer in every way. In this book, she brings to light all that is possible when serving an extraordinary and supernatural God, even in the most challenging situations. As you read this book, ask God to lead you into new levels of surrender. Watch and see what incredible things He will do through your little life of love.

Dr Heidi Baker
Founder and CEO, Iris Global

I have known Paula O'Keefe for quite a few years and have observed her passion and costly unceasing commitment to the cause of King Jesus. It is a privilege to know her and to recommend this book to you.

Roy Godwin
Author: *The Grace Outpouring,*
The Way of Blessing and *The Blessings Course*

This is a true story of what God has done in Paula's life in the midst of war and devastation, and of the amazing miracles she has experienced. May it challenge you to know Jesus and what He wants to do in and through your life.

I admire Paula's life and dedication to serve Jesus in places and circumstances not many would dare to go. But I assure you, if you allow her life to inspire you to embrace your destiny, then her story will become yours as well. Obey Jesus like Paula has done and you are heading to the greatest adventure of a lifetime...

Mel Tari
Author: *Like A Mighty Wind*

Miracles in the Midst of War is an important and dangerous read. Important, in that it confronts you with the truth of why we exist. Dangerous, in that it challenges you to the core to think differently about what we are doing with our lives.

Paula courageously shares her story and the story of others. Chapter after chapter she takes us with her on adventures with God. We go with her as she steps into harrowing situations from Russia to Chechnya. We see what the gospel truly looks like, and witness God's transforming love at work through costly discipleship.

We are left with a choice. To choose mediocrity or, like Paula, to say yes to God. And the miracle of our yes is that we can be a part of something bigger than ourselves. A participation with Him to a lost, broken and dying world. Experiencing and witnessing His miracles is a given. A serious, must read book for everybody who wants to be a follower of the Lord Jesus Christ.

Dr Lesley-Anne Leighton
Missionary and Founding Director Diadem International,
Holy Given International School of Missions

This is a gripping account of God at work in amazing ways in a war zone. It is like a modern-day version of the Book of Acts – with miraculous escapes, healings, troubles, divine appointments and using every opportunity to share about Jesus. *Miracles in the Midst of War* describes what can happen when you decide to go with God's flow. Some parts of the story may seem incredible, but I believe this record is true, because I have known Paula for about thirty years and have witnessed some of her story first-hand.

I became a Christian through *The Cross and the Switchblade* and grew in my faith through reading autobiographies such as *The Hiding Place*. I am now sharing Paula's book with my son, who is the same age I was when I began my Christian journey. This book could help a new generation to grow in their Christian lives.

If you want to know where God is in a war-torn world, I recommend that you read *Miracles in the Midst of War*.

Dr Debbie Hawker
Clinical Psychologist Executive Committee of the
Global Member Care Network

At times one reads stories that challenges one to the very core. *Miracles in the Midst of War* does just that. Paula, more than anyone else I know, combines both a reckless, abandoned love for the Lord with an uncompromising love for those living in the most challenging of contexts.

This is an honest, yet beautiful account of Paula's years of service in Chechnya. Whilst her account will undoubtedly be outside the experience of most of her readers, Paula invites us into her story. Time and again we are invited to see that her story is in fact His story. It is indeed an extraordinary story of God's goodness and faithfulness as He demonstrates His love for the lost and the most broken. It is a raw story of deliverance to those who are suffering and struggling to keep going and survive in the most desperate and dangerous situations. Time and again the power of prayer and worship is the key to bringing such deliverance.

Uncompromising faith and obedience are the hallmark of Paula's story and this book. Yet it remains a deeply honest account of Paula's own struggles of remaining in a place of faith and peace through some of the darkest and challenging times. It is indeed a practical account of the toll that such radical obedience can take.

For those who want to be brave enough to ask the Lord to help them live a more abandoned life in service of the One who gave everything, this is a radically challenging read. Indeed it is a must read!

Anne de Leyser
Director, Local Houses of Prayer, Ffald-y-Brenin

I was responsible for introducing Paula to Russia in the early nineties and encouraging her with her ministry in Russia. With a God-given gift of faith Paula has served Jesus with extraordinary zeal and courage. This becomes obvious as you read her amazing account. Her life is a challenge to all who read this book.

Bill Rice (DipTheol, Cert Ed)
Leader, The King's Church Poole Joint Director,
Poole Healing Rooms

I first met Paula O'Keefe at the NETS school (at Ellel Pierrepont) in 1999. I was drawn to her vivacious English mannerisms and mesmerized by her radical faith. She took Jesus literally, made evident in the stories she shared of her work in Russia. When I asked her what mission she was with, she said she wasn't with one. She was on her own under the covering of her local church. When I commented on how lonely she must be, she quickly responded,

"I'm not alone – there are four of us: the Father, the Son, the Holy Spirit and me." She really meant it.

As you read this book you will experience the love of the Father, the redeeming presence of Jesus and the supernatural power of the Holy Spirit made manifest on every page.

While reading I had to put it down every few chapters, forced to do some soul searching. This book puts your own trials in perspective and is like pouring disinfectant on the wound of western materialism – it smarts!

Paula is an amazing woman of faith and obedience yet, as you work your way through this book, she doesn't come out as the heroine, but rather as one who obeys Jesus and pushes past her own weaknesses and struggles to make room for His miraculous work.

Repeatedly while reading through the book, I had to fight the urge to forward it to various individuals who I know would be blessed; everyone from young adults who have their whole life ahead of them to veteran missionaries who would find such solace in a fellow sojourner.

I believe this book is timely in our increasingly 'weird and wacky world.' I believe God is calling His church to be 'first responders' as disasters in our world increase. This book will stir up your heart to become ready to join Paula and many others in making necessary sacrifices of obedience to be a beacon of hope to an increasingly desperate world.

Rev Kathryn D Klassen
Christian and Missionary Alliance, Eastern Canadian Director
of Relational and Spiritual Vitality, Deeper Life Coach

A FAITH ADVENTURE

MIRACLES
in the Midst of
WAR

PAULA O'KEEFE

Sovereign World

Published by Sovereign World Ltd
Ellel Grange, Bay Horse, Lancaster, Lancashire LA2 0HN

www.sovereignworld.com
Twitter: @sovereignworld
Facebook: www.facebook.com/sovereignworld

ISBN 978-1-85240-8329 (Printed edition)
ISBN 978-185240-8343 (POD edition)
ISBN 978-1-85240-8336 (Kindle edition)

British Library Cataloguing-in-Publication Data
A catalogue record for this book is available from the British Library.

This is a true story. Most names and some details have been changed to protect the
anonymity of those involved.

Typeset by Envydesign Ltd

To my amazing mum.
You did a fantastic job of letting me know I was loved
from as far back as I can remember,
over lengthy chats at dinner,
leisurely walks around the pond,
crazy swims in any available body of water
and cosy bedtime stories and prayers.
I outsmarted you at chess and you beat me at tennis.
We laughed until our sides hurt
and clung on to each other through grief and loss.
Thanks for always being my greatest fan
and believing that, with God's help,
I could do anything I set my mind to.
Your tenacity to keep going
through all the challenges, your passion for Jesus
and your kindness to those forgotten by the world,
have been an incredibly inspiring example to follow.

I love you, Mum.

CONTENTS

ACKNOWLEDGEMENTS

First of all, I want to express my overwhelming gratitude to my sweet Jesus, for your amazing friendship and never-ending love. I'll always be blown away that you chose me – a weak, skinny English girl with so many unresolved issues – to partner with you to see lives transformed. What an incredible privilege and joy!

To all my courageous friends from Russia. Many of you have already finished the race, but I'm indebted to you for allowing me to share your stories with the world. It has been phenomenal to do life with you and I'll never be the same. You are my heroes!

To my lovely Mum, what can I say? Without your help in holding down the fort, cooking healthy meals and bringing me endless cups of tea, this book probably would never have been completed. To my amazing children and grandchildren, thank you for bringing so much love and joy into my life, and to my dear daughter Lera for your helpful suggestions as I edited the book.

To my beautiful aunt Penny, a talented writer yourself, your professional advice and valuable feedback, especially in encouraging me to include difficult experiences from my childhood, has made this book so much richer. And to my precious cousin Gina for your editorial input. You were more like a sister to me than a cousin and I relished discussing earlier drafts with you and laughing over shared memories. You tragically left this earth too early, but I look

MIRACLES IN THE MIDST OF WAR

forward to giving you a big, big hug, when I get to heaven. I love you and miss you, my sweet Gina.

To Sovereign World Limited and especially to Peter Horrobin for encouraging me to put my story into writing and to Rosalinde Joosten, for your tireless work in bringing it all together. To my editors Thomas Wray and Michele Hackney for your professional, creative and efficient work.

To all at Karuna Action (and previously Kingscare), for your fantastic administrative support for our ministry and in particular to George Dowdell, for your help in finding digital copies of old newsletters and photos.

A huge thank you to Betsy Frost, Pam Robertson and Jan (and more recently Colin) Hession for your faithful prayers and support over the years, for providing me with a home away from home, and for lovingly storing diaries, newsletters and photos. You all deserve medals for your patience with my seemingly endless requests to search for something else amongst my things! To Catherine Hammett for painstakingly typing up excerpts from my diaries and newsletters. To Jan Hession, Julia Pierce, Kathy Klassen, Connie Bradfield, Judy Johnis, Ariana Shekhonina, Elaine Story and Julia Stevens for reading draft after draft ad nauseam and offering valuable feedback. To Katya for carefully poring over the manuscript to check the accuracy of historical and geographical information and helping with the correct transliteration of Russian words. To all my dear friends who took time out of your incredibly busy schedules to read my book and write such wonderful endorsements for me. I'm blessed beyond words to have so many fabulous friends all over the world.

And, finally, a big thank you to all of you who've touched my life in countless ways through kind words, a reassuring touch, financial support, a place to stay, heartfelt prayers, being a listening ear or offering advice. No matter how seemingly small or insignificant your contribution has been, you've played a part in getting this book completed and I send you all a big thank-you hug!

I am the Lord, the God of all mankind.
Is anything too hard for me?

Jeremiah 32:27

PREFACE

They overcame him by the blood of the Lamb
and by the word of their testimony.

REVELATION 12:11 (NKJV)

I'd been invited to preach in Geneva to a prestigious congregation and was feeling extremely inadequate. What could I possibly share with these diplomats and other officials in high places?

The Lord gently assured me: "As you share your testimony from your heart, life and healing will flow to others."

While I preached, an elder wept; others were visibly touched.

Whenever I share my testimony, God touches those listening. Truly, there is power in talking about the miracles God has done in our lives.

As a little girl, I devoured books about missionaries, sparking a fire in me to use my life to make a difference in this world. After years of serving on the mission field, I felt the Lord prompting me to write a book to encourage others in a similar way. Then in 2005, when Peter Horrobin (International Director and Founder of Ellel Ministries and Director of Sovereign World Publishers) suggested I get my story down, I realised it was time to start writing.

A lot of this book has come out of the comprehensive diaries and detailed newsletters I wrote while in Chechnya. It's a true story based on the way I remembered situations and recorded them at the time. Of course, memory can be fickle and other people in the story may have different memories of the same occasion. Where

I've been able, I've asked those featured in the book to have a look at the text and correct anything they felt was inaccurate.

I also asked a few family members and close friends to read earlier drafts of the book and some found it too harrowing. Even though I wasn't in Chechnya during the worst moments of full-blown war, I've still seen some awful things in my life and heard countless horrendous stories.

There's a fine line between describing enough of the situation so the reader can understand the context, and traumatising anyone reading it. It's a delicate balance to get that just right. So I've cut out certain stories.

I trust that as you read the testimonies in this book, life and healing will flow to you.

INTRODUCTION

Most Christians long to see miracles,
but they don't want to be put in a situation
where they will need one.

ATTRIBUTED TO RICK JOYNER[1]

Miracles await us in the most desperate moments of our lives. If only we have eyes to see. And hearts to believe.

When life is beautiful and everything runs smoothly, miracles are often far from our thoughts. We can manage quite well without God and His help, thank you very much.

A miracle, by definition, demands a hopeless situation. Desperation humbles us, bringing us to our knees, begging a supernatural God to intervene on our behalf. If He doesn't come to our aid, we're sunk.

We long for miracles and wonder why we don't see them in our comfortable everyday lives.

Stepping out of our comfort zones and sharing God's love with the poor, lost, and broken will significantly improve our chances of seeing God's supernatural hand at work. When we share the good news, the Lord confirms His word with accompanying signs, just as in the New Testament (Mark 16:20).

This is especially so when we're in virgin territory where the good news has never been preached. There we'll invariably come up against a whole host of obstacles the enemy puts in our way, accentuating the need for miracles to overcome them. Not just miracles of healing, but also of provision, protection, transportation, multiplication – you name it. Whatever is needed so the gospel can be preached, He'll do it. The Father will go to any lengths so that His lost sons and daughters can hear the good news and find the way home.

The more desperate the need, the more likely we'll see miracles. Just living in a war zone can take us off the chart in terms of desperation, creating an atmosphere ripe for miracles.

In the middle of writing this introduction, I stopped to prepare lunch. A glass saucepan lid fell off the counter and, without thinking, I put out my foot to break its fall and stop it from smashing to pieces on the tiled floor. The blow to the top of my foot by the metal handle was in the exact place I'd fractured it years before. By the evening the pain was excruciating.

There I was, so beautifully discoursing about miracles, and suddenly I found myself again desperately in need of one!

Those around me prayed and watched the bruising and swelling go down, but it was still extremely painful as I fell asleep. I woke up and apprehensively waited for the pain to hit me. But there was no pain. I moved my foot. The pain was gone. Hallelujah! I almost cried with joy and relief. I tried putting weight on it; there was still a little pain, but within a few days it was back to normal. Completely normal. Jesus had answered our prayers and done another miracle. Yay, Jesus! He's simply the best, so kind and good.

I pray that this book will inspire you to believe for miracles in your hour of need. Big miracles and small ones. And as you see God stepping into harrowing situations and performing miracle after miracle, may you realise He can turn things around in your life too.

The miracle might not come in exactly the way you expect; sometimes God, in His wisdom, will answer in a different way. Instead of taking you out of the problem, He may grant you the grace, strength and ability to walk through it. In those moments you can be certain that He has a purpose in mind and that treasures, worth their weight in gold, are waiting for you that couldn't be found any other way.

Regardless of what happens, rest assured that if you take your eyes off the problem and look at Him, a host of blessings lie in store: His comforting presence, grace, and strength (Philippians 4:13), an open door, a fresh perspective, transformation. A peace that passes all understanding (Philippians 4:7) will fill your soul as you trust Him that He will somehow bring good out of the situation (Romans 8:28) and turn it around for His glory.

In the pages of this book, may you be encouraged that God uses ordinary people just like you and me to change the world.

As we reach out to others in their desperation, God will do the miraculous. Our lives, and the lives of those we serve, will never be the same again.

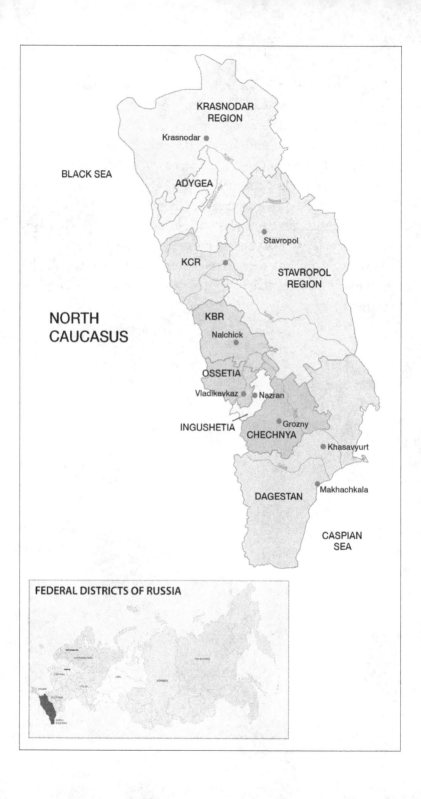

KRASNODAR
REGION

Krasnodar ●

BLACK SEA

ADYGEA

Stavropol ●

KCR ●

STAVROPOL
REGION

NORTH
CAUCASUS

KBR
Nalchick ●

OSSETIA

Vladikavkaz ● ● Nazran

INGUSHETIA

● Grozny
CHECHNYA

● Khasavyurt

DAGESTAN

● Makhachkala

CASPIAN
SEA

FEDERAL DISTRICTS OF RUSSIA

Chapter 1

DANCING IN THE FACE OF TERROR

God is our refuge and strength,
an ever-present help in trouble.
Therefore we will not fear.

PSALM 46:1-2

The heaviness is tangible. Tension from recent events hangs in the air. A car bomb exploded at the local market only the day before, killing the Chief Mufti[1] and narrowly missing our team by minutes. Two doctors, due to help us with the camp, were kidnapped in a neighbouring town. Rumours of another invasion by Chechen fighters are buzzing endlessly.

It's hard to take our minds off the ever-present brutalities of war and to just focus on Jesus.

"Lord, we desperately need a breakthrough."

I strum my trusty guitar as I struggle to lead our traumatised refugees[2] deeper into the presence of God. Out of the corner of my eye, I suddenly see the door opening. I sense that something is wrong, terribly wrong.

My heart misses a beat.

A burly Chechen fighter stumbles into the room, with five others on his heels. Fumbling as they push their way through the stuffy basement crammed to capacity, they make a beeline for me.

"Lord, help," is the best prayer I can muster.

"*Tiiii* – you – stop playing that guitar," the ring-leader yells at me, slurring his words. "*Perestan seichas* – stop right now!"

He reeks of sweat, cheap cigarettes, and vodka. This, combined with the nauseating stench from a nearby broken toilet, causes my stomach to heave.

An eerie hush descends on the room. The only sound I hear is my pounding heart threatening to leap out of my chest. A thousand thoughts race through my mind.

"Is this my last day alive?"

"Will we meet the same fate as our friends at the Baptist Church?"

I'm bombarded by gruesome images of Muslim terrorists beheading the leader Alexei and brutally raping members of the congregation.

"Why on earth did I organise this camp?"

The sweltering heat is unbearable. It's forty-five degrees Celsius and sweat is streaming down my face, leaving an unpalatable salty aftertaste in my parched mouth. Breath comes in short gasps.

Although only in my mid-twenties, I suddenly feel bone-weary from all the atrocities and deprivations I've witnessed as a missionary in a war zone.

"I can't cope with much more of this."

Dripping with my perspiration, my modest blue dress clings to me, outlining my bones. The meagre diet of watery soup, bread, and potatoes hasn't done much for my figure.

After a few seconds that seem like an eternity, indignation rises up inside me against Satan, my real enemy.

"How dare you forbid me to worship my Jesus!"

Bursting out into exuberant praise in my prayer language, I strike the strings of my guitar once again with a passion. Our congregation of about eighty instantly follow my lead and bellow out at the top of their lungs. I feel joy, energy, and a profound peace welling up from somewhere deep within. The heavens open and the Lord graces us with His sweet presence. In that moment, the euphoria of being with Him is all I'm aware of. It no longer matters whether I live to see another day.

I see the colour slowly draining from the fighter's face as

he glances first at me, then at our gathering, and finally at his colleagues. Unnerved to the core, he apologises, turns on his heels, and careers out of the room, closely pursued by the others.

The term 'high praise' takes on a whole new meaning for me on that unforgettable evening in August 1998.

Refugees and missionaries, both young and old, leap unashamedly before the Lord, as King David did.

Whooping and whirling ... Swinging and swirling ... Twisting and twirling.

As we dance and praise in the face of terror and persecution, the years of hardship and the horrors of war all melt away into the fullness of joy in His presence.

This weeklong camp was held in Dagestan, a Muslim republic in southern Russia. I was the director. Deprived families from a refugee camp joined with families from our underground church to have the time of their lives; a kaleidoscopic world was waiting to embrace them, a mere three hours away from their homes in war-torn Chechnya, but a lifetime away in terms of experience.

The children's shrieks of raw delight at their first glimpse of the sparkling blue sea was something I would never forget. Their wide eyes of sheer bliss hungrily drank in the beauty and wonder of it all. They'd seen so many ugly things in their short lives, and this was better than anything they could imagine. The Caspian Sea was a glory of shifting colours, the dark blue deep beyond rolling gently near into a happy light-blue calm that suddenly crashed into frolicking beige-white waves, cheerfully breaking over the little ones' toes. Golden-yellow sand glistened enticingly in the brightness of the blazing sun, perfect on this lazy afternoon for creating sandcastles and exquisite palaces, and, of course, for burying playmates.

The unhurried carefree days, fresh sea air, deep soul rest, and nutritious food did everyone the world of good.

This beautiful haven wasn't completely sheltered from the conflict raging close by, but it was a small foretaste of heaven in the midst of the storm. Many were healed from the trauma of war; peace and joy returned to their hearts in a way they never thought possible.

A vision of a bright light descending from heaven set one guest free from occult involvement in her past, and she stopped hearing voices.

A heart problem, flu symptoms, and a lump on someone's breast disappeared after prayer.

Lives were changed forever by the power of a loving, heavenly Father.

On the night before the last day of the camp, Luba, the camp administrator, and I were up working well after midnight. This was often the case during camps, as there was always so much to do. Ultimately, the director was responsible for making sure timetables were working efficiently – so that water buckets were kept filled, guests were happy, meetings were led, food preparation was going smoothly, expenses were paid, conflicts were sorted out, and volunteers were found to help when the unexpected cropped up. The list sometimes seemed to be never-ending.

Luba was one of my closest friends, a strong-minded brunette who looked and acted much older than her twenty-four years. Her mother – while pregnant with Luba – had been brutally beaten by Luba's drunken father, and this more than likely caused Luba to be born with scoliosis and blindness in one eye. She hadn't let these disabilities hold her back; in fact, they'd made her more determined.

From an early age, she'd looked after her mother and drunken relatives, and later her mentally ill stepfather. This had given Luba a strong sense of responsibility. When she met Jesus in her teens, He brought her a new life and filled her with a deep peace she'd never known. She wanted to use her life to serve Him with her very all. As the first full-time helper on my team, she travelled back and forth from her home in Dagestan to help me.

Luba and I finally turned in for the night, slipping quietly into bed so as not to wake up our other roommates. Lipa, one of the leaders in the Chechen church, was asleep in the room across the hall with her children and another Chechen believer, Lilia.

Lipa was a young mother in her thirties. She'd been introduced to her heavenly Father the previous year by Vera, at the time a member of our church and her colleague at work. Lipa's life had been transformed as she'd seen visions of Jesus and angelic beings.

She immediately started composing songs, their lyrics filled with love and passion for Jesus, and set to hauntingly graceful traditional Chechen melodies. Her heartfelt simple worship – as she played the accordion and sang with a voice pure and sweet as an angel's – brought tears to my eyes.

Lipa was her husband's first wife. They'd had four healthy sons together but not satisfied with just one wife, he'd ended up bringing an attractive teenage girl into their home to become his second wife. After a few tense months of living together as a big but not-so-happy family, he threw Lipa and her boys out of the house.

When Lipa was baptised, she understood she could lose her sons, as Chechen women had few legal rights at the time. But she still joyfully chose to be baptised, coming out of the water with her face glowing.

When she returned home and her husband found out she'd become a believer in Jesus, her worst fears were realised as he showed up at their rented flat, told her she would never see her boys again, and forcefully took them away. Her youngest son, then still barely a toddler, was dragged away screaming, ripped out of his weeping mother's arms.

However, a few months later, the second wife became fed up with looking after Lipa's children. Her husband brought them back to Lipa, much to her great joy and relief saying, "My wife can't bear them crying. You can keep them and do what you like with them. I don't want anything more to do with you or them."

So, on that fateful night at the camp, Lipa was rudely awakened by loud knocking at the door.

"It must be one of our people," Lipa thought, opening the door without asking who was there. Three Chechen men pushed past her, mumbling, "A robbery has taken place in the camp, and we're checking documents."

In a flash, one of them was already almost on top of Lilia.

Lipa wasted no time, racing into the corridor shouting, "*Pomogite* – help, please! Help."

Abruptly jolted from sleep, I shot bolt upright, heart pounding. I rushed out of bed and dashed into the corridor.

Even in the middle of the night, Lipa looked presentable, beautiful and vulnerable as always. Her silky black hair had been hurriedly tied back and was covered with a headscarf in the usual Chechen way. Only on rare occasions had I been privileged to see it loose and flowing down to her waist.

Luba hurried for the base director, and soon a shouting match ensued as the director escorted the men off the base. He gave one of them a good beating when they were out of our sight.

As I again drifted off to sleep, I thought, "I hope that's the end of it."

Little did I know...

Chapter 2

HISTORY OF CHECHNYA
AND SURROUNDING REGION

And this gospel of the kingdom will be preached
in the whole world as a testimony to all nations,
and then the end will come.

MATTHEW 24:14

Russia, the largest country in the world geographically, has eleven different time zones spanning its vast landmass. While business men in Moscow are enjoying their mid-morning coffee, residents in Kamchatka are already turning in for the night.

If you head to the southwestern part of Russia, you'll discover the beautiful *Kavkaz* (Caucasus) mountain range which stretches from the Black Sea to the Caspian Sea, marking the crossroads between Europe and Asia. These mountains contain the highest peak in Europe, Mount Elbrus, which rises up majestically to a full 5,642m[1].

Sochi, host city for the 2014 Winter Olympics, is situated on one side of the Caucasus mountains on the Black Sea coast, and on the other side in the northern part of these mountains, next to Dagestan on the Caspian Sea, lies the small republic of Chechnya.

Chechnya is a part of the Russian Federation. Having courageously held off Russian invaders for centuries, she finally surrendered in 1859. For a brief period during the civil war Chechnya enjoyed a spell of independence before forcibly being brought under Russian rule again in 1920.

During the Second World War thousands of Chechens fought

valiantly in the Soviet army against Nazi Germany. In spite of this, in 1944, Stalin falsely accused them of collaborating with the Nazis and ordered the deportation to Kazakhstan of the entire nation. Over 60% of the population died as a result. Those unable to travel were shot. Thousands perished during the unspeakably inhumane deportation – very similar to the Nazi transportation of Jews to the concentration camps – where men, women and children were crammed, with only standing room, into cattle trucks and given little food or water for weeks. Some survived the horrendous journey only to succumb in Central Asia because of the harshness of life there. In 1957, survivors were allowed to return to Chechnya, settling alongside Russians, Ukrainians and others who'd been resettled in the region.

With the collapse of communism, the Soviet Union started to crumble as republic after republic sought independence. On 1 November 1991, Dzhokhar Dudayev, Chechnya's elected president, also declared his country independent. In 1992 he renamed her the Chechen Republic of Ichkeria.

While letting some of the other republics go without a fight, Russia was determined not to lose Chechnya. Not only rich in oil and natural gas, Chechnya provided a direct route to the Caspian Sea with significant oil and gas pipelines from other republics running through her territory. A militant Islamic state was also the last thing Russia needed on her southern border.

So on 11 December 1994, twenty-five thousand Russian soldiers crossed into Chechnya and nine days later the first Russian bombs rained down on Grozny. The city centre was shelled, and the majority of its 350,000 inhabitants fled for their lives.

A bloody twenty-one month war ensued in which around 100,000 people were killed, thousands made homeless, and much of Grozny destroyed.

After a ceasefire was agreed upon, the Russians pulled out, leaving Chechnya to govern herself. This was the state of the country when I started working there in the autumn of 1996.

Not only were tensions with Russia high at the time, but after the collapse of the Soviet Union, ethnic conflicts started springing up throughout the whole Caucasus region. The Chechens are one of the Caucasus' larger people groups. This myriad of hot-blooded ethnic tribes were known in ancient times as 'Scythians'. 'Scythians' are even mentioned in the Bible by the Apostle Paul in Colossians 3:11:

> Here there is no Gentile or Jew, circumcised or uncircumcised, barbarian, Scythian, slave or free, but Christ is all, and is in all.

These ethnic groups are known for their hospitality and generosity but also for their independence and brutality. The Chechen motto epitomises this – 'we are your best friend or your worst enemy.'

A host of diverse languages resound throughout the Caucasus mountains, some sharing common roots, like Chechen and Ingush, others completely unrelated.

Sunni Islam is the majority religion. Exceptions include Armenia, Georgia and parts of Ossetia, who are Christian and extremely proud to have withstood the Islamic onslaught in the eighth century. In later centuries Islam became associated with resistance to Russian invaders which encouraged other tribes to wholeheartedly embrace Islam. In the Northern Caucasus, the Dagestanis were the first to convert to Islam, the Chechens the last, mostly converting between the 16th and 19th centuries.

Intense enmity between some of these neighbouring peoples reminds me of the conflict between neighbours in other places: Hutus and Tutsis, Serbs and Bosnians, Greeks and Turks. Like estranged family members, grudges are kept and rehearsed for generations.

During the seventy years of communism, these hatreds simmered just below the surface. They re-emerged with a vengeance after the collapse of the Soviet Union. People groups, peacefully co-existing under communism, suddenly took up arms against each other:

- Armenians and Azerbaijanis
- Ingush and Northern Ossetians
- Chechens and Russians
- Georgians and Southern Ossetians
- Dagestanis and Chechens
- Avars and Dargins

Neighbours slaughtered one another as the horrors of ethnic cleansing swept from region to region.

The increase of Islamic fundamentalism after the fall of communism also led to bloodshed. In the early 1990s a Saudi Arabian fighter named Khattab brought a new strain of Islam – *Wahhabism* – to Chechnya. It became increasingly popular among the disillusioned youth.

Under communism, most Chechens weren't religious. But the combination of seventy years of atheism and the horrors of war created a spiritual hunger in people's hearts. As a result a desire for understanding their roots and returning to their religion led many to study Islam. In 1998 Islamic Sharia law was introduced into the country.

After the First Chechen War boys who'd known nothing but war returned home to a devastated country to resume civilian life. Many had lost family and homes. The infrastructure of the country had fallen apart. The few jobs available paid only meagre salaries. Some workers were not paid for months or years. Islamic fundamentalism seemed an attractive way forward.

Under communism, Chechnya had been one of the most beautiful and prosperous regions of the Northern Caucasus. By 1998, however, the country had spiralled into lawlessness, corruption, and anarchy.

Like most of the peoples of the Caucasuses, Chechnya had

been totally unreached for the gospel until the early 1990s; the combination of being a Muslim republic in the Ten-Forty Window[2] and seventy years of atheistic communism had made preaching the gospel practically impossible. In the 1990s after hearing the gospel for the first time handfuls of Chechens became believers in Jesus. Home groups sprang up in various villages and towns all over Chechnya.

By the time of this summer camp in 1998, I had been living in Chechnya for a year and a half. I co-pastored one of these fledgling home churches, counselled traumatised women and children, and brought food, clothing, and basic necessities to those in desperate need.

Six years before that, in 1992, never having heard of Chechnya, or the Caucasus for that matter, I went to Russia for the first time to be obedient to the call to preach the gospel to the ends of the earth. I was a mere twenty-one years old. I felt all grown up and mature, but looking back, I was still barely a child. So how on earth did I, a young English girl, end up coming to this little known part of the world in the first place?

Chapter 3

LET THE LITTLE CHILDREN COME TO ME

Let the little children come to me, and do not hinder them,
for the kingdom of God belongs to such as these.

MARK 10:14

There is a God-shaped vacuum in the heart of each man
which cannot be satisfied by any created thing but only by
God the Creator, made know through Jesus Christ.

SEVENTEENTH-CENTURY FRENCH
MATHEMATICIAN PASCAL [1]

My childhood was one of contrasts, mixtures and extremes.

I grew up in a single-parent family with no siblings; but most of my childhood was spent in community, living with extended family, church family, in homeless hostels and on council estates. I was immersed in different cultures, living in both the USA and UK, half-English and American, with a frugal, disciplined, stiff-upper-lip Scottish grandfather and an extravagant, passionate, emotional Brazilian grandmother. I had family members who were brigadiers and university professors, and rubbed shoulders every day with fellow school girls from wealthy, privileged families but I also lived for certain periods of my childhood in homeless hostels and council estates amongst the most needy members of society. I met Jesus at a young age and saw Him answer prayers and move in power but I lived with the reality of being sexually

19

abused and witnessing drunkenness and conflict amongst family and neighbours.

My mother's father, whom we affectionately called 'Daddy John', came from an illustrious family, filled with academics and clergymen. He grew up in the UK, the youngest son of a vicar and had gone on to study engineering and join the British army. He'd fought bravely in the war and had worked his way up to Brigadier. Then he'd joined the British Council and had taught engineering in various countries.

He'd met my grandmother, whom we called 'Vovo,' (which means 'grandmother' in Portuguese) just before the Second World War in London. Vovo was the youngest of seven children and had grown up in Brazil. She'd been dazzlingly beautiful in her prime, elegant, sparkling and fun.

My grandparents had two daughters, and because of Daddy John's work, brought them up in a number of different countries.

As a teenager, Mum fell off a horse, suffering a head injury. A few weeks later she had a mental breakdown and was diagnosed with schizophrenia. If it had happened today, when we can much more accurately diagnosis and treat head injuries, she may well have recovered much more quickly. But in the 1950s her accident and subsequent diagnosis led to years of being in and out of mental hospitals. Her family were very supportive and did everything they could to help her and she eventually recovered enough to leave hospital.

With the help of family and friends she managed to qualify as a nurse. Around this time, my grandfather was offered a job in Colombia and Mum was excited at the opportunity of moving there with her parents and she soon became fluent in Spanish. Two years later, a job opened up for Daddy John to teach at the university of Rio de Janeiro, the city Vovo had grown up in and where many of her family were still living. One evening, soon after relocating to Rio, Daddy John brought his colleague, a good-looking American professor, home for a meal and introduced him to my mum saying, "This is my eldest unmarried daughter!"

My mum and dad hit it off immediately, talking well into the night and soon fell in love. After courting for a few months on the romantic beaches of Rio, they decided to move to the USA and get married.

After a year of marriage, Mum was delighted to find out she was pregnant with me, their first and only child.

But six months into her pregnancy, during a freezing January snowstorm, she nearly lost me. My father was away on a business trip. Mum felt so weak and ill that she didn't even have the strength to lift up her hand to brush her hair. Completely alone in a foreign country with no one to turn to, she desperately cried out: "Lord, please send someone to help me get to the doctor, I'm feeling so bad."

The Lord answered by sending an angel of mercy, in the form of a neighbour, who popped in to see how she was doing. Taking one look at Mum she said, "We need to get you to the hospital, my dear, as soon as possible." She promptly fetched another neighbour with a car and rushed her to the hospital through the fierce snowstorm.

"I'm afraid you're seriously ill with toxaemia. Your blood pressure is way too high, and you could have a fit. We need to keep you in for the moment," the doctor told Mum gently but firmly.

Every half hour the nurses checked her blood pressure and my heartbeat. After one of these checks, the nurse hurried away looking worried. The doctor appeared and said soberly, "The baby's heartbeat is half what it should be and if it gets any lower, I'm afraid we'll have to do a caesarean section. I'll be honest with you, I'm not a Catholic doctor so I'll do everything I can to save your life. I'm afraid your baby, at twenty-four weeks, isn't likely to survive."

"But," he added brightly, "don't worry, Mrs O'Keefe, you're young and can have lots of other children."

"I don't want lots of other children, I want this one," Mum thought.

A cleaning lady working in the hospital mentioned that she had a Catholic priest who could come in and pray for Mum. So, in the hustle and bustle of a busy hospital ward, with the room being vacuumed around them, God came and did a miracle. The priest was full of faith and read out a set prayer from a sheet: "Lord, I ask you to heal this mother and baby. I bind the powers of darkness stopping this child from seeing the light of day. In Jesus' name. Amen."

After sharing communion with Mum, he added, "Don't worry, dear, no one who I've prayed for has ever lost their baby."

The crisis passed. Mum recovered enough to go home. But the doctor wasn't prepared to let her go until there was someone in the house to look after her. Vovo was sent for and arrived from Brazil. After being on complete bed rest for three months, at full term after a quick, easy labour, Mum gave birth to a healthy baby girl. And a rather plump one at that – all eight pounds, ten ounces. However, within a couple of years my puppy fat dropped off and I've never put it back on since!

Soon after, my parents' marriage fell apart.

Mum and I moved in with a friend of my father's, Irene, who happened to be a 'born-again Christian.' At the time Mum was a devout Catholic.

Just as an aside, I believe it's not important which church you go to, or whether or not you even go to church. What really matters is that you have a personal relationship with Jesus and seek to follow Him as His disciple. Some true disciples of Jesus are not part of a traditional church at all. There's room for all sorts, shapes and sizes in God's Kingdom.

In most Christian denominations, as well as people who really know, love and serve Jesus, there are others who are just religious, going through the motions and doing all the right things, but who haven't met Jesus personally as yet. Mum was one of those who'd had some experience of God as a child, but she didn't actually know Jesus personally. She only knew of Him, honouring Him and loving Him as best she could. But she had no idea there was more awaiting her. So much more.

At first Irene tried to explain this to Mum, but Mum just didn't seem to get it. So God gave Irene a different strategy: to stop talking about it and just to love Mum and serve her.

It wasn't long before Irene felt the Lord say that the time had come to invite Mum to her church. Mum really didn't want to go to an evangelical church but, after all that Irene had done for us, she felt it would be rude not to go. So she gritted her teeth and went.

To her surprise Mum heard the gospel in a way she could understand for the first time in her life. She realised it was what she needed and promptly asked Jesus to forgive her for the wrong things she'd done and to come into her life. She was born again and her life was transformed forever.

A deep peace permeated every fibre of her being. It was similar to what she'd experienced when taking tablets for mental illness but much, much better! Meeting the One who created her, who loved her more than anyone ever had in her entire life, changed everything. It was as if she'd come alive to a new world. This is what she was created for. All the bad things she'd done had been wiped away. The slate had become clean. Her priorities had changed and she no longer wanted to do things that would hurt Jesus. The Bible opened up and came alive in a way it never had before.

Soon afterwards she was baptised by full immersion in a local river.

As Mum pushed me in my pram, she would spend hours talking to her new friend, listening to His voice in the stillness of her heart and singing songs to Him. These were some of the happiest days of her life, even though she was going through a divorce. And Mum's new-found love reflected on me as my first words were 'Mummy' and 'Jesus.'

When I was eighteen months old, my mum and grandparents decided it was time to return to England. We all moved into a big house in Fleet, Hampshire, about forty-five minutes by train from central London.

As in all families, there were good times as well as difficult ones.

I grew up with no contact with my father or his side of the family, except for his sending regular maintenance cheques. I always knew my family on my mother's side loved me, but they all had issues they were dealing with.

Mum loved me with all her heart and always told me that, apart from Jesus, I was the best thing that had happened to her. I knew she would have done anything for me. She was tall and sporty with silky black hair loosely tied back in a ponytail. Her kind brown eyes, behind big seventies prescription glasses, lit up her face whenever she smiled – which was often, and which revealed a chip in her two front teeth, the result of a bike accident at the age of eight.

When she wasn't working, and in the holidays, we spent hours walking and chatting, playing tennis and going swimming. She'd played tennis on local teams in her early twenties in Columbia and encouraged me to take part in sports. She took me to lots of different training sessions. I was on a swimming team at eight, played tennis for my county at eleven and as a teenager we played badminton every Sunday afternoon with our church friends. I later was part of the badminton team at university.

Mum was amazing in the many things she managed to accomplish – including holding down her nursing jobs – but her mild brain damage had left her challenged in certain ways. I ended up helping her do the things she struggled with including keeping the house tidy, finding our way to places, mending things that had been broken and putting things together.

She also suffered from a lot of unresolved emotional pain. Often, I was the only one left to look after her, a burden too heavy for a little girl to carry. But at the time I was proud that my role in life was to be the strong one in my family, protecting and caring for Mum and others.

Mum was determined to get healed and I am so proud of the way she has kept going and really come through so many difficulties in life. She has been on the mission field with me for many years since retiring. She is truly a walking miracle!

On returning to the UK from the States, Mum asked the Lord which local church she should go to. Soon afterwards a local Christian, Pam Robertson, came to our door to tell us about Jesus. Pam was an evangelist in her forties with a young family. She had a lovely open face and was chatty and warm. Mum excitedly told Pam that she was already a Christian. Pam invited us to come to the new church that she and her husband, Alan, were starting in their home. We loved it from the first time we went and joined this small fellowship which later became known as the 'Fleet Christian Fellowship'.

Our little fellowship was a 'happening' place, linked to Chard Fellowship and the exciting outpouring of the Holy Spirit taking place in the early 1970s in southern England.

When I was a toddler, Mum ventured out on her first mission trip, leaving me at Pam and Alan's. She arrived back to find I'd been potty trained by their eldest daughter, Christine, who at the time was doing a childcare course!

One morning when I was two years old, Mum was quite concerned for me as I was having trouble sleeping and had become quite disturbed because of the divorce and all the drinking and quarrelling. As Mum prayed for help, she felt the Lord reassure her, "I'm going to send you a lady called Eileen who will help you with Paula."

That night, when Mum and I arrived for the house group, Pam introduced us to her friend Eileen who'd come to minister that night.

"Wow, you won't believe this," Mum exclaimed full of excitement, telling them what God had told her earlier in the day. Later that evening Eileen prayed extensively over me for healing as I slept on Pam's daughter's bed. She then invited us to come to her house for a visit.

Mum's thirtieth birthday was soon approaching, and she asked the Lord for a special present from Him on her birthday. And she certainly got one!

We spent the day at Eileen's house where she asked me: "Would you like to invite Jesus to come and live in your heart and be your friend?" I nodded and Eileen led me in a prayer.

So at the grand old age of nearly three, I asked Jesus to come into my life. Mum noticed I had a new sense of peace and security that I hadn't had before.

A week later, in the bath, I apparently remarked, "Mummy, you don't know Jesus properly until you've asked Him into your heart, do you?" I had truly met Jesus and was privileged to grow up with Him as my friend.

For Reflection and Application

Have you met Jesus personally? If you don't know Him in the way I've described but would like to, take a look at Appendix 2, at the back of the book, for further help in this.

Chapter 4

MOULDED BY THE MASTER POTTER

And we know that in all things God works
for the good of those who love him, who have
been called according to his purpose.

ROMANS 8:28

I will restore to you the years that the
swarming locust has eaten.

JOEL 2:25 (NKJV)

Mum was an evangelist; she longed for others to also meet Jesus
and have their lives transformed just as hers was. She shared her
new-found faith with friends, neighbours, and anyone she met.
Around her neck she proudly wore a sizeable metal cross, in the
hippy-style of the seventies.

Mum was constantly talking about Jesus to her family but instead
of being interested, they were very concerned, thinking she'd joined
a cult and worrying about the influence it would have on me. Because
of this there was a lot of conflict and quarrelling in our home.

By the time I was born, Vovo was not only unwell, but also
depressed – she hated being away from her family, her culture and
the beautiful sun in Brazil. Unfortunately her way of coping was to
drink too much.

But when she was feeling well, we enjoyed playing cards together,
listening to her stories of her wild childhood in exotic Brazil and

cooking together. I could hear when she was coming by the jingling of her bangles as they dangled on her wrist. I loved it when she sang to me.

Daddy John helped me with my homework and enjoyed singing with me as I played the piano. In the summer he took me on outings and sometimes let me join him as he played golf. He taught me chess and we would spend hours playing. In the end I became so good at it that he was the only one in my family who could occasionally beat me at it. I played on the chess team at school when I was eleven.

My uncle was in the US Navy and so, when he was away at sea (which was for about six months of the year), my mum's sister Penny and my cousin Gina lived with us. When Gina's daddy was around, it really brought home to me the fact that I didn't have a daddy. My family came up with a lovely solution – to call our grandfather, 'Daddy John' and my uncle, 'Daddy Bob'. When Daddy Bob was around, I loved the way he would play with us girls and spoil us. And often when he took Gina on an outing, he would take me too. Unfortunately, as is often the case with military men, he also drank too much.

Gina and I were like sisters, doing everything together. The day before we were due to be angels in the school Christmas play, we were very naughty and cut off each other's gorgeous locks! Another time when Gina was pulling my hair, my aunt came into the room and heard me saying, "Gina, I love you very much!"

When we were toddlers my mum and aunt would take us for walks in our double pram and people would often stop and admire these blond curly-haired 'twin girls!'

My aunt was an attractive, elegant woman, creative and full of fun. We loved listening to her singing, playing the guitar and enjoyed the pictures and caricatures she painted of us. She was the one who taught me my first chords on the guitar. Unfortunately she was also unhappy a lot of the time I was growing up and she had a tendency to bury her sorrows in drink.

When I was eight, a minister came to our church. He advised Mum it would be good for her to move out of her parents' house, to get away from all the drinking and conflict. Although it was an excruciatingly painful decision for all involved, Mum felt that it was probably the right thing to do. That night a family in the church agreed we could live with them.

It was a very stressful time for everyone. I couldn't understand why we weren't living with my grandparents who were heartbroken. The family who took us in were a newly-married blended family with children from both partners' previous marriages. The last thing they needed in their crowded house, was a third family (Mum and me) living with them.

I've always loved reading and studying and I remember during this time I had one book with me – by Enid Blyton – which I read and reread until it was worn out. During my childhood, I always had my nose in a book. As a young child I especially loved children's adventure novels and missionary autobiographies. As I got older, I could get lost for hours in non-fiction books on anything that took an interest. When things were difficult, or just plain boring, I would pull out a book and disappear into a different world.

After six months of living with that family, they felt it was time for us to move on and gave us three weeks to find somewhere else to live. We couldn't find anywhere. I remember the day when Pam packed up our belongings into the back of her car with my toy castle lying on the top of the pile. She drove us to the council offices where they offered us a place at the local homeless hostel.

When we walked into our allocated room in the attic of the hostel, Mum and Pam were shocked beyond words. The hostel was in a condemned building: smashed glass was in the window, floorboards were decaying so badly that in one place you could see through to the floor below and there was no furniture, except a stove.

I, however, thought it was really cool. In my vivid imagination, I could now be the heroine in a cowboy or detective movie in this derelict house!

Our first meal in our new home was without plates, sitting on the floor on the two cushions Pam had given us from the back of her car. We slept on the floor with the blankets Pam had brought for us. But it was our own place and we were free to do whatever we chose and it was peaceful and quiet. The freedom felt exhilarating.

Through the generosity of friends and family and the staff at the nursing home where Mum worked, soon we had everything we needed: glass in the windows, zed beds to sleep on, a kitchen table and plates. After a few months, the house was demolished and we were transferred to another homeless hostel. Soon after that, the council gave us a two-bedroom flat of our own.

Unfortunately in all of the places we lived we were surrounded by neighbours who drank and got into fights. None of them had a phone and they would sometimes hammer away at our door in the middle of the night to phone the police. Mum and I were terrified, but Mum always let them in because she felt sorry for them. On occasion they carried on fighting in our house.

As a child, I wasn't able to talk to anyone about these things, so I just bottled up my emotions inside myself. But as a teenager, my friend, Adriana, took me along to Al-Anon, a group for friends and relatives of alcoholics where I gained an understanding about alcoholism and its effects. There I learned that it was okay to share what was happening with me. Through this, I received support in a way I'd never had before and started to receive healing from the effects of growing up around alcoholism.

Because of all the moving around, I changed primary schools a number of times. This actually turned out to be a blessing as, in my first school, the teacher had told Mum that I had learning difficulties, and in a couple of the schools the children teased me unmercifully for any and every reason they could think of.

As I approached the age of eleven, Mum prayed about which secondary school to send me to. One morning she awoke sensing the Lord encouraging her to send for the prospectus for a local private girls' school. Mum was more than a little surprised wondering how on earth she would pay the fees.

Later that evening, on picking up the local paper, her eyes were drawn to an advertisement entitled: 'Assisted Places for Gifted Children at Farnborough Hill.' Only two years previously, in 1980, unbeknownst to Mum, the government had started an Assisted Places Scheme, making scholarships available for children from families unable to afford private education.

After passing the entrance exam, I received a full scholarship which included the school uniform, transport to and from school and free lunches. I was so grateful to be able to go to Farnborough Hill. Not only did it have a high academic standard, but also a Christian ethos, a firm belief in the power of prayer and in helping the poor.

The school truly believed that girls weren't second class citizens and wholeheartedly prepared us to go out into the big, wide world with the expectation of following our dreams, achieving our potential and, in the process, changing the world.

By the time I went to Farnborough Hill, Mum and I had lived in two homeless hostels and were now living in a council flat the government had given us. As you can imagine, going to a private school while living on a council estate was not without its challenges. I was teased by some of my schoolmates for being 'poor', and by neighbourhood kids for being 'posh'. Part of our school uniform was a green beret with a red pom pom which we were supposed to wear until we got home. But when I approached our street, I would take it off to avoid being teased. Of course it was still blindingly obvious which school I attended: the green and brown stripped blazer, green skirt and brown knee-length socks and shoes stuck out for all to see!

Those around me knew I was growing up with certain challenges, but there was more going on under the surface which I was unable to tell anyone about at the time – sexual abuse. An attractive little girl, friendly, affectionate and open, the circumstances of my childhood made me particularly vulnerable. It wasn't until I was twenty-eight, when I went to the Ellel NETS school, that I began to receive healing from the consequences of sexual abuse and other traumas in my childhood. God promises to restore all that the locust has eaten (Joel 2:25), and He's done so over and abundantly in my life, taking away the pain, fear and horror and replacing it with His love, peace and joy.

His hand has truly been on my life from my earliest years and I stand today as a living testimony of a life transformed through God's love and healing power. Not one moment of the suffering I've been through has been wasted. The Lord has turned it all around for good. Like a master potter, He has used everything that happened in my childhood, both the good and bad, to tenderly mould me into the person He's created me to be, perfectly designed for my unique destiny. I can feel at home in diverse cultures with both the poorest of the poor and the wealthy and have a passion to share God's heart with the poor and to see the broken-hearted healed. I now have a determination and authority that comes from having walked personally out of the pain of abuse and trauma into freedom.

For Reflection and Application

If you are also a survivor of childhood abuse or trauma and are still struggling with the consequences of it, I encourage you to reach out for help to someone you trust. It may be a relative, friend or spiritual leader. There is healing for you no matter what you've been through. Ask the Lord for wisdom with whom you should share and for courage to step out.

Chapter 5

MY CALLING
INTO MISSIONS

At the end of our lives, we will not be judged
by how many diplomas we have received, how
much money we have made, or how many great
things we have done. We will be judged by,
"I was hungry and you gave me to eat.
I was naked and you clothed me.
I was homeless and you took me in."

MOTHER TERESA OF CALCUTTA [1]

For as far back as I can remember, I'd wanted to be a missionary.

From an early age, I watched Mum and our church family reach out to help those around them. Mum took me with her nearly everywhere she went, which often included church events. At the age of three, I helped her give out tracts from my pram. I often fell asleep on laps or other people's beds at house groups or prayer meetings. I saw Mum sharing what Jesus had done for her everywhere she went.

Alan and Pam also loved to tell people about Jesus. They often took needy people into their home, sacrificially giving their lives to bring God's love and healing to those around them. Every Sunday the whole church gathered in their living room for fellowship and a shared meal. Being part of a close-knit, loving, Christian community – and Alan and Pam's love, care and example had a deep impact upon me. We spent a lot of time with them, going on camps, outings and picnics together.

When I was five, I spoke in tongues for the first time. One night, Mum was praying and reading the Bible with me. The Lord told her to speak out in tongues. "But Lord there's only me and Paula here," she replied, a little confused.

Then she realised who she was speaking to and decided to be obedient. Suddenly she heard that I'd joined her speaking in tongues with a real flow, much more that she'd had! I never looked back.

Around that time I was fond of gathering my dolls and teddies together and preaching to them. One day I'd assembled my 'congregation' together in our *salita* ('living room' in Brazilian Portuguese). With my back to the door, I preached my heart out, then prayed in tongues over them. Vovo came into the room, unbeknown to me, and stood listening. Not sharing our beliefs, she was unnerved by my speaking in tongues. "Stop it immediately," she said.

With my cute innocent look, I smiled and replied, "But Vovo, it wasn't me speaking in tongues, it was her!" pointing at the 'guilty' Tiny Tears, my favourite dolly.

Vovo burst out laughing, and so did I, relieved not to be in trouble.

"You funny girl, you," she chuckled, tickling me and smothering me with kisses, her deep brown eyes twinkling mischievously.

Around the same time I surprised Mum one morning when I pinned a 'Jesus saves' badge on my cardigan to go to school. I told her I wanted to wear the badge to let my friends know about Jesus' love for them and that He wanted to be their friend. I wore that badge to school for months.

I'd desperately wanted to be baptised in water for as long as I could remember and kept asking Mum if I could be. Finally, just before my eighth birthday, Mum, Alan and Pam all felt that I was now mature enough and really understood the serious step I was taking: to make public my commitment to follow Jesus for the rest of my life. I was baptised, along with my dear friends Joanne, Danielle and Betsy plus a few others, in the Basingstoke canal on a rainy spring day. I'll never forget the deep peace that enveloped me as I emerged out of the murky water. The baptism was in the local paper and I showed the article to my class at school.

When I was eight a school friend, Sarah, came round for tea after school. For some reason we were under the kitchen sink in our *salita*, and I was telling her about Jesus. "Jesus really loves you and wants to come into your heart. It's really wonderful having Jesus as your friend." I smiled reassuringly. "We can pray together and ask Him to come into your heart if you want."

She nodded her head. "Yes, I'd like that."

Huddled together with my eight-year-old friend under our kitchen sink, I led her in a prayer inviting Jesus to come into her life. After we prayed, Sarah remarked excitedly, "I feel good inside. Really good." She added, "I saw Jesus moving into my heart, carrying His suitcases with Him!"

Our annual Good News Crusade Camp, which Mum and I attended most summers, reinforced my calling into missions. Impassioned speakers, who were out in the world 'doing the stuff,' both inspired and challenged us into mission with amazing stories of God at work. David Abbott, the children's leader, sincerely believed that children weren't just the future of the church but also the present. Accordingly in our children's meetings we spent time praying for people, evangelising, and moving in the gifts of the Holy Spirit.

I started going by myself to Christian children's camps when I was eight. After that, most summers I would look forward to, and was really impacted by, these camps, including Chard, Good News Crusade and Swindon camps. I enjoyed making new friends, playing, having fun, and doing sports, as well as amazing times of worship and experiencing the presence of the Lord together. Through the teaching in the camps and at church, and as I grew in my own walk with Jesus, the Lord started to reveal to me His heart of compassion for His lost sons and daughters.

Mum worked as a nurse and I would go with her to work before and after school and during the holidays. As I watched Mum gently caring for those unable to care for themselves, I learned to do the same. As a small child I spent time around girls with learning difficulties and as a teenager spent many hours in various nursing homes gently stroking the heads of dying patients, holding their hands and helping them with their transition into eternity. The difficulties I went through myself as a child also gave me a determination that, when I grew up, I would do all I could to alleviate the suffering of others.

One Easter Monday, when I was twelve, Mum and I travelled to a meeting at the Royal Albert Hall in London where Reinhard Bonnke, the famous evangelist to Africa, was speaking. I don't remember what he spoke about, but I know that when he gave an appeal for young people who wanted to go into missions, my heart burned within me. I leapt out of my seat and scrambled to the front. I made it right up to the stage, and it seemed hundreds followed behind me. Reinhard Bonnke prayed for us and laid hands on a few, and I was so excited when his hand touched my head for a few seconds.

By now I knew beyond a shadow of a doubt that God was calling me to be a missionary. The profound joy and fulfilment I'd experienced, from an early age, when I could do something, even if it was only very small and seemingly insignificant, to alleviate another human being's suffering led me to realise that this was what I wanted to spend the rest of my life doing.

I read all the books I could about missionaries and was especially impacted by Patricia St John's books about her life as a missionary nurse in Morocco. I determined I would become a missionary doctor and give up my life to serve the poor. I wasn't sure where exactly it would be but suspected it would be either in Brazil or Africa. Little did I know!

In 1984, when I was thirteen, our church joined up with a local Baptist church to become the 'King's Church.' This opened up new opportunities for mission, both in the UK and overseas. Bill Rice, one of the leaders there, was zealous for Jesus and mission and challenged us young people to give up our lives for the gospel. I was so blessed to have Bill's influence in my life starting in my teenage years. And for the opportunity, alongside other young people, to go with him on a number of life-changing mission trips.

Soon after we joined the King's Church, my beloved Vovo had a debilitating stroke and for the next eighteen months was bedridden. She spent time in different hospitals, but then we were pleased to be able to look after her ourselves in my grandparent's house and also in the nursing home where Mum and Betsy worked. Three months before I took my O Levels, she died.

During that time Penny and family moved back to the USA permanently where Penny finally overcame her battle with drinking. A few years later Bob also managed to give up drinking. I'm so proud of them both as they have stayed sober ever since.

My sixteenth year was really hard. My immediate family was depleted to only Daddy John, Mum and me. Most of my close friends left Farnborough Hill to go to various colleges. I was lonely and depressed and taking A' Level subjects which weren't my favourites (biology, chemistry, physics and maths) in order to become a doctor.

Mum was so kind to me when she said, "If you want to give up your education to become a cleaning lady, sweetheart, I would still be proud of you." This really took the pressure off, but I was determined to succeed. All my life I'd wanted to be a missionary doctor and so I struggled on through. Friends and relatives lovingly helped me: Mum's cousin and friends from church spent hours coaching me in physics and maths.

Around that time I joined a young people's house-group at our church. My house-group leaders, Andy and Lorna, were on-fire followers of Jesus in their mid-twenties, and their house group was dynamic and fiery. Some weeks we evangelised on the streets; other times we would pray and prophesy over each other. Several people from the house group became missionaries, including Andy and

Lorna themselves and my dear friend Heidi. When I was sixteen, I was thrilled to be invited to go on my first mission trip – with Bill to minister in a church in Wales.

I also started making new friends as I reached out to single parent families in our church: supporting the mums as they shared their stories with me, playing with the children and helping with baby-sitting and other practical things they needed. When I was seventeen, I decided to take as many of them with me as I could to our summer camp. I organised the whole trip, with the help of Mum and others in the church, and we found tents and all the camping equipment we needed, plus a minibus and driver to take us all to camp. We had a wonderful week together.

Around the same time, Francis McNutt, a former Catholic priest with a healing ministry and his wife Judith, a psychologist, were speaking. Mum invited me to come and I was interested, but when it was time to go, was engrossed in a TV programme. I told her I didn't want to go. She left a bit disappointed, but soon returned to the flat as she felt the Holy Spirit prompt her to come back and ask me again if I wanted to go. As I heard her coming back in, I felt an urgency in my spirit that I needed to go. I jumped up, got ready quickly and we dashed out.

The moment we walked into the meeting, I was struck by the atmosphere of peace, warmth and comfort. Almost as if the Lord had wrapped His arms around me in a beautifully tangible way. I'd never met a Christian psychologist before or even knew that they existed. As they gently and lovingly shared story after story of lives transformed through healing and deliverance, the thought crossed my mind: "Maybe if I don't become a doctor, I could do this."

For my seventeenth birthday, instead of being sad that I didn't have much family left to celebrate with, I decided to take my cake out onto the streets and share it with the homeless. Reaching out to others again brought joy to both me and those in need around me.

Later that same year, in the middle of my A' levels, the Lord spoke clearly to me: "I want you to lay down three things for me."

"What is that, Lord?" I replied. "You know I love you and want to be obedient to you." I meant it with my whole heart.

"Being a doctor, getting married, and watching TV."

My heart started to pound. Two of my lifelong dreams were being a doctor, and getting married and having a family. And now the Lord was asking me to surrender them. I also couldn't imagine being alone without TV on the long nights when Mum worked nightshifts.

It took me a week before I was able to wholeheartedly say yes to Jesus. The first thing I did was get rid of the TV. Mum came home from work and looked around, surprised. "Where's the TV gone, sweetheart?"

"It's in the cupboard, Mum." I let her in on my secret and explained why.

"How wonderful," she declared brightly. "I'm so glad. You know how much I hate that TV. It brings so much rubbish into the house and is such a waste of time. Darling, that's really made my day!"

Around the same time, we were overjoyed to be given a lovely tape recorder and our very first worship tape. I'd heard them at other people's houses and thought I'd love to have one. So instead of the TV being on, worship songs now filled our home. When I was alone at night, I was able to go to sleep much earlier and with much more peace. Throwing the TV away turned out to be a real blessing; God broke my addiction, and I've never wanted to own a TV since. The Lord always knows what's best for us.

When I was seventeen, my church organised a mission trip to Germany. It hadn't even crossed my mind to go on the trip, as I was interested in the Third World, and not Europe particularly.

A friend from my church, Sonia, came up to my mum and said, "I'd like to use some of my inheritance money to pay for Paula to go on the Germany trip."

God also provided for Mum; we both went to Germany for two weeks with a team of about ten from our church. Other teams joined us from the USA and Sweden, and we shared rooms with them in a hostel. The deep fellowship we experienced opened my eyes to what God was doing in different countries. During the trip, I shared my testimony publicly for the first time. Completely unexpectedly, I had a microphone thrust into my hand: "Paula, share with the people here what Jesus means to you."

It was amazing how people responded as we ministered on the streets and prayed with them. We also had wonderful times of prayer in the morning, which I so loved. Brad, the missionary leader there, had a powerful prophecy one morning about God wanting to use me.

We also took part in Suzette Hattingh's intercession team in a 'Fire Conference' with Reinhard Bonnke. I learned to intercede in a deeper way than ever before and see the power of prayer in reality: the things we'd prayed about specifically in the afternoon we saw answered dramatically in the evening meeting. During that time God revealed to me His heart for the teenage prostitutes and I wept for hours, crying out for them to know God's love and healing in their lives.

It was a life-changing trip. I came back from Germany totally on-fire for God and for mission. Knowing my calling in life was to share with as many as I could the joy of knowing Jesus personally. To see suffering relieved and the broken-hearted healed. To lead souls, lost and disorientated in the darkness, into the light of His presence.

For Reflection and Application

Has God ever spoken to you so strongly about something that your heart burned within you? If so, have you been obedient to what He asked you to do?

Have you been baptised in water by full immersion? Water baptism is a powerful step of dying to your old life and being raised up again to a new life in Christ.

Have you experienced the baptism of the Holy Spirit? Do you speak in tongues? Speaking in tongues is a gift the Lord wants to give to each of His children. It builds us up spiritually and helps us to pray when we don't know how to.

If you would like to be baptised in water or in the Holy Spirit, ask the Lord to lead you to disciples of Jesus who can help you in this.

Chapter 6

CALLED TO RUSSIA

I have but one passion: it is He, it is He alone.
The world is the field and the field is the world;
and henceforth that country shall be my home where
I can be most used in winning souls for Christ.

COUNT NICOLAUS LUDWIG
VON ZINZENDORF[1]

The late 1980s and early 1990s were a time of great change in the world.

The Berlin Wall came down, and communism collapsed in the Soviet Union. I remember watching the news with trepidation as a lone, brave young man stood in front of a column of tanks, on 5 June 1989, the morning after the Chinese military had suppressed the Tiananmen Square protests. I can still recall how excited I felt, on 9 November 1989, as I watched East and West Berliners using hammers and picks to knock away chunks of the wall and enjoying amazing street parties and celebrations. My friend Heidi travelled out there to see for herself and came back with a piece of the wall for me as a souvenir. What an exciting time it was to be alive and to be involved in missions.

In 1990, as I travelled around the USA, Russia came onto the radar everywhere I looked. A number of times while visiting churches in various cities I found them raising money to send Bibles to Russia. In trains and at friends' houses I met Russians or people who'd just come back from Russia.

Mum forwarded me a letter from Keele University, where I

would begin studying that autumn. I had a strange combination of A' Levels – physics, mathematics, English, and religious studies – because when I'd decided not to study medicine, I'd given up chemistry and biology and taken up English and religious studies instead. I applied to Keele University where they had a four-year course with a foundation year, during which you could try out different subjects before deciding what to take for your degree. I wasn't sure what subjects I would be studying in this foundation year, except I hoped to do psychology and a language. My preference would have been Portuguese or an African language, to prepare me for being a missionary in Africa or Brazil.

Keele didn't offer either. The choice of languages turned out to be French, German, or Russian.

As I travelled by car from Chicago to Washington DC, I read my letter out loud to my friend Tim. We happened to be driving through West Virginia.

When I mentioned the Russian language, Tim interrupted, "Wow, Russian, how interesting. You should study it. I did Russian for a semester and thoroughly enjoyed it."

It had never crossed my mind before to study Russian, but French and German seemed boring in comparison, so I thought maybe I would try it.

Bill was preaching my first Sunday back in England. He was talking about being called into missions.

"Someone here is called to go to Russia," he suddenly announced in the middle of the sermon. As soon as the words left his lips, my heart sank.

"No, not me, Lord. I don't want to go to Russia. It's cold there and filled with communists. I want to go somewhere hot and tropical."

At the end of the meeting, I greeted Bill, having not seen him for nearly a year.

"Why did you say someone was called to Russia?" I queried.

He looked puzzled, "I didn't mention Russia, did I?"

I realised it was God speaking to me again about Russia.

"Oh no, Lord; I don't want to go!"

When I arrived at Keele, I attended the various introductory subject meetings. The Russian teacher turned out to be a fascinating native girl, fun and full of life. I also found out the course had a year-long residential exchange programme with a university in Russia.

"I'd love to spend a year in Russia! And I can always study Russian now, then later go and study Portuguese."

I also ended up studying to be a teacher. My neighbour, Sonia, was on her way to the teaching introductory meeting, and as I'd nothing else to do, I joined her. I found out it was possible to study education simultaneously with my other subjects.

"How useful it would be to have a teaching certificate!"

God had led me to give up medicine, but He hadn't clearly spoken to me about what to study instead.

I thought I'd just drifted into my three subjects – psychology, Russian, and teaching – when in fact God's hand was guiding me. An English medical degree would have been useless in Russia, because to practise medicine there would require that I take another six-year medical degree in Russia. God knew it was much better for me to become a psychologist and teacher for my future career, as this would open many doors for me in Russia. Not to mention the bonus of being able to speak Russian. I'm so glad He guides us, both through hearing His voice and through circumstances.

I thoroughly enjoyed my time at Keele University, both the studying and the social life. I threw myself completely into the life there.

I started a Russian Society, and some nights helped to man the student emergency phone lines as a listening ear for people struggling with suicidal thoughts or other serious issues. I was often up late into the night helping friends through various crises, and I introduced some of them to Jesus.

I served in the Birmingham University Officers Training Corps for a year and a half of my time at university. I thought it would be a fun way to earn extra money.

I remember once, on a weekend exercise, lying in the snow in wet clothes during my two-hour night watch, wondering if I would freeze to death.

Another time, after a long exercise, we came back absolutely exhausted, having not slept for days and with filth, mud, and camouflage caked on our faces.

"There's no hot water here," the officer warned us. In the icy cold shower I cried with exhaustion, cold, and frustration as I scrubbed my face to remove the dirt. After lunch, we were allowed to lie down, and I fell asleep immediately.

"Wake up. Attention. Come on, get on with it, you lazy load of wasters."

Struggling to wake out of deep sleep after being asleep only a few minutes, I somehow managed to throw my weary, aching body out of bed and to attention.

"You're to head to Officer Green's house now and put down his new carpet."

We girls wearily obeyed. We'd just finished moving all his furniture, including heavy wardrobes, out of the room and rolling up the old carpet when the officer came back in. "He's changed his mind about the carpet," he stated curtly, "put everything back where it was." Fuming under our breath, we forced our bodies, with our last ounce of energy, to obediently do what we were told.

What I was experiencing – the discipline, unquestioning obedience to authority, and ability to survive without complaining in horrendous conditions with next to nothing – turned out to be perfect training for what I would be doing in the future. Our heavenly Father knows best!

I was involved in the leadership of the Christian Union and found a lovely church 'Emmanuel Christian Fellowship' where I immediately felt at home. I will never forget, not only the warm welcome I received the moment I walked in, but also the sight of Paul, the leader, dancing unashamedly for joy before the Lord with his gorgeous curly-haired four-year-old daughter in his arms, her large spectacles bumping up and down on her tiny nose!

When his wife Vicky invited me home for lunch that first Sunday, I was so shocked I didn't know what to say. She thought I was hesitant because I didn't want to come: "You don't have to if you don't want to!"

Having spent my teenage years in a large church I was no longer used to leaders talking to me, let alone asking me for lunch! I agreed to go, and during lunch I was more than a tad surprised when Mark, their eldest son, unceremoniously put some ice cubes down my back! I retaliated by putting some down his. I had been initiated into the family!

I spent time with them most weekends.

In my final year they invited me to live with them. It was so fun and healing to be a part of their family.

In those years of studying the Russian language and watching the news unfolding day by day, the Lord was giving me a heart for Russia. This is what I wrote in my diary on the 29 November 1990: 'In Russia the crisis is terrible and there is now no food in the shops – people are starving. We have to do something.'

At the time, I didn't realise I would be an answer to my own prayer!

Over the Christmas holidays that year, the country I was studying ceased to exist. When I left for the holidays, the country was still called the Soviet Union; when I returned, it was now called the Russian Federation. What an exciting time to be studying Russian!

At around the same time, I had the opportunity to see Reinhard Bonnke, the African missionary, a second time. Again I sprinted forward when he made an appeal for those who wanted to give their lives in missionary service. I reached the front before anyone else, as he was naming different countries. As he laid his hand on my head, he called out, 'Russia.' At the time, I thought it was a coincidence. Years later, I realised the significance of the Lord commissioning me through Reinhard.

In my first year at Keele, my mum studied at our church's
Bible school. One of the school outreaches that summer was to
Lithuania, in August 1991. At that time, the doors were just opening
up for foreigners to enter the former Soviet Union and preach the
gospel. My mum signed up for the trip and asked the leaders for a
special favour: "My daughter would love to come and help out as an
interpreter. Would you make a special allowance and let her come,
even though she isn't a Bible school student?"

They agreed, and I worked all through the year to earn the money
to go. I also received a scholarship from my university to pay some
of my way. We planned on teaching in a Bible school for a month, as
well as helping in orphanages and doing evangelism. I was so excited
to finally be going to a non-Western country to minister. We filled
up the church minibus with clothes, games, and toys almost up to
the ceiling, and drove for two days across Europe until we reached
Sweden, where we were due to take the ferry to Lithuania.

As we arrived at the border, we learned that a coup had taken
place in Moscow, and the communists had taken over again.

"Great timing!" I thought.

All borders into Lithuania were closed until further notice. We
waited in Sweden in a hostel hoping the situation would improve
quickly, spending hours praying for the former Soviet Union. Many
of us had visions as we cried out to God.

At a nearby lake, we swam and played together in water so
bitterly cold it took our breath away. Food was extremely expensive,
so we survived on a diet of rationed bread and jam. We'd planned
to visit one of the cheapest countries in the world, only to spend
two weeks in one of the most expensive countries!

One day our leader, Julian, gathered us together. He quoted from
Job 1:21 (NKJV): 'The Lord gave, and the Lord has taken away,
blessed be the name of the Lord'. After two weeks in Sweden,
with the borders still closed and our money running out, he broke
the news to us that our church leaders in England had decided we
should return home.

I was so disappointed. I dashed out of the meeting and locked myself in the bathroom. Sobbing on the floor, I cried, "Lord, I don't understand." I'd faithfully prepared to come for a whole year, and even received money from my university. Here we were so close, and yet so far.

He gently reassured me, "Don't worry, Paula; you will make it to Russia."

His encouragement brought peace and comfort to my heart. I calmed down and returned to the meeting. Little did I know that I indeed would go to Russia and live there for twenty years!

For Reflection and Application

Is the Lord laying a particular country on your heart? If you aren't sure, ask Him. If He shows you a country, ask Him what the purpose is. It could be to pray for that nation's people on a regular basis, to support missionaries or a charity working there, or to go there as a missionary.

What steps can you take to be obedient to what God is asking you to do concerning this country?

Chapter 7

EARLY DAYS IN RUSSIA

Multitudes, multitudes
In the valley of decision!
For the day of the Lord is near.

JOEL 3:14

A year later, in 1992, my home church organised another mission trip to Russia, with Bill leading.

The events of the previous year had birthed a deep longing in me to go to Russia. I prayed for Russia throughout the year as I studied the nation's language, literature, history, and culture. I worked hard to collect the money for the trip. We planned to spend a couple of days in Moscow sightseeing, then head south to Krasnodar, one of the largest cities in the Northern Caucasus, with about a million people.

When I finally landed on Russian soil for the first time in July 1992, I was bursting with excitement. Russia far exceeded my expectations. It felt like the book of Acts was coming alive right in front of us as a wind of spiritual renewal – a revival – was blowing across the former Soviet Union. I'd never experienced anything like it before.

Doors for sharing the gospel were wide open. Seventy years of brutal religious repression by the state – with an estimated 200,000 religious leaders murdered and another 500,000 persecuted – had finally come to an end. Communist leader Khrushchev, who had boasted that he would destroy all faith and parade the last living Christian on TV, got it completely and utterly wrong.

In fact, instead of destroying all faith, repression had done just the opposite. A lifetime of being told there is no God and having atheism forced down their throats had created an incredible spiritual hunger in people's hearts. Desperate to hear about God, hundreds gathered expectantly every day as we stood on the street and preached the gospel. And every day, hundreds were coming to know Jesus.

You didn't need to do anything here to draw a crowd. In the West, we painted our faces white and did mimes. Although we'd prepared mimes for our time in Russia, we soon realised this wasn't needed; all we had to do was to stand and preach, and a crowd hungrily gathered.

The first time Bill handed me the microphone to preach is indelibly imprinted on my memory.

The atmosphere was electric with anticipation. A crowd of men, women, and children – as far as the eye could see – were hanging on my every word. At the end I made an appeal: "Would anyone like to come forward to give their lives to Jesus?"

The whole crowd took a step forward. Everyone wanted Jesus.

"They don't understand that it's a life-changing decision. I'd better explain it again," I thought.

"Hang on a minute. Listen, this is a serious decision. Being a follower of Jesus is life-changing; it's for the rest of your life. It's something you can't take lightly. You need to seriously think about it." I paused, letting the words sink in. "Okay. So if you're really ready to repent of your sins, turn away from your old life, and follow Jesus, please come forward now."

Again the whole crowd, as if one man, took a step forward together.

Having come from the West, it was hard for me to imagine how desperate these people were for Jesus. But they really were.

We led them in a prayer of repentance. I'll never forget a disabled Afghan veteran with only one leg weeping in Bill's arms.

Exuberant joy fell on all as young and old, including a few

babushkas – grandmothers – let their hair down completely, dancing unreservedly with us.

On another unforgettable day, we did a March for Jesus, walking down the main street in Krasnodar, singing and sharing about Jesus. As we marched, a police car escorted us, declaring through a loudspeaker, "These people have something important to say. Listen to them!"

Once, in a café, Mum had been prompted to give someone a tract. The lady was absolutely overjoyed. Bursting out she exclaimed, "I've been searching for God all my life." Her face beamed with delight as she continued: "And now you've shown me how to find Him. I can't thank you enough."

Hospitals, schools, and orphanages all opened their doors for us to share the gospel, give out literature, and pray for people. When we let the administration of one hospital know that we wanted to pray with their patients, the head consultant declared, "You're not leaving this office until you pray for me first. Then I want you to pray for the rest of the staff. Once you've finished with us, then you can pray for the patients!" We spent hours praying there.

I fell in love with the Russian people – so open, generous, and loving. I couldn't wait to come back.

Olya, an Orthodox believer who taught at the local university, offered to arrange for me to spend my year abroad there.

Back in England, I tried my best to earn the money to go but failed miserably. I needed $2,000 to pay for my tickets and university course. Most of my friends' parents had paid for them to go, but Mum wasn't in a position to help me out at that time; in fact, I helped her financially when I was able to, working and sending some money home.

Mum felt bad about it and spoke to our heavenly Father: "You're her Dad; please help her go to Russia."

Soon afterward, my friend Heidi came up to me one Sunday morning in church. "God's asked me to give you $2,000 to go to Russia," she said. "It's from my inheritance money."

I knew Heidi didn't have much money, and I wasn't used to accepting large gifts, so I told her, "It's too much. I'm sorry, but I can't take it."

When I arrived home, God rebuked me: "Paula, you asked me for the money, and I laid it on Heidi's heart to give it to you. Now you need to accept it!"

The next week, I spoke to Heidi. Looking at the ground and wishing it would swallow me up, I mumbled sheepishly, "Sorry about this, Heidi, but I wanted to ask you: Do you still have the money? It's just that I've changed my mind."

"Yes, of course, my dear," she replied, laughing. "God told me to put it aside for you anyway. I'm thrilled to give it to you."

In September 1993, I arrived in Krasnodar for my year abroad. Olya had arranged a place for me to stay with a *babushka* and to have Russian language lessons at the university.

Two weeks after I arrived, there was another coup. My friend Sonia joked that I must have an anointing for coups!

That historic day, my host and I were watching her favourite television programme – *Prosto Maria*, 'Simply Maria,' a Mexican soap opera dubbed into Russian. Without warning, the story was abruptly cut off by Boris Yeltsin's face materialising on the screen. My Russian was still pretty dreadful at the time, but from the tone of his voice I picked up that something was happening. Something serious.

The Mexicans suddenly returned, pressing on with their grand displays of passion. The poor heroine barely had time to respond to her knight in shining armour before the leaders of the coup unceremoniously made an appearance. They'd taken over the TV station.

A little while later, the TV station was again back in the government's hands. Yeltsin came into view assuring the people that all would be well.

Frustrated with not understanding what was happening, I tuned the radio to BBC and listened every hour to the news in English. What a baptism by fire into life in Russia!

Doors for preaching the gospel were still open, and I visited orphanages, prisons, and hospitals.

I was reading about Smith Wigglesworth[1], and I decided to follow his example by walking around the streets, praying that God would show me the person He wanted to receive His love that day.

Once, on a bus, I talked to a young Armenian refugee carrying an adorable baby girl. She promptly invited me to her house and met the Lord in a powerful way. We became friends. I visited her once a week and discipled her.

A man on a bus saw me reading the Bible and asked what I was doing. I gave him a Bible and invited him to church, and he gave his life to Jesus and started to come to church regularly.

The church I attended grew from three hundred to a thousand members in one year. Every day, people were coming to Jesus and on most Sundays around sixty responded to the altar call. It was a special time for Russia, with many new on-fire believers sharing the gospel and worshipping everywhere they went.

One time we were travelling by tram, and Dasha, my new friend from church, asked the driver, "Could I have the microphone to tell the people something incredibly important?"

"Why yes, of course," the driver replied, handing Dasha the microphone.

"Repent, repent for the kingdom of God is at hand," Dasha boldly proclaimed. People in both carriages started looking around, wondering where the voice was coming from. "This is not a joke," Dasha added, before giving back the microphone and sitting down calmly and peacefully.

My courageous friend, with her medium-length, raven-black hair, had a profound impact on me the first time I met her. She was publicly testifying in church about her mother, who had been mentally ill and struggling, and now was improving. Dasha's striking brown eyes radiated her delight in Jesus, who she'd only recently come to know. I ran straight to her after the service. "I just wanted to tell you, my mum's been healed of mental illness, and I'll pray with you for yours."

Dasha and I hit it off immediately. I'd found in her a kindred spirit I could share my heart with. I was also thrilled to discover she spoke English fluently after living in Canada for a time.

After three months of living with the *babushka*, I moved into Dasha's flat, which consisted of a single main room with a sofa opening up to become a double bed and a kitchen, toilet, and bathroom. Running water, both hot and cold, switched itself on and off at regular intervals during the day. The electricity was also intermittent. Although it wasn't quite the same as life in the UK, our standard of living was better than that of the majority of Russians living in villages who still had no running water or indoor bathrooms.

Chapter 8

FALLING IN LOVE
WITH RUSSIA

Shall I abandon, O King of mysteries, the soft comforts of home?
Shall I turn my back on my native land, and my face towards the sea?
Shall I put myself wholly at the mercy of God, without silver,
without a horse, without fame and honour?
Shall I throw myself wholly on the King of kings, without
sword and shield, without food and drink, without a bed to lie on?
Shall I say farewell to my beautiful land,
placing myself under Christ's yoke?
Shall I pour out my heart to him, confessing my manifold sins
and begging forgiveness, tears streaming down my cheeks?
Shall I leave the prints of my knees on the sandy beach,
a record of my final prayer in my native land?
Shall I then suffer every kind of wound that the sea can inflict?
Shall I take my tiny coracle across the wide sparkling ocean?
O King of the glorious heaven, shall I go of my own choice upon the sea?
O Christ, will you help me on the wild waves?

PRAYER OF A PILGRIM, BRENDAN (B 486)[1]

Russia was a world apart in terms of culture, language, and traditions, and I had a lot to learn.

During my first year there, getting used to the language and culture provided many laughs as well as more than a few embarrassing situations.

I had lessons at the university every day, and for the first three months, I didn't go out much, instead spending all my spare time studying Russian. After those first three months, I was able to communicate adequately. When Mum came out to celebrate Christmas with us, I was just about able to translate for her.

I vividly remember seeing in the New Year at church. New Year's Eve is the most important holiday of the year for Russians. Families get together enjoying all-night celebrations. Russians love creativity, games, and music, and at celebrations they enjoy skits, singing, and reading poems.

Dasha and I took turns translating for Mum well into the night, until I saw she'd fallen into a deep sleep with her head almost in the *shuba* – a traditional Russian New Year salad made of beetroot and herring. *Shuba* means literally 'fur coat'; all the food on top of the herring was like the fish's coat.

I quickly learned that hospitality, the receiving of guests, whether expected or not, is a high priority in Russia. Feeding guests is especially important. We sometimes jokingly called it 'aggressive hospitality,' as hosts insisted on feeding you even if you weren't hungry. In the Caucasus culture, it was polite to refuse food up to three times, and then the third time it was okay to admit you were hungry. When we Westerners uttered the word 'no', we meant it, whereas our local hosts thought we were hungry and just being shy.

The *babushka* I'd lived with always encouraged me to eat more than I wanted, as did friends when I popped in to visit them. It was their way of showing love.

The raised voices and animated gestures of the local people meant that I first thought people were constantly angry with each other. I soon learned this was just their way of communicating. They were decidedly blunt; you knew whether people loved you or hated you. And everyone felt it was their right to boss you about.

This was a completely different world from the one I grew up in. As a twenty-one-year-old Westerner, used to doing as I pleased, I'd already lived away from home, at university for two years, and in the USA for a year. Yet my host *babushka* would treat me like a small child, scolding me for not wearing enough warm clothes and coming home in the dark.

My daily commute to university was a cultural experience in itself. It was during rush hour, with hundreds of people trying to cram into a small tram. People elbowed each other out of the way, and the trams were so jam-packed the doors almost couldn't close. The first tram seemed way too crowded, so I waited for the next one. That was also packed; so were the third, fourth, and fifth.

"I could wait forever at this rate," I thought.

If I wanted to go anywhere, I had to assertively push my way on like everyone else. This went against everything within me, but I managed it somehow.

I once got stuck in the door and nearly crushed. Another time, during intense summer heat, I was squashed between so many people that I could hardly move my chest, and I struggled for breath. As everything was going black, the doors suddenly opened and I staggered out of the tram and fell onto the grass, lying there for a few minutes before I recovered.

I often chose to walk instead of taking public transport. My daily walk was past a market. During my first week, I casually wandered past a car with the boot open only to nearly jump out of my skin when I saw a grizzly pig's head staring at me from the boot! People slaughtered their animals at home, chopped them into pieces, and sold the whole animal from their car boot.

Both Dasha and I loved animals. One day we were given a lovely kitten, Nushka. Russians fed their cats and dogs leftovers, since life was hard and most people lived extremely frugally. I'd bought some *kolbasa* – Russian sausage – and gave some to the cat. Dasha was mortified: "Many people here can't afford to buy sausage, and here you are feeding the cat with our precious *kolbasa!*" In actual fact, most people survived on soup, bread, and potatoes; meat was a special treat.

Alcoholism was an acute problem in nearly every family, and the results of this were visible everywhere. Drunks lay unconscious in the streets, especially when it was cold. Once on my way back from university, an inebriated man got his leg cut off when a tram ran over him. I stood there, helpless, watching with the crowd that had gathered, praying he would meet Jesus before he died.

One evening an old friend of Dasha's knocked on our door. Stumbling into the flat with his light-brown hair all dishevelled, he mumbled, slurring his words, "D-a-a-a-s-h-a, my dear, I-I-I've come to celebrate New Year with you."

He was shocked when she explained, "I don't drink anymore. I've become a believer in Jesus. I'm a completely different person now."

She spent several hours telling him about Jesus. When he sobered up, she asked him, "Do you want to ask Jesus to come into your heart and give you a different life?" Her brown eyes burned with intensity.

He fell on his knees, sobbing, and accepted Jesus there and then on our living room floor. He got up off the floor a changed man. A new sparkle in his eyes and a cheeky grin lit up his face, attractive in his own way, in spite of years of drinking. He became involved in the church and soon was married. Tragically, a few years later he backslid, and was murdered while in a drunken state.

As I woke up one morning, Dasha told me, "Don't go outside, Polochka[2] ; there's a dead body on the doorstep."

We waited until the police arrived. It turned out our neighbour had drunk too much and passed out, then froze to death on the doorstep.

The family took his body into the house to prepare it for burial. Russians believe the spirit hangs around after death for three days, so most burials are on the third day after someone's death.

We knew these neighbours, having had *chai* (tea) with them several times. I'd even stayed one night at their house when Dasha had gone to another city and forgotten to leave me the key (we only had one key to the flat).

As was the custom in Russia, the family came around collecting money for the funeral; we gave what we could to help. There was a real sense of community and sharing in a way I'd not experienced growing up in England.

It was almost impossible to get a telephone installed into one's home at that time in Russia. Some people had been on the waiting list for as long as twenty years. Our neighbour, on the fifth floor, had a phone and would let us use it. I arranged for a time when Mum would phone me once a week, and I waited for her call in my friend's house. Many people would be using the phone. I felt sorry for the owners constantly running up and down the stairs, fetching people to receive calls.

Although Dasha had been a believer for only six months when I moved in with her, she was already leading a small house group in her home. The group consisted of neighbours who had recently become believers. We spent hours discipling them. The lady who owned the phone and her son became believers.

An Armenian refugee family – a father, his sons, and nephews – lived in an upstairs flat the same size as ours, with only two sofas. Often other relatives appeared and stayed for weeks on end, taking turns sleeping on the worn-out sofas. The Armenian father along with one son and a nephew became believers and came to our home group. The elder brother was a Mafia boss, large and threatening. He owned three cars, which meant he was extremely well-off for those days, when most people didn't have a car. He was kind to us, however, and when Dasha had some money stolen, he offered to go and beat up the people involved and get the money back. Dasha declined the 'kind' offer!

The younger brother was the complete opposite – a skinny, shy poet who'd never done a decent day's work in his life. He fell in love with me and was constantly writing me love poems. When Mum came to visit at Christmas, without warning me, he asked in Russian, "I'd like to ask for your daughter's hand in marriage." His love-struck brown eyes looked up expectantly as he waited for me to translate his words.

I was horrified. "I'm not translating that for you," I told him, "and I'm certainly not planning on marrying you!" My poor Mum wondered what in the world was going on.

One day he came in our flat for a cup of *chai* and stayed for four hours. In their culture, it's rude to tell someone you're busy, so I was wondering how on earth I could tactfully escort him out the door. He suddenly asked, "Are the *sosiski* cooking?" I realised he was waiting for me to feed him. I cooked him some *sosiski* (hot dogs), which he ravenously devoured as if he hadn't eaten in months, and then he left.

It was a completely different mindset, and in some ways hard to get used to. But the sense of community, generosity, directness, and simplicity were like a breath of fresh air.

I was falling in love with Russia.

Chapter 9

CHECHNYA CALLING

For my own part, I have never ceased to rejoice
that God has appointed me to such an office.
People talk of the sacrifice I have made
in spending so much of my life in Africa.
Is that a sacrifice which brings
its own blest reward in healthful activity,
the consciousness of doing good, peace of mind,
and a bright hope of a glorious destiny hereafter?
Away with the word sacrifice.
Say rather it is a privilege.
Anxiety, sickness, suffering, or danger, now and then,
with a foregoing of the common conveniences
and charities of this life, may make us pause,
and cause the spirit to waver, and the soul to sink;
but let this only be for a moment.
All these are nothing when compared with the glory
which shall be revealed in and for us.
I never made a sacrifice.

DAVID LIVINGSTONE, PIONEER MISSIONARY
TO AFRICA (B 1813)[1]

After my year abroad, I returned to the UK to finish my degree. Russia had won my heart, but I still thought I was called somewhere else full-time; I just wasn't sure where.

During that time I seriously considered a couple of tempting offers: a university scholarship for a PhD in psychology, and becoming a youth pastor with a decent salary and a car in the church I attended at Keele. But having no peace about either, I turned them down.

Then Krasnodar University offered me a job teaching English, and my heart leapt within me. "This is it."

I knew God was opening a door for me. I needed to go back to Russia and teach for a year. Then He'd show me where to go next, where to settle down, what my life's calling was – or so I thought.

I took time out after finishing my degree, working for a few months and then travelling. I visited my family in the USA and then went to Brazil where I met some of Vovo's family for the first time. It was such a joy to meet them, they were so loving, warm and open. After praying for healing for my cousin Deidre's hands, she felt warmth and comfort and went around telling everyone I had healing hands! I reassured her it was Jesus healing through my hands. After that, many different people started coming to be prayed for. I shared and prayed with my great uncle who was blind; he so liked the prayer inviting Jesus into his life that he asked me to write it down so that his wife could read it to him every day. Five months later, he died.

Next, I went to Sri Lanka, to see my dear friend Heidi and the work she was doing out there. Having set up mobile clinics, she would treat needy people in tea plantations and other remote areas where there was no medical help. I learnt how to do wound dressings and give injections. A few times I was put on the spot, being asked to share or preach at church meetings and at a rehab centre.

I also saw my first war zone, as it was quite a tense situation at the time, with many checkpoints, terrorist explosions and house to house searches. One night a group of soldiers came banging at our door, looking for Tamils.

I remember how Heidi looked fiercely out of the window and shouted, "You can come in if you want, but if you wake my baby up you'll have to stop him screaming and rock him back to sleep yourselves."

Horrified at the idea of babysitting, they made a hasty exit!

Sleeping in the same room as Heidi's baby Nathan, one night I was awoken by the sound of loud explosions nearby. Grabbing Nathan, I laid down under the bed thinking the glass would shatter at any moment. When the noise finished and the glass didn't smash, I realised it was just fireworks and felt extremely stupid!

In the spring of 1996, I travelled back to Russia. God was so faithful in helping me with the journey and transition even in little ways. I gave a report in my newsletter in April 1996:

When I arrived at Moscow airport, I met some English Christians standing in the Passport Control queue. They invited me to stay overnight with them at their mission house, so I didn't have to find a place to stay.... I shared a taxi with them and didn't have to carry my luggage across Moscow alone. The next day...because of bad weather conditions I didn't arrive into Krasnodar until 11 pm, ten hours late, and there was no one to meet me. The Lord provided me with a free lift to a friend's house and I didn't have to spend the night alone at the airport.

The Lord has also provided me with an amazing place to live...with two lovely YWAMers ... Because it is the YWAM[2] office in Krasnodar ... we have the privilege of having many mod cons which are a rarity in Russia, a computer, fax machine, email, telephone, washing machine, TV and video. It's even got a piano, I'm just praising the Lord for His wonderful provisions!

I arrived to start my new job only to find the job hadn't materialised. Due to the economic crisis, the university had no money to pay a foreign teacher. And they'd forgotten to let me know. Great. I'd come all this way, given up my plans for a year, and this. Suddenly it dawned on me and I looked up and laughed.

"This looks like Your hand, Lord!" I thought. He'd cleverly used the job offer to get me back to Russia. "Now I just have to work out what You want me to do here. Please show me clearly, Lord."

I threw myself into evangelism, going regularly to a children's hospital and orphanage. We loved sharing God's love with the children and seeing them blossom as a result. And also showing the staff by example that these children needed to be loved and touched, and encouraging the staff to do the same.

Two little ones particularly stole our hearts.

Nine-year-old Luba was so excited to hear she had a Father in heaven that every time we talked about God after that, she'd shout out, "He's my God" or "He's my Father."

When we arrived to play with them every Sunday afternoon, two-year-old Diana – a black toddler with the most endearing smile – would come running with outstretched arms, delightedly shrieking, "Mama!" I tried unsuccessfully to adopt her for a few years until she was eventually adopted into an American family.

Generally, however, I found people in Russia were no longer quite as open as they had been. So many different religions had flooded Russia, including Jehovah Witnesses and Mormons, and people started to become suspicious and overwhelmed. Spiritual hunger was being replaced by the newfound materialism, consumerism, and Western lifestyle.

Though people were no longer coming to the Lord in droves, they were still coming to Him individually. God led us to those people of peace[3] who were open and searching.

One clear example occurred one day when a YWAM team was staying at our flat. One of them noticed a sad-looking African girl in her early twenties, resting her weary head on the bus window. She seemed to have a deep sadness about her, as if carrying the world on her shoulders. Only much later did we find out why.

"Are you a Christian?" the YWAM team member asked her. After chatting with the African girl for a bit, he remarked, "Jesus has laid it on my heart to give you some money." He kindly offered her $20.

She looked puzzled, then politely refused, "No, thanks, I'm okay." She'd been taught not to take money from strangers.

"No worries. But we're staying with missionaries. Would you like to come back to the house and meet them?"

She readily agreed, and she met my roommates.

"Just my kind of people," she thought, feeling right at home.

They invited her to come back whenever she wanted. A few days later she popped in for another visit, and that's when I met her.

Christabel was from Cameroon and studied medicine at the local university. She invited me to come to her student dorm. When I went for the first time, I realised she had no food, so I started to pop in and bring her food regularly. We became good friends. I talked to her about Jesus and invited her to come to church. She wondered why I was always talking about Jesus and reading my Bible. But soon she met the God of all comfort face to face. Renewed hope lit up her beautiful face, and her deep brown eyes shone with fresh joy. She knew everything would be okay now that Jesus was on her side. And it was.

God provided funds for her to complete her studies. Mum had just come into some inheritance money and paid for Christabel to finish her degree. On a trip to the UK to visit us, Christabel met her future husband, and is now married with four beautiful children and living in London.

Later on, she related to me the story about the life-changing day she'd met the missionary on the bus. Her only sister had died a few years before, breaking her heart. Adding to her heartache, she found out her father had become seriously ill. Just before he died, he let her know he was praying that God would lead her to a missionary who would help her.

After her father's death, she was left stranded in Russia with no finances and no way to return home. Starving and desperate, the final straw came when her toes froze from the holes in her boots. She decided enough was enough. That was it. She was going to kill herself: get drunk on vodka, then throw herself out of her seventh-floor dorm room window. On her way home to execute her plan, she was shocked when the missionary talked to her. Remembering what her father had told her, she came home to our house. And the rest is history.

You never know when being obedient to a prompting of the Holy Spirit may change somebody's destiny. Jesus literally saved Christabel from killing herself that day. Through the obedience of one man on a bus. Who'd been sent all the way from the USA to Russia. To save one desperate girl from Africa. As an answer to the prayer of a desperate, dying father.

Isn't it wonderful how God goes to so much trouble, sending people from one end of the earth to another, just to save one person! How does He manage to coordinate these divine appointments so smoothly? Doesn't it just make you love Him even more? I know it does me.

While I was in the UK finishing my degree, Dasha felt the Lord call her to Chechnya. In the summer of 1995, she and two friends from church had dreams and visions, independently of each other, to run a camp for young people from the war zone.

They took a train to Grozny and, as the Holy Spirit led them, invited thirty mostly Russian youngsters to come to a camp. During the ten-day camp, nearly all decided to follow Jesus. This meant Dasha and her friends suddenly became responsible for a newly formed church. God led her to move to Chechnya soon afterward and to disciple these new believers. At the time, she'd been a believer for only just over two years herself.

When I relocated back to Krasnodar in the spring of 1996, Dasha came every two months to stay with us. She shared about the church in Chechnya, and we prayed together. I started to feel God was calling me to go to Chechnya as well.

At first, I quivered in my boots at the thought of going alone, a single young girl, to a war zone.

One night I couldn't sleep, so I was reading a book about reaching out to Muslims. All night I wrestled with fears, especially of being killed. Finally, just as the first peek of sunlight sent shimmering rays over our slumbering neighbourhood, I surrendered. Totally and completely.

"Here I am, Lord, I'm willing. Send me wherever You see fit. And if I perish, I perish."

Just as the inky darkness was quickly dispersing with the light of day, so the fear I'd been contending with lifted. Almost in an instant. In its place, I could feel a river of joy, peace, and excitement welling up inside me, bubbling over. The Lord was filling me with His presence – and with strength, courage, and determination that I would need for the journey ahead.

"What an amazing privilege and honour, Jesus, to serve You on the frontlines. No matter what."

Then one day in March, the Lord spoke to me clearly: "When your mum is happy about it, I'll send you to Chechnya."

"Well, that's not very likely!" I remarked to the Lord. "Mum would never be happy for me to go to a war zone. Whose mother would want that for her young single daughter?"

I didn't tell anyone about it; I just pondered it all in my heart.

That summer, I ran out of money, so I returned to the UK and worked in a boarding school teaching English to gather the funds to go back to Russia. While there, I received from Dasha a letter telling me about the situation in Chechnya. It ended with these words: "There are bombs going off all the time, everything is destroyed, many people are in need. I think you would really like it here, I think it's the right place for you!"

I knew God was speaking to me, but I was still a bit freaked out by the idea.

The following Sunday, I had a day off and decided to go to church. In the phone book I found a friendly village church. After the service, a local family invited me and another girl in her twenties to lunch. Chatting over lunch, they asked me, "So what do you do?"

"I'm a missionary in Russia." I filled them in a bit about what I was doing. Then for some reason I surprised myself by saying,

"A few days ago I had a letter from a friend inviting me to work in Chechnya – where the war is at the moment. I'm a bit scared at the thought of it, but I'm praying about it."

"Oh, how amazing," the other guest burst out exuberantly, "I'm a missionary in Bosnia. I just got back from Sarajevo. There's been terrible fighting there."

She recounted her story to us, excitedly sharing testimonies of how God was working in the midst of war. Then they all prayed for me.

I left feeling tremendously uplifted by the encouragement. Both through people and through the Lord in His kindness providing another unexpected confirmation about me going to serve Him in Chechnya.

In late summer that same year, I travelled back to Russia.

My pastor Bill came out to visit, and I had a long conversation with him about my desire to go to Chechnya.

"Are you 100 percent sure God is asking you to go?" he asked.

"No, only about 95 percent sure, I think."

"Only when you are 100 percent sure should you go," he said.

I agreed. But I thought, "That's never going to happen. How can you ever be 100 percent sure?"

I later realised that you can, in fact, be more than 100 percent sure about something.

In late September, I organised a camp for the young church in Chechnya. This was the first time I'd been director of a camp and organised it myself. I was twenty-five at the time.

The campers had just endured a month of intense fighting, living in basements being continuously bombed. My mum and a team of five young men came from our church in the UK to minister at the camp.

Miracles started before we even arrived. Travelling there was an experience in itself for six English people, most of whom had never been to Russia before. The carriage was full of drunk Russian soldiers heading off to fight in Chechnya. We'd locked our compartment and had just fallen asleep when there was a loud banging on the door. An intoxicated Russian voice hollered through the door: "Dima, give me back my *vodka*, I know you're in there."

"There's no Dima and certainly no vodka in our compartment," I shouted back. "You've made a mistake."

All night the poor soldier was convinced his vodka was in our compartment and kept knocking. We were very relieved when morning arrived and no soldiers had broken or shot our door down in the night to reclaim their 'lost' vodka!

God also did miracles escorting the church out of Chechnya. Only one person actually had the right documents.[4] The two without passports weren't checked by guards at any of the checkpoints; everyone else had their documents inspected.

I will never forget how excited the guests were when they finally arrived. The sight of bananas and ice cream thrilled them. Most of them had been surviving on very little during the intense fighting.

The 'camp' was held in Vladikavkaz, the capital of the Republic of Northern Ossetia-Alania, a three-hour bus journey from Grozny, in the tenth-floor apartment of my friend, Pastor Valera. Thirty people slept in the four-bedroom apartment. A broken lift and no running water meant hauling buckets of water up ten flights of stairs.

In spite of this, the fellowship with each other and the Lord was sweet. God did a thorough work, bringing healing from deep traumas.

His presence was so strong and an extraordinary miracle happened a few hours after we'd departed. Valera had two young sons, blond and mischievous with adorable smiles, the kind that melted your heart and made you forgive them immediately. The evening we left his youngest boy choked on a piece of food. The family tried to dislodge it, but to their horror, the gorgeous little boy died in his distraught father's arms. Valera held his blue lifeless son, for what seemed an eternity, crying out for mercy and speaking life into him. His wife, Alla, couldn't bear to be in the room and went outside heartbroken, already thinking about funeral arrangements. After half an hour the boy came back to life again, and soon he was running around happily playing as if nothing had ever happened.

During the camp, Mum and I shared a room with some of the guests. God gave us a special love for one of them, Mila, as we listened to her stories and prayed for her. A middle-aged widow with chestnut brown hair, she'd survived two abusive marriages and was now bringing up her four children singlehandedly. Passionate and animated, Mila loved to discourse about any subject at length. Lovable and vulnerable, she was sensitive to the Holy Spirit, and wept profusely whenever she felt His comforting presence. It was a privilege to spend time with her.

Toward the end of the camp, Mum approached me excitedly. "I've got something important to tell you."

"What's that, Mum?"

"If God calls you to go to Chechnya, I would be happy about it."

"Mum, you don't know what you're saying!" I took a deep breath.

She continued: "What I mean is that I can see that there's a deep love between you and these precious people. It's amazing to see the way you really love Mila and family, and how they love you back. More than anything, I want you to be obedient to what God is calling you to do."

This was all the confirmation I needed. I was now 150 percent sure God was sending me. I wrote to Bill to let him know I was completely sure.

Within a month, I moved to Chechnya.

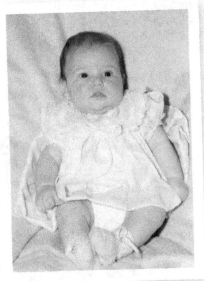

Left: Paula at three months.

Right: Enjoying her tricycle.

Left: With Mum on their favourite mode of transport.

Right: Paula on left with her cousin Gina.

Left: Clutching her favourite 'Tiny Tears' doll.

Right: Five-year-old evangelist with her 'Jesus saves' badge.

Bedtime Bible reading with her cousin Gina on right.

Members of the Good News Fellowship line the canal bank as a baptism takes place.

Baptisms in cold waters of the canal

EIGHT people were baptised in the waters of the Basingstoke Canal on Sunday afternoon.

Members of the Good News Fellowship of Fleet gathered along the banks of the canal at Pondtail Bridge, Fleet, while Mr. David Benson and Mr. David Hanson, submerged in their wates in the murky water, carried out the baptisms.

One by one the candidates, young and old, were fully dressed, bravely dip-toed into the cold water.

They confessed Jesus as their saviour and acknowledged that in the baptism they were burying their old mortality life and its habits and embracing by faith a new way of life.

They were then fully submerged under the water.

A family baptism was carried out when Mr. Michel Vandromme (33), his wife Carol and their children, Justine (7) and Danielle (4), of Beaufort Road, Church Crookham, all took the plunge.

The others were Paula O'Keefe (7), of Glen Road, Fleet; Anthony Couttanr (18), of Wakeford Park, Ewshot; Mrs. Betty Frost, of Wellington Avenue, Fleet, and a young boy who did not want his name mentioned.

As the ceremony began the heavens opened and the rain bucketed down drenching everyone.

Baptisms are carried out all over the country in this way. The Good News Fellowship usually uses a swimming pool in Fleet, and last year a group was baptised in the sea at Little-hampton.

It is not the first time the Basingstoke Canal, recently dredged and cleaned, has been used for this sort of ceremony. Baptisms were baptised in the canal in Crookham Village over 100 years ago.

Mrs. Carol Vandromme is baptised by Mr. David Benson.

Left: Newspaper article about the baptisms in the Basingstoke Canal on a rainy spring day in 1979. The two photos show friends being baptised, the top one also showing members of the Fleet Christian Fellowship watching. Paula, almost eight, is in a white coat with hood up (on front row, far left, behind white board) waiting for her turn to be baptised.

Below: Paula, in brown jumper, with grandparents and cousin Gina, enjoying a day at the beach.

Left: Paula, in middle, on her 10th birthday with, from left, Aunt Penny, cousin Gina, her grandparents and cousin JP.

Right: Primary School Netball team. Paula – back row, far left – aged 11.

Left: Sharing sandwiches with the pigeons in a London park aged 12.

Left: In Farnborough Hill school uniform aged 15.

Right: Graduating from Keele University.

In Sri Lanka with Heidi and baby Nathan at an elephant orphanage.

Left: Mum in Moscow on their first mission trip to Russia in 1992.

Right: The mission trip team with pastor Bill Rice (on right in the orange shirt) enjoying Russian food at the local 'Intourist' hotel.

Left: Crowds listening to the open-air preaching.

Right: Mass baptisms. Those being baptised are dressed in white as is the tradition in Russian baptist churches.

Left: March for Jesus in Krasnodar with the police escort in front blaring through the loudspeaker, "Listen to these people, they have something important to say!"

Left: A large crowd marches down Krasnodar's main street singing praises to Jesus during the March for Jesus.

The King's Church

Paula O'Keefe

... working for the Church in Krasnodar, Russia

RUSSIA

Moscow

Kiev

UKRAINE

KAZAKHSTAN

Krasnodar

Grozny

Black Sea

Istanbul

TURKEY

Caspian Sea

IRAN

Left: Church Fund Raising Brochure from 1993.

Right: The house group made up of neighbours meeting at Dasha's flat (with kitten Nushka on Paula's lap).

Left: Ukraine in the bleak midwinter.

Right: In an unheated electric train with temperatures outside of -30°c with gloves on her feet in an attempt to warm up!

Left: Paula's African friend Christabel holding a friend's baby.

Right: At the New Year's Eve church party in the middle of translating for Mum, Paula turned to see her fast asleep with her head just missing the salad!

Chapter 10

FIRST GLIMPSE OF CHECHNYA

In the vast plain to the north
I have sometimes seen, in the morning sun,
the smoke of a thousand villages
where no missionary has ever been.

ROBERT MOFFAT, WHO INSPIRED
DAVID LIVINGSTONE[1]

We were finally on our way to Chechnya, and I was so excited I could hardly contain myself.

We arrived in Vladikavkaz and spent the night at Pastor Valera's house. As the birds filled the dawn air with their bright chorus, trilling and warbling and chirping, we took the first bus.

Vladikavkaz is surrounded by majestic snowcapped mountains, visible from almost everywhere in the city. The road we were taking today, however, was heading away from the mountains. The terrain levelled out into flat, green, dust-filled plains.

Before reaching Chechnya, the bus was due to wind its merry way through the Republic of Ingushetia. Dasha and I squeezed into the rickety old bus and soon were winding through the Ossetian countryside.

Not long afterward, a bullet-riddled house came into my view, followed by a burned-out building, then another. We were passing through some sort of deserted ghost town, devoid of people and livestock. Ruins, fallow fields, and an eerie silence seemed to be all that was left.

73

"*Stranno* – How strange," I whispered to Dasha, a little confused. "We haven't even reached Ingushetia yet, let alone Chechnya."

"It's from the Ossetian-Ingush war[2] in 1992," Dasha quietly explained. "We're in East Prigorodny, where the worst fighting took place."

She whispered into my ear: "Even though the Ingush and Ossetians are neighbours, they really hate each other. It's awful to see such an intense level of hatred. It seems they've been enemies forever. Well, for centuries at least. Both sides believe in blood revenge and in actively remembering the past. That really doesn't help matters at all. Hatred gets passed on from generation to generation. Every Ossetian and Ingush family I know has stories of unspeakable atrocities committed against family members at the hands of their neighbours. They seem to love going over all the awful stories again and again. And from time to time, conflict flares up. Then gangs of armed civilians attack a village and murder whoever they find, raping and pillaging as they go. It's horrendous, and of course creates new victims. And the cycle continues. It's tragic. Truly tragic. We really need God to intervene and change people's hearts."

We prayed quietly together for both people groups to meet Jesus and to be able to forgive and let go of the past.

After crossing the border into Ingushetia, we motored through another uninhabited village, also devastated by war.

"Everyone fled from both border towns when the war started," Dasha said. "It seems people are still too scared to return."

We soon coursed through a few sleepy Ingush villages. *Babushkas* in headscarves and long-sleeved dresses whiled away the day chatting with neighbours on benches, putting the world to rights. Chickens and geese squawked as they sprang out of the way of oncoming cars. Little huts[3] lined the main roads. Metal fences painted red, green, and blue added a touch of colour.

Finally the border with Chechnya came onto the horizon, marked by barbed-wire fencing, sandbags piled high, tanks and war-weary soldiers poised and alert, and blood-red words daubed menacingly on the walls: *Strelyaem bez predupresdenie* – 'We shoot without warning.'

As we penetrated deeper into Chechen territory, signs of war were everywhere: blackened, bombed-out buildings, half-burned trees, upturned wrecks of cars and tanks.

None of this fazed me. I was so excited, knowing I was 100 percent in the centre of God's will.

When I saw Russian soldiers with tanks, I wanted to hug them and dance a little caper, whooping for joy. It was an amazing feeling to be in Chechnya at last, after a year and a half of preparation.

The exhilaration didn't last long, however; the first time I heard bombing close by, I nearly jumped out of my skin. The ten-story building swayed with each explosion, and I was petrified.

For the first couple of weeks, I stayed with a family from our church. Carrying buckets of water up ten flights of stairs each morning was exhausting, making me feel I might collapse.

No running water in Chechnya and intermittent electricity added a heavy burden to a people already wearied by war. Those with money or somewhere to go had fled a long time ago.

Most factories and workplaces had been destroyed. Wages were often delayed for at least six months. Payment, when received, was not always monetary; sometimes it was in the form of food or goods from the workplace. People survived in bombed-out buildings or in metal huts or basements, on a meagre diet of bread and potato soup.

Dasha soon introduced me to all her friends. She was well loved and respected, having faithfully been through the war with them. Since I was her friend, they also welcomed me with open arms.

Larisa, a close friend of Dasha's and the leader of the church there, was in her late thirties, divorced, and longing to be whisked away into the sunset by her knight in shining armour. Her long slender figure, at first glance, could mislead you to underestimate the physical strength she actually possessed, gained from years of hard labour. Her large, expressive eyes, kind heart and warming giggle, revealing a row of gold teeth, made it difficult not to love her. I remember laughing on one occasion for what seemed like hours when she modelled an unsightly hat for us.

She'd become a mother early to Maryam, her lovely daughter, after a brief marriage. Her husband left her for another woman, and she returned to her parents who helped her bring up Maryam. Just before the war, Larisa's father had been stabbed and left for dead, and she and her family nursed him at home until he passed away. Soon after that Larisa's younger sister, Aminat, who lived in a town outside Chechnya, offered Maryam the chance to live with her and her family and go to college there. Although it was hard to see Maryam go, it was a blessing that she was in a safe place and missed most of the horrors of war. We caught up with her every summer when her aunty Aminat would bring her to our annual summer camp.

Larisa's other sister, Malika, lived in the same apartment block as Larisa, on the eighth floor. A widow with two daughters, her husband had also died soon after the war started.

By the time I met them, Larisa lived alone with her mother, Aunty Asya, a petite, well-read, and sprightly lady in her mid-seventies. For most of my time in Chechnya, I lived with them. Aunty Asya's joys were cooking and history books. She cooked scrumptious meals from scratch, making the best of whatever ingredients she had. She especially prided herself on her homemade bread. She had an extensive library of history books, and when she was in a talkative mood, she could take an unwitting listener to London and back as she shared all the intimate details of the economic situation in the 1920s or the intrigues of the war cabinet in the 1940s.

Larisa had grown up in a Muslim home. All her life, she'd been searching for God and had dabbled in various religions. She vowed to herself, "I won't be content until I meet the true God face to face."

One night, as her mother slept peacefully nearby, a man dressed in white appeared to her in a vision coming down on a white cloud.

"Who are you?" she asked Him.

"I'm Jesus, the Son of God."

"You can't be the Son of God. You just can't," she contested, convinced as Muslims usually are, that God couldn't possibly have a son.

"Yes, I am the Son of God. But I'm also God," He added.

"But you just can't be!" she reiterated, completely baffled.

He lovingly reassured her, "Yes, I am indeed both God and the Son of God."

After leaving it for a moment to sink in, He gently continued, "And my dear girl, you're not worshipping the true God. I'm the only true God. Are you prepared to leave everything and follow me?"

"But I'm a Muslim," she thought to herself fearfully, imaging all the awful things that could happen to her if people found out. "So perhaps I could follow Him in the next life?!"

As if reading her thoughts, He responded immediately, "No, I want you to follow Me in this life."

"Da – yes – take me," she willingly agreed, thinking He would take her up to heaven.

"Not yet," He said and then to her surprise, showed her a vision of herself being immersed fully in water.

"How strange," she thought, wondering what that was all about, as she'd never seen a baptism before.

Soon after that, she was attracted to a poster inviting people to come and hear a talk entitled, 'Jesus, my life.' She went along to the talk where she heard the gospel for the first time. She invited Jesus into her life and was given a New Testament, which she started to study and soon after bought herself a Bible at the market.

A few years later Dasha appeared at her church and invited her to the summer camp. She enjoyed herself at the camp and made many new friends. When a church was planted out of that camp, she was invited to help pastor it.

When I arrived, I helped her and Dasha to lead the new church. After a few months, Dasha felt God calling her to another ministry. I stayed to continue the work she'd started and to support the fledgling church. God's planning and timing turned out to be perfect for both of us.

That winter I immersed myself in pastoral work: visiting people, listening to their tragic stories, praying for them, and leading meetings.

I also prayed a lot. I discovered that living in a war zone greatly improves your prayer life! Hearing shooting and bombing close by caused me to fall to my knees often, crying out to God for mercy for the land, in a way that nothing else could.

I also did as much as I could to help alleviate the overwhelming poverty all around me. George Dowdell from Kingscare, the charity based in my home church and now supporting me, came out to see how he could help. I met him at the airport in Mineralnye Vody, and we travelled together into Chechnya. George didn't speak any Russian and looked very English.

No seats were available together on the crowded bus, so we put George as far away from the door as possible, in between other passengers, warning him to keep his mouth shut. At the checkpoint into Chechnya, a soldier climbed onto the bus, glancing at all the passengers and taking some of the men's passports.

"Lord, please don't let them check George," I prayed quickly.

Miraculously they didn't, and we made it safely into Chechnya.

George came with us to visit our people and the refugee camps, to assess how Kingscare could help.

On one occasion, we had a scary moment. George and I were treading our way through the rubble in downtown Grozny when suddenly a soldier, a reasonable distance from us, beckoned us to come over. I whispered to George, "Just keep walking. Calmly but fast."

As we continued, pretending not to see him, shots were fired, seemingly in our direction. A supporting wall loomed in front of us, the remnants of a once towering high-rise building. Hurriedly stepping into the welcome safety of this solid wall, we were sheltered from the ricocheting bullets. Dashing away, we soon reached the central market and disappeared into the crowd.

When George arrived back in the UK, he raised money and awareness for the work. Kind friends and even strangers who heard about the ministry donated generously. Soon we were able to distribute food, clothes, shoes, eyeglasses, and schoolbooks, as well as cover the costs of dental and medical treatment, sort out documents and passports, donate $2,000 worth of medical equipment to a local hospital, install gas into freezing metal huts in the refugee camp, and set up small income-generating businesses.

During this time, I felt like I was doing so little. But I was encouraged by Mother Teresa's wise words[4]: "We ourselves feel that what we are doing is just a drop in the ocean, but if that drop was not in the ocean, I think the ocean would be less because of that missing drop."

Chapter 11

OUR UNDERGROUND CHURCH

I will build my church, and the gates
of Hades will not overcome it.

MATTHEW 16:18

Our little underground house church, 'The Peace of Christ,' met regularly in different homes. Living in a Muslim republic under Sharia law, Muslims accepting Jesus faced the threat of martyrdom on a daily basis.

Before the mid-1990s, most believers in Chechnya had been of Russian descent. But as a result of the war and ethnic cleansing, most Russian believers had left the republic or were planning on leaving. As a result by the time I was working there most of the churches were either very small or gone.

The Pentecostal Church had received a prophetic warning that a war was about to start, so most of its members left Chechnya before the fighting began; only a handful of Chechen believers were still left. After the second war, most of them left too.

A small Charismatic church had fallen apart when the young courageous pastor had been forced into a car by armed Chechens and was never seen or heard of again. A handful of his people joined up with us.

A once thriving Baptist church was completely destroyed in 1999 when the building was razed to the ground. By then, most of the leaders and congregation had left or been killed. The two elders who stepped in as impromptu leaders had both been kidnapped and killed.

We'd met both these elders on a few occasions when we'd brought aid to the church. Alexei, a short, kind, bald single man in his late thirties, had gently and lovingly looked after his disabled mother. Sasha was a true Russian Baptist in his fifties always standing firmly for his traditions.

A small Orthodox church was still functioning at that time; a handful of elderly ladies attended.

Our church started out with about twenty young people, mostly Russians, who'd accepted Jesus in July 1995 at the summer camp Dasha had organised. We met a few times a week. Apart from the main meeting on Fridays, the Muslim day off, we held a weekly prayer meeting and three home groups, one for young people, another for older people, and one in the urban refugee camp. We could have up to fifteen people, but often only a handful. Our meetings had to be in the daytime because of a curfew after dark. For everyone to be home before dark in the winter (sundown could be as early as 3:30 pm), we had to finish our meetings in early afternoon; occasionally we held all-night prayer meetings when everyone would stay the night.

Most gatherings were simple and homely. We drank tea and ate together, prayed for one another, sang worship songs, and shared from the Bible together. We tried to encourage and lift one other out of the despair and trauma which was like a heavy blanket trying to drag us all down.

Sometimes the family hosting the meeting were in a state when we arrived. In that case, we ministered to them before we could even start a meeting. Relationships in families can be difficult at the best of times, but when war, deprivation, and trauma are added to normal family problems, the tension and conflict can be devastating. Tempers grow fraught with each added trauma. Many families seemed to be angry and at odds with each other one moment, then forgiving one another and covering each other's backs the next.

One day I found the host in a terrible state when I arrived at their house for a meeting. The mother had managed to find two potatoes and one onion, and she was making soup. As she chopped the onion, with each violent chop of the knife, she talked about killing herself or her son. She'd had a fight with him, and they weren't talking.

I managed to help her calm down before the other believers came. Eventually she let me pray with her, and she put down the knife. During the worship time she wept as the Lord touched her; with His help, this mother and son were able to forgive one another and be reconciled. Sometimes I didn't know which was worse – the tension inside families or the tension in the country as lawlessness and violence increased.

Many came to the meetings depressed. In a good week, perhaps only one person from the church had been robbed at gunpoint, beaten, or raped; or lost their home, possessions, or a loved one; or seen these things happen to family, neighbours, or friends. In a bad week, most of the church could have had something similar happen to them during the week . If you didn't intentionally lift the conversation to something more positive, people would constantly be talking about awful situations. Sometimes there seemed to be absolutely no good news whatsoever. Life just seemed to be one nightmare after another. And the doom and gloom could become worse with each new topic of conversation.

Hurt and traumatised people clashing with other hurt and traumatised people caused a lot of distress and friction even within the church.

One older, Armenian lady, Vera, got offended with Larisa and ended up taking half of the church with her. It felt like a divorce, ripping our heart in two. They met in Vera's house, until she and her family also fled the country.

Andrei, one of our regulars – a young man with learning difficulties and a crooked smile revealing the few black and de-caying teeth he had left – met Jesus at that first summer camp. He'd been adopted as a baby, only to have his new mother abandon the family. His father brought him up but was tragically killed during the bombing. Soon after, his uncle was kidnapped, reappearing five years later after having been forced to work in a labour camp in the mountains.

Andrei had a violent streak. When he was in that state, for some reason he always seemed to turn on our shy, sweet Karina. During one meeting, he tried to push her down the stairs; another time he chased her down the street with an axe. Luckily, she wasn't physically hurt either time, just shaken. But this wasn't the witness we needed to attract non-believers to faith!

I can still picture one particular day when I was on the bus going to see Vera. The bus made its way through the centre of town, where devastation was at its worst. Piles of rubble littered the ground, and not one building was left standing. The desolation caused by the war was obvious everywhere I looked.

I felt the Lord clearly reveal a profound truth to me: "The people have been just as devastated as the buildings; it's just not as obvious at first sight. And just as it takes time and effort to bring restoration physically to the city, so it will take time and effort to bring healing to my people." This insight gave me a new compassion, and particularly helped me to extend grace to Vera and Andrei.

I would always set off for the meeting via the market to pick up food for that week's host family, as well as tea, sugar, and cakes to enjoy after the meeting. On birthdays or public holidays – or whatever special occasion we could come up with – we had parties, games, and fun together. To survive in the midst of such high levels of despair and pain, it was vital to have fun and let down our hair as often as we could. Larisa and Dasha both had a great sense of humour, and so we shared much hilarity as we played, had fun, and erupted with laughter as often as we could in the midst of all the drama and trauma.

Celebrating birthdays wasn't a Chechen tradition, so for many it was the first time they'd ever had a birthday cake or been made to feel so special. Many Russians living in Chechnya had also never had birthday parties, due to poverty and dysfunction in their families. What a tremendous delight it was to behold their beaming faces grinning from ear to ear, and their tears of happiness.

For Hava's birthday, I bought a cake and balloons, and brought chocolates as a present for her. I reached Mila's house and caught up with the family's news. Our dear church family soon started coming in – Larisa first, followed by Andrei.

That Friday, rumours of a second war were fresh in everyone's minds. After discussing it at length, we progressed onto other equally depressing topics, things that had happened around us that week. As we discoursed, a sickening feeling rose in the pit of my stomach. The fear and despair were contagious and beginning to drag me down too. For the sake of our sanity, I knew we needed to look to Jesus.

I exhorted them: "Let's focus on the Lord and worship Him."

Just as I said that, Karina arrived carrying her adorable baby son, brown locks sticking up and ruffled. The presence of children always brought life and joy, as they skipped cheerily and giggled throughout the house, thoroughly delighted to be together, and with the toys laid out for them.

The front door squeaked open again. Hava rushed in breathlessly, headscarf sliding off her dyed blonde hair, revealing grey roots. Breaking into a delightful smile, she was bursting to share her wonderful news: "I had an amazing time in the village I visited yesterday. I witnessed to some ladies, and they accepted Jesus into their lives." Our Hava was a breath of fresh air, radiating life and excitement and dispelling fear and despair.

Next to arrive was a young lady named Adel. She'd come to know the Lord through a dream: heaven opened and a stairway led up toward heaven. As she climbed up the stairs, she felt her soul leaving her body. Jesus stood at the top with outstretched arms. She took hold of His hand, and He showed her the New Jerusalem, then a terrifying glimpse of hell. As Jesus led her away from hell, a little boy grabbed her foot, but as her hand was firmly in the hand of Jesus, she thankfully managed to struggle free from the boy's grasp.

As I led worship on the piano, the Lord bestowed His presence on us. Larisa and Hava danced joyfully before the Lord. Everyone sang from their hearts. Some clapped. Mila and Farida wept as the Lord brought healing to deep wounds. Hope was renewed as God's light came in and strength was given for the journey ahead.

As I later shared from the Word, the Holy Spirit encouraged and uplifted us.

During my time in Chechnya, worship became a lifeline for me. Both corporate and personal worship times strengthened and renewed me. Sometimes when Larisa and I worshipped together at home, God would fill us with an incredible joy, the likes of which I'd never experienced elsewhere. We truly knew His joy as our strength, and we would dance unashamedly before our Lord, oblivious to bombing or gunfire in the background.

When alone on buses in dangerous situations, I found it helped (when it was possible to do so) to just close my eyes, listen to my Walkman, and be caught up in worship, knowing that my life was in His hands, regardless of what was happening around me.

Our dear Chechen friend Farida, from the refugee camp in the village nearby, was a regular attender, and on this particular Friday she rolled in embarrassingly late – as she often did, since she was running on 'Chechen time'! She'd brought her friend Hadizhat with her from the refugee camp.

I'd fallen in love with Nadia, Farida's gorgeous toddler, from the first moment I'd laid eyes on her. Little Nadia had fine, coppery hair and hazel-brown eyes. She was always so excited to see me, running with tiny hands held up, beaming at me expectantly, her sparkling brown eyes melting my heart. I would have done anything to make her life happier. I would pick her up, smother her with kisses, and carry her around on my hips for the rest of the visit. Often when new people came to our church, they thought Nadia was my daughter because she was always in my arms. I loved her as if she were my own.

That day little Nadia put her sticky little hands up to me as usual and I picked her up, threw her into the air, and then kissed her little tummy as she squealed with delight.

However, Farida showed me little Nadia's bottom which had a gaping hole in one of the cheeks, the result of a scar from an injection becoming infected. The needle had obviously not been disinfected properly; doctors and nurses worked in primitive conditions without the necessary equipment. We prayed for tiny Nadia, then Mila found some iodine and cleaned the wound.

A corporate ministry time ensued, when anyone who wanted prayer could be prayed for, which was usually the majority of our motley gathering.

Finally it was time to eat. We sang happy birthday to Hava and presented her with the chocolates and cake. She sliced it up with joyful anticipation. We encouraged Hava by sharing with her the things we liked about her and spoke blessings over her. Her entire countenance lit up as she felt so accepted, honoured, and special. It was the second time she'd ever celebrated her birthday; we'd also had a party for her the year before.

For the children (and for some of the adults), the best part of the meeting was the food. They stuffed their little faces as if there was no tomorrow. Nadia and the other toddlers would cram in so much that their tummies extended while we watched. I knew they didn't have much to eat, so I let them eat to their heart's content, even if it wasn't good for them.

After the food, the toddlers' bowels would relieve themselves. Since they weren't potty-trained and they had no nappies, they would defecate in their underwear or tights. A mighty stench would fill the house as they would all relieve themselves around the same time.

The mothers would then wash and disinfect the clothes by boiling them on the stove. Once at Mila's house, I went to pour myself some soup only to see that the boiling pot had cloths, underwear, and tights in it, not soup!

At the end of the meeting, we played a balloon game together, which the children especially relished. Hearing the children squealing with sheer delight always lifted our spirits, no matter what was happening.

Finally, about an hour before sundown, we all went our separate ways, uplifted and ready to face the coming week.

Our tiny church, in all its rawness, was a rare beacon of hope in a world gone crazy. Attracted to the light of Jesus, people were slowly but surely coming to faith.

The church didn't grow in numbers, however. People would become believers, spend time with us growing in faith, and then God would open a door for them to leave Chechnya. It was almost as if we had a revolving door.

In this way, most of our original church family left Chechnya. But small groups of new believers started springing up all over Chechnya, as seeds sown grew into a harvest.

For Reflection and Application

Pray for believers in the persecuted church. Pray for the Lord to encourage them, provide for them, protect them and give them His boldness and courage to keep sharing the good news no matter what the consequences.

Pray for fresh fire and boldness for yourself and for the Lord to open up opportunities for you to share the gospel where you live and work.

Chapter 12

THE BIBLE COMES ALIVE

I remember my affliction and my wandering,
the bitterness and the gall.
I well remember them, and my soul is
downcast within me.
Yet this I call to mind and therefore I have hope:
Because of the Lord's great love we are not consumed,
for his compassions never fail.
They are new every morning;
great is your faithfulness.
I say to myself, "The Lord is my portion;
therefore I will wait for him."

LAMENTATIONS 3:19-24

While living in Chechnya, I found the Bible coming alive as never before.

Most of the Bible was written to persecuted believers and I realise that, until you've lived under persecution, it's hard to understand the depths of comfort, peace, and joy to be found in the Scriptures.

In my first week in Chechnya, Dasha asked me to share at our church. As I prepared to speak, the Lord led me to the short book of Lamentations – and I found that it had never spoken so clearly to me before. It had always seemed such a depressing book, full of awful horrors. Suddenly, living in the middle of a war, I realised how comforting it actually was.

I sat in Mila's house looking around at the little group gathered as we opened our Bibles to Lamentations. I explained the book's background. "The story is about the final days of Jerusalem before the armies of Babylon destroyed her in 586 BC. Days extraordinarily similar to the worst horrors of the war here. Dark days full of terror. Let's read it through together and then see what verses jump out at us or speak to us. I want us to look through the book and see the similarities to our lives here."

We read selected portions of the book and discussed it together. I added more background information: "As the armies of Babylon advanced through the land of Judah, the word went out to enter the fortified city. Thousands of people entered Jerusalem, which was then besieged. The siege lasted from the winter months in Zedekiah's ninth year as king to the summer of his eleventh year, about eighteen months in an increasingly terrible situation. Just as the food supply failed, the siege engines of Nebuchadnezzar broke through the city walls, and the war was over. Most of the survivors were packed off to Babylon, but the poorest of the poor were left in the land."

When leading small-group Bible studies, the aim is to facilitate a discussion and create an environment where everyone feels safe to share their thoughts. Asking the right questions encourages everyone to look deeper into the text, allowing the Holy Spirit to reveal to each individual how to apply the truth revealed in the passage to their own lives. I've seen how much more effective this is in changing people's lives than if I just spoon feed them my thoughts on the subject.

Continuing, I invited them to look at the passage with me: "So let's look at some of the similarities between their time of siege and our own situation. First, the population of the city increased overnight. Imagine the impact of such drastically increased numbers, especially during a long siege. The makeshift shelters. People everywhere you looked. Does it remind you of the refugee camps? People living in bombed-out buildings and makeshift shelters? Making do wherever they were able to lay their heads to rest.

"What about water? Thankfully, Jerusalem had its own internal water supply. But for that number of people, it had to be rationed, and there wasn't enough. How do we know that?"

"You can see they were totally parched," Dasha observed. "Look at chapter 4, verse 4: 'Because of thirst the infant's tongue sticks to the roof of its mouth'."

"I've felt like that," Karina commented, "when we were out of water for days."

I went on. "Also, in the heat of summer, people wouldn't be able to keep themselves clean. Or their plates. Or their clothes. Or anything. Look at chapter 4, verse 8: 'But now they are blacker than soot; they are not recognised in the streets'."

Larisa noted, "Sounds like what we looked like during the height of the war, when the oil wells were burning, black smoke was in everything, and the fighting was so bad we couldn't go for water. It's amazing how similar it is to what we've experienced."

"Yes," Hava added, "we didn't recognise ourselves in the mirror, our faces were so black."

"And it's just like us having to wait for the Red Cross water truck to come round," Lilia said. "Sometimes it doesn't come every day, and then we're really stuck." They lived in a part of town where there was no fresh water anywhere. No pumps, wells, nothing.

"Food was also a big problem," I added. "No food could be brought into or out of the besieged city. Food was limited to whatever supplies the city had stored for such an emergency, and we know supplies ran out. Completely. For a long time. What verses tell us that?"

Larisa remarked, "Look at chapter 4, verse 10: 'With their own hands compassionate women have cooked their own children, who became their food when my people were destroyed'. They had it much worse off than us. Even in the darkest times, I never heard of that happening here." She shuddered at the thought.

"Another similar thing is the rubbish everywhere," Dasha observed. "I guess no one could really collect and take rubbish outside the city for disposal. Just like here, with piles of rubbish everywhere, since no one has taken it away for years, it seems."

"And probably," Marina noted, "smoke from burning rubbish choked the people in the besieged city. It's bad enough when our neighbours start to burn the rubbish, but I can't imagine it inside the walls of the city."

"And what about sickness?" I asked. "Imagine you have a city crowded with makeshift shelters of unwashed, malnourished people. You have a recipe for the rapid spread of disease. Just like in the refugee camps. Smallpox, diphtheria, whooping cough, measles – such diseases could erupt with nothing to stop the spread. And the worst part is the corpses. People died, some of natural causes, but many of diseases. What do you do with the dead?"

"Sounds like during the worst part of the war," Andrei commented, "when bodies were lying around everywhere." He shook his head at the remembrance. "We buried my dad in the backyard, and then reburied him when the fighting stopped."

"Yes, terrible," I gently responded. "No one should have to go through that. In Lamentations we don't know what they did with the bodies, but it was pretty desperate too. Perhaps they threw them over the city wall. Basically, the situation in the city became extremely desperate. Especially when food finally ran out."

I continued: "Someone, probably Jeremiah, who was there through the siege and fall of Jerusalem, wrote the book of Lamentations. He saw the destruction and the famine and the disease with his own eyes. He saw women eat their own children. In writing Lamentations, he was attempting to come to terms with those memories and God's place in it all. Lamentations is like a universal poem of grief, but also one of hope."

I brought it even closer to home, "Let me ask you: How did you feel when you saw bombs landing on your city? When you came back to the smouldering ruins of your home? Your region of the city? Imagine the city of Jerusalem burning, and that it was your home, and that it was the place where God's presence had resided in the Temple. And then Nebuchadnezzar had burned it all. How would you feel? How could you come to terms with it? And how did the author come to terms with all that was happening around him? Let's look at chapter 2, verse 19. It's one of the keys. Can someone please read it for me?"

'Arise, cry out in the night, as the watches of the night begin; pour out your heart like water in the presence of the Lord. Lift up your hands to him for the lives of your children.'

"So," I asked, "what do you think are the keys?"

"Cry out to the Lord," Karina answered.

"Pour out your heart to Him as water," Dasha replied.

"What do you think that means?" I asked.

"Well," Dasha added, "I guess it's telling Him how you feel, pouring out your pain and trauma and stress to Him."

"Yes, it's so important to pour out our hearts to Him and let Him know how we feel in reality – what is really going on. He can take it. We don't need to be afraid to be real and honest with Him. As we share our pain with Him, He's then able to take it and replace it with His comfort, peace, and joy. What else do we see the author doing in that verse?"

"Lift up your hands to Him," Larisa commented. "I guess that means worshipping Him and thanking Him in the midst of the trial."

"Yes, I think that's what it means," I agreed. "It's so important to take our eyes off the problem and onto Him, and to worship Him. Then we're able to enter His presence. As it says in Psalm 100:4, 'Enter his gates with thanksgiving and his courts with praise'."

I continued, "And I think the key to the whole book is found in the middle – in chapter 3, from verse 19 – 24: 'I remember my affliction and my wandering, the bitterness and the gall. I well remember them, and my soul is downcast within me. Yet this I call to mind and therefore I have hope: Because of the Lord's great love we are not consumed, for his compassions never fail. They are new every morning; great is your faithfulness. I say to myself, "The Lord is my portion; therefore I will wait for him."' What can we learn from this? What is the author doing here?"

"He's calling to mind the Lord's love."

"Remembering the good things the Lord has done previously."

"Thinking about His faithfulness in the past."

"Yes, it's all those things. What's amazing is that he remembers the bad things; he's living in horrendous reality, and yet in the midst of it, he's able to call to mind God's love. And that gives him hope. He takes his mind off the problems and onto God. And if that's possible for him in the midst of hell on earth, then how much more is it possible for us!"

I concluded with this: "Let's pray and ask the Lord to help us to do that. Let's pour out our hearts and grief to Him now. Give Him our pain and anguish. Be real and honest with Him. And then let's call to mind His love, worship and thank Him and allow Him to fill us with new life and strength."

As I sat and played the piano, our church family did business with the Wonderful Counsellor, the best counsellor in the world. Some were sobbing, others silently pouring out their hearts. And as we gave Him our grief, His comfort and joy filled us in the deepest places of our lives, giving us the strength to go on.

If Jeremiah could do it during the siege and destruction of Jerusalem – then so could we.

And so can you. With His help.

Chapter 13

EVERYDAY LIFE
IN CHECHNYA

He is no fool who gives what he cannot keep
to gain that which he cannot lose.

JIM ELLIOT[1]
(missionary martyr who lost
his life in 1956 trying to reach the
Auca Indians of Ecuador)

One icy December morning in late 1996, I was truly shocked as I looked in the mirror.

"I don't think my hair has ever been this greasy in my entire life."

It had been about ten days since I'd washed my hair or even had a proper wash.

Even by local standards, it was bitterly cold, with temperatures falling as low as twenty degrees below zero (Celsius). The flat was freezing; there was no heating, and the radiators were broken. A neighbour had created a makeshift fire for us, consisting of two open burners, hooked up to the gas, alight day and night in the living room – It would never be allowed in the UK!

Houses often burned down when makeshift fires were knocked over. Chest problems, from breathing in fumes, were rampant. Huddling around the stove and heater in our scarves and gloves, we tried to warm up.

The war had caused the infrastructure of the city to fall apart. By Soviet standards, Grozny used to be a modern city with a good standard of living. High-rises were purposely built when electricity, gas, and running water were the norm.

Living without running water in a modern city is complicated. The plumbing in most houses was designed to have hot and cold water flowing freely through the pipes. Entrepreneurs had taken advantage of this, selling buckets, water containers, basins, scoops, and bowls by the side of the road everywhere.

It was a common sight to see people carrying buckets of water from taps or pumps in the street to their homes. Everyone who lived in high-rises in Chechnya had their own tried and tested system of storing water. Having learned firsthand from being days without water during the first war, most kept reserves at hand.

Our flat was no exception. The whole house was full of covered buckets of water, and it was highly important to know which buckets were for which purpose, and not to get buckets or scoops mixed up. Each bucket had its own special plastic scoop. The kitchen had an almost spotless bucket, where water was used only for cooking purposes. The purest water was put in there. Next to it stood a jug of boiled water – our drinking water. In the bathroom was a bucket of clean water for washing. By the side of the toilet was a bucket where water was saved for flushing the toilet.

No water was ever wasted; every drop was precious when it had to be lugged up seemingly endless flights of stairs. The aim of any activity involving water was to use as little as possible.

Washing up economically and successfully was an art in itself. First, you waited until a number of dishes had piled up in the sink before doing the washing up. Once a pile had gathered, you could heat up the water in a metal bowl on the stove. When it was hot, you separated it into two bowls; in one you washed the dishes, in the other you rinsed. The ritual was incomplete until you poured the grimy dish water into the bucket in the toilet to be used for flushing.

There was a similar ritual for washing clothes. The only difference was that you needed more water, and at the end you poured the murky water into the bucket you used for washing the floor. Once you'd washed the floor with it, that water then got put in the toilet bucket. It added a whole new dimension to the concept of recycling.

Our designated shower day was a big event involving a lot of organisation. The first thing we did was to reorganise the buckets. We transferred water from one bucket to another so we could have four empty buckets to take downstairs. Next we put the kettle on so that in the event of the pipes being frozen, we could pour boiling water on the pipe to thaw it enough for us to collect water. Sometimes one kettle full of boiling water wasn't enough. When we found the pipes were frozen yet again, we poured boiling water onto the pipe and thanked God if this was enough to start the water flowing.

Rinsing out each of our buckets thoroughly was an important step before filling them up. As we filled up our four buckets, other people started to queue up for water.

If we arrived back at the house and found that the electricity was still not on, that meant the lift wasn't working – which solved the usual dilemma of do we or don't we take the lift. (When it was working, it was always a toss-up. On the one hand, it was wonderful not to have to carry weighty buckets of water up five flights of stairs. On the other, if there was a power cut after you'd already got into the lift it was no fun being stuck in the lift for hours or even days. At least if you were going to get stuck, it was better with full buckets of water than empty ones.)

On shower days, we had to go three times to fetch water instead of two. The first trip with two full buckets didn't seem too bad; the second time, you wondered if you'd make it; the third time, you had to stop every few seconds to rest.

With all the water gathered, Larisa would immediately start transferring water and putting one metal bucket of water on the stove to heat up for our shower. I really didn't know how she did it. I'd no energy to do anything except sit down.

While we waited for the water to heat up, we had *chai*, which warmed us up, giving us some energy.

Larisa and her mother had the first showers. Then it was my turn.

It was so cold in the bathroom in winter, I couldn't take all my clothes off in one go. I poured some hot water in the bath so I could bear to stand barefoot on the porcelain. Next I made up a hot bowl of water, taking water from both the hot and cold buckets. I washed the top half of my body first, with my clothes still on my bottom half. Then I reversed it. I had as good a wash as I could under the circumstances. Finally, when I was fully dressed again, I leaned over the bath and washed my hair. I came out of the bathroom freezing and almost squeaky clean. Well, clean enough for another ten days or so, unless of course I could have a bath at Mila's house.

Mila lived outside of town, meaning she often had running water. A boiler in her bathroom heated up the water splendidly. It was such a luxury to lie in a steaming bath, which I always thoroughly enjoyed.

For Reflection and Application

Do you have hot running water and an indoor toilet in your home? If so, thank the Lord for these blessings in your life that millions around the world do without.

Pray for any regions you know of that are lacking these basic necessities. Pray for God's Kingdom to come, for righteousness and justice to be established and for long-term solutions to break the cycle of poverty there.

Chapter 14

MILA'S FAMILY

All they asked was that we should continue
to remember the poor, the very thing
I had been eager to do all along.

GALATIANS 2:10

Mila's place soon became my second home.

Her house was situated just outside the city in a peaceful village. Well, peaceful most of the time. I enjoyed the company of Mila and her children, chatting and praying with her and playing with the children, and it was a great place to have a break, to soak in a lovely bath, and to wash my clothes in hot running water. She was the only person I knew with that luxury.

Mila worked at a local factory and, like most of the city, had not received any wages for months. Often when I arrived at their house, there wasn't much food around for such a growing family of five. The family did have a garden, with fruit trees and vegetables. They also had sacks of flour and sugar we'd bought them, and a few chickens, providing eggs and occasionally meat.

In 1996, when I first met Mila's son, Maksim, he was a shy, gangly thirteen-year-old. Still only a child, the responsibility he felt for his mother and sisters rested heavily on his slender shoulders. Every time I stayed the night, he prided himself on baking me an apple cake. Simple yet delicious, it touched my heart that a young boy would do something like that for me.

On special occasions, Mila slaughtered a chicken. Once, when

Mum came to visit, Mila found that her rooster had bleeding feet. "Oh no," she said, "the rooster must feel poorly, as the hens are pecking at it, poor thing. I'm going to have to kill it for us to eat now."

Mum, perturbed, pleaded, "Please don't kill the poor thing. We'll pray for it instead."

After praying for it, we left it in the corridor for the night to recover. We awoke the next morning to find it truly deceased. Cold and stiff. Not only had we not been able to eat it, but it died anyway. What a bummer.

Maksim was the only Russian boy left at his school. One morning when I stayed the night there, he came back from school half an hour after leaving the house.

"Why did you come back, son?" Mila asked him, concerned. "What happened?"

Pale as a sheet, he gave nothing away. He shook his head, uttering, "I'm never going to that wretched school again."

And he never did.

Later, he told us that Chechen schoolmates had threatened to kill him.

Maksim loved to be with us and was at every church meeting and outreach. Studious, he buried himself in any books he could get his hands on. I gave him an English-Russian dictionary, and he learned a few words every day until he picked up English.

I loved to worship using Mila's piano; the rest of the family also loved it, and we would often worship together. Maksim wanted to learn to play, so I taught him what I knew, and soon he'd learned to play beautifully.

When portable computers came in, Maksim was particularly interested when he saw mine, as he'd never touched a computer before. Again I taught him the basics, and soon he overtook me in his knowledge of computers.

One Friday we asked him to preach, and he did an excellent job, having researched his subject thoroughly.

Soon Maksim became our bodyguard, walking Larisa and I home

in the dark, even though it meant another hour-and-a-half walk for him back to his own home.

Irina, Mila's eldest daughter, was a shy, slim girl with chestnut brown cropped hair. During the first war, she had fallen pregnant and now was trying to cope with being a single mother in difficult conditions. Unfortunately, baby Varya was weak and malnourished and had problems in her back. I arranged for her to have surgery in Makhachkala.

The day of the surgery Irina, Varya, and I climbed onto the bus and started our journey to Makhachkala, usually only three hours. But not that day. Little did we know.

By the time we reached the border, it was firmly closed.

No one was allowed in or out of the country; the government was taking no risks after an attempted coup the day before.

We waited for an hour in the heat and dust among the crowds of men, women, and children, and the long queues of buses and cars.

I was in the midst of a long fast, and suddenly felt quite weak. I was drinking only fresh apple juice I'd made that morning, with juicy apples from their garden.

"Lord, please get us through soon. Please, Lord."

As Irina fed baby Varya by the side of the road, I watched the world go by: people trying to cross on foot and being turned back, a bus attempting to cross facing warning shots before it came to an abrupt halt.

Eventually we heard someone saying, "They're letting certain people through who have the right passports."

"Presumably Dagestani ones," I concluded to Irina. Feeling a prompt from the Holy Spirit, I suggested, "Let's risk crossing the border now." She nodded in agreement.

I prayed, "Jesus, please get us through without having to show documents or answer any questions." We headed toward the border as nonchalantly as possible. Everyone was being stopped and checked. We walked straight past all the soldiers, who paid no attention to us whatsoever, almost as if we were invisible.

"Thank You, Jesus," I cried.

An old man in a car showed up after the first border. We hailed him down and asked, "We need a lift, have you any room?"

He agreed to take us to the next border into Dagestan. That border was also virtually closed and crowded with people, buses, and cars. We waited in the queue as they endlessly checked all the people, lorries, and cars in front of us. When we reached them, they waved us through without checking us or our documents.

"Thank You, Jesus, for again doing a miracle for us."

Irina's baby had her operation and recovered remarkably well.

We bought a goat in another city for Mila's family, which she took back with her on the eight-hour train journey to Grozny. The goat provided milk. Not only did baby Varya flourish, but the rest of the family gained much needed weight from drinking fresh goat's milk every day.

Mila's second daughter was living in another city with her aunt and studying at a local school there. Mila's youngest daughter, who was eight in 1996, was severely disturbed and had learning difficulties. I spent time playing with her, reading to her, and praying over her for healing as she slept.

Mila's family were living testimonies of the fact that provision sometimes comes in unexpected, miraculous ways. One week when the bombing and fighting were particularly heavy, and they were down to virtually nothing, she cried out to the Lord for help. She had only seven thousand roubles left to her name (about a dollar and a half at the time). Only enough to buy three loaves of bread. She prayed, casting her cares upon the Lord, then put her remaining money on top of the broken television set.

In the middle of the night, she was wakened by a masked man with a machine gun trying to kidnap one of her daughters. As she jumped out of bed to rescue her daughter, she cried out in desperation to the only person she knew could defend her.

"O God, help!"

While begging the intruder to let go of her daughter, she

managed to grab him, pull him into the bathroom, and lock the door.

"I want a ransom in return for the life of your daughter," he demanded.

"I've sold all my jewellery to buy food," she told him. "All I've got left in the world is seven thousand roubles. It's on the TV set, you're welcome to take it."

He seemed surprised, "Is that all you have to feed your family?"

"Yes, I'm afraid it is."

"Alright, then, let me out of the bathroom and house."

Stepping outside, he handed her his machine gun. "Hold this for a minute," he said, searching his pockets.

"O God, he's looking for a knife to slit my throat," she thought.

After a few seconds, he pulled out a fifty-thousand-rouble note, handed it to her, and stated, "Buy some food for your family."

Taking back his machine gun, he apologised for disturbing her, and made a swift exit.

"Thank You, Lord, for Your protection and Your answer to my prayer for provision. I wasn't expecting it in such a dramatic way!" Mila said as she praised the Lord.

On another occasion, Mila was talking to the Lord: "I'd really like something tasty to eat, Lord, something like cheese, for instance." Dairy products were rare at the time, and she hadn't had cheese for months.

She headed out with her children on the hour-and-a-half walk from her house to our flat, where we were meeting for our service that week.

Spring was setting in, the long awaited, lovely, fickle, hesitant spring of southern Russia. Even in the midst of war, it brought miracles of new growth. Buds, fresh and green, popped out their cheery heads, birds chirped their merry songs, and welcome, fresh, yet warmer days lingered in a glory of colourful sunsets.

There was a rather unfortunate side of spring, however, in war-torn Grozny. The glorious, picturesque, spotless snow unceremoniously turned into deep puddles of murky, dank water, causing roads to become extremely hazardous. Cavernous bomb craters were hidden by the pools of water, and you could suddenly, without warning, disappear up to your eyes in water. At other times you tripped over rocks, concrete, and twisted metal lurking menacingly beneath the water, waiting for unsuspecting victims.

As the family slid along the road, the mellow rays of the sun reflected off a plastic bag. It seemed to contain a large object and was floating, minding its own business, in the middle of the puddle.

Mila turned to Maksim. "Go and get the bag for me, son, and see what's inside it."

Maksim, fifteen by this time, let out a snort of disdain. "It's not cool to go snooping in puddles for strange plastic bags. If you want it so badly, get it yourself."

Teenagers like to be cool even in war zones.

Wading through the puddle, Mila picked up the bag and discovered a large round piece of goat's cheese, deliciously mouth-watering, still unopened in its wrapping. Arriving at church, they shared the cheese with everyone, and all marvelled at God's amazing provision.

One time I sent Mila to Russia for an Ellel conference on healing and deliverance. I looked after her children while she was away.

Late one night, Maksim and I were having tea in the kitchen when we saw soldiers running in our direction. We heard gunshots, explosions, and loud metal bangs.

"Oh no, intense fighting has started up in our neighbourhood," I thought.

We quickly turned out the light in the kitchen so they would think there was no one in, and Maksim and I got under the kitchen table and waited, trembling in the dark. The shooting, explosions, and banging seemed to go on for ages, then finally stopped.

We emerged from under the table and drank our now cold *chai*. The next day, we found out there had been an eclipse of the moon, and the soldiers had been shooting, banging on all the gas pipes in the area including ours, and firing explosives into the air for superstitious reasons to keep the evil eye away.

Another time, I was relaxing in the bath, and a bomb exploded close by, rocking the whole house. Fear gripped me as I prayed that we would be okay, and that nothing would happen to Mila's children. I didn't know how I'd be able to look her in the eyes if anything happened to them while they were in my care. God answered my prayers, and the bombing stopped.

Unfortunately, one day in 1996, soldiers broke into their next-door neighbour's house. A Russian mother and daughter lived there. The soldiers murdered them and took their house. Mila and her family heard them screaming but could do nothing to help them. The following day, Mila found their poodles wandering around distressed and hungry and took them in.

Because of the dangers for Russian families living in Chechnya, I felt compelled to do something to help. I prayed and shared with the outside world what was happening. I believed God would somehow provide for these families to move to a safer place.

For Reflection and Application

Are you living in a country without war? If so, thank the Lord for the blessing of peace and safety. Pray for those living in war-torn countries to meet Jesus in the midst of their suffering and to find the true peace that only comes in Him.

Chapter 15

LOVING THE ONE IN FRONT OF YOU

Ministry, however, is simply
loving the person in front of you.
It's about stopping for the one
and being the very fragrance of Jesus
to a lost and dying world.

HEIDI BAKER[1]

Frantic knocking at the door wakened me.

"It can't be morning already, Lord."

The night had been too brief. It seemed we'd only just gone to bed. Hava, my friend from church, and I were up until about two in the morning, praying for Chechnya.

"*Otkroyte* – open up – it's only me," a familiar voice shouted frantically through the door.

My heart sank: "Oh no, what's happened now, Lord?"

Hava pulled her headscarf in place with one hand and put on her dressing gown with the other as she hurried to open the door.

"Have you seen the news?" her neighbour cried. "It's terrible. Absolutely terrible."

It was 17 December 1996. Six Red Cross workers, all doctors and nurses, were killed in cold blood – shot, effectively executed – while they were sleeping.[2]

I suddenly felt nauseous and very, very tired.

"Come and see the news."

We joined his family in crowding around the TV set. For the short time we had electricity, we all sat and cried together – locals, both Muslims and Christians, and one English missionary – horrified by the futility of it all.

Yeltsin declared that if the lawlessness didn't stop, he would send in troops again. Suddenly the TV screen went blank, the room dark. The electricity had gone, taking with it our precious contact with the outside world.

Hava was a fiery evangelist who shared her faith at every opportunity possible. Although hardship had aged her prematurely, making it hard to guess how old she really was (perhaps thirty-something or could she be fifty?) her open face and enchanting smile put you at ease immediately.

At eighteen, she'd been deeply in love with a friend from school and was hoping to marry him. But she'd had the misfortune of being kidnapped in true Chechen style and being forced to marry her kidnapper. She'd attempted to run away, but her family had taken her straight back to her husband as they deemed him more suitable than the man she loved. He in turn was heartbroken and they lost touch when he moved away to work in Siberia.

The marriage, as you can imagine, had not been a happy one but she had been blessed with four healthy children along the way. Her husband had been killed at the beginning of the first war. Although sad to be widowed, she was relieved to be free at last. No more abuse or control.

Her children were in the village being brought up by their grand-parents. According to Chechen tradition, in the event of death or divorce, the father and then the father's relatives have rights to the children; the mother has no say whatsoever in the matter. Hava made the most of the situation by throwing herself into prayer and evangelism.

She'd become a believer through a healing miracle. Having been diagnosed with a progressive debilitating disease, after various forms of treatment had failed to cure her, she'd been sent as a last resort to hospital for an operation.

The doctor had warned her, "There's not much hope of you completely recovering, you know, medically speaking." But he added, "I'm a believer in Jesus, and I know that God can heal you. Can I pray for you in the name of Jesus?"

She was shocked to the core that he, a Muslim man by birth and culture, could declare that he was a believer in Jesus. But she agreed to let him pray for her. He did, then gave her a Bible and encouraged her to read it.

Hava made a swift recovery, much to the surprise of everyone except her doctor. Reading the Bible, she found it made sense.

When the bombing started in her town, she realised she needed to get serious about God and started to look for a church. On her way to church, she bumped into dear Larisa, who explained to her how to get right with the One who loved her so much, who'd died to give her new life. As shells exploded around them, they knelt down and prayed together, and Hava made her peace with God.

Just as a tiny pebble tossed nonchalantly into a humongous pond is unaware of the far-reaching ripples it will create, in that moment Hava couldn't even begin to imagine the impact this simple decision would have on her own life and on the scores of men, women, and children who would be touched through her witness. As she got up off the ground, all she knew was that she felt lighter than she'd ever felt in her entire life. Her face radiated the newfound joy welling up within her.

Her faith was tested almost from the start. When her family found out she'd become a believer in Jesus, they decided – as is too often the case in fundamentalist Muslim families – that she needed to be put to death because she'd betrayed the family name. News reached her that her brother was on his way to kill her. She fled to Larisa's house. Quickly Larisa arranged for her to go to Moscow. She ended up studying in a Bible school there for a year, which she thoroughly enjoyed.

When her brother found out she'd gone to Moscow, the family gathered together to discuss what to do. Her father managed to persuade her brother that she was just a silly woman and that it was only a phase she would grow out of. After a year of being away, she realised the storm had blown over, and it was now safe to come home. Her family no longer wanted to kill her.

She invited us to go to her village to share with her parents. We went with much fear and trepidation.

But it was so much better than we'd expected. Her parents, a kindly elderly couple, received us warmly into their home and hearts. We offered to show the *Jesus* film, which they watched with great interest. Her father, in particular, was powerfully touched when we prayed for him.

On the way back home from the village, as we stood by the side of the road waiting for a bus, we heard people discussing how three foreigners had been kidnapped from that very bus stop the previous day. "Thank You, Jesus, that we're here today and not yesterday. And please help those kidnapped to meet You in a real way."

In the darkest places, the light shines more brightly, and I knew I was there to shine the light of God's love. So on that clear and frosty winter morning when we heard of the loss of the Red Cross workers, even though my heart was grieved for them, and I was unable to do anything about the political situation, I knew I could make a difference in the lives of those He'd put in front of me.

I could be the love of God to Hava in a concrete way. Being Jesus' hands and feet to her, I helped her fetch water and carry it up to her fourth-floor apartment. I could also be Jesus' hand of provision for her by going to buy bread, *chai,* and sugar for breakfast.

When I'd arrived at Hava's place the night before, she had absolutely nothing at all to eat or drink in the house.

"I'm fasting," she explained.

I knew she was fasting not purely for spiritual reasons but because she had nothing in the house. So I was glad the Lord sent me at just the right time when she needed provisions.

After breakfast, we walked to the refugee camp on the outskirts of town, stopping at the market to pick up food for the camp. Again

I knew I could be Jesus' hands, feet, and mouthpiece that day in the refugee camp, by bringing them food, His love, and His Word.

Every week, Larisa and I conducted a Bible study in one of the small metal huts. We discussed different topics from the Bible that were relevant to our lives and prayed for each other to experience His touch. Afterward we enjoyed the tea and treats we'd brought. As we drank *chai,* we listened to their stories, prayed with them, and were a shoulder to cry on. Every week we went around to different huts visiting the many precious people whom we'd come to love so dearly.

One elderly man in the camp had an interesting comment one time when I arrived: "Have you heard the ancient Chechen prophecy that Chechnya would be saved through the English?"

"*Niet* – no, I haven't actually."

"Well, maybe it was talking about you. I've been waiting for salvation to come through the English."

Isn't it extraordinary that such a prophecy would be uttered, which may have prepared the hearts of some Chechens to believe the message. Over the years, I heard from a number of elderly Chechens about this prophecy.

There was a lot of work to be done in Chechnya. The harvest was plentiful and the labourers few (Luke 10:2). God had equipped me for the momentous task and was teaching me to receive from Him day by day, so that I had something to give these precious people with such overwhelming needs. To love the person in front of me. And in that way allowing His love to change the nation. One person at a time.

Chapter 16

THE CALMER
OF STORMS

Who is this? Even the wind and waves obey him.

MARK 4:41

When a train goes through a tunnel and it gets dark,
you don't throw away the ticket and jump off.
You sit still and trust the engineer.

CORRIE TEN BOOM [1]

After the visit to the refugee camp that afternoon, I decided to visit a friend an hour's walk away. Maka, an intelligent stylish woman in her fifties, lived in the centre of town, a region badly damaged by bombing. Although a Muslim by culture, she was interested in knowing more about Jesus.

Her daughter and son-in-law were killed in the first war. Taking in her orphaned grandchildren, she couldn't face telling them their parents had died, so she made up a story: "Mummy and Daddy have gone away on a business trip, and you'll be staying with us for now." A year and a half later, they still couldn't bring themselves to tell the children the truth about their parents.

Soon after their tragic loss, when Maka thought things couldn't become any worse, she was slapped in the face again. By a bomb. Blowing her own house to smithereens. She and her husband lost nearly everything. Home. A lifetime of irreplaceable things. Their extensive library. All their photo albums. They were especially sorrowful at having no photos left of their beloved daughter or of their son-in-law. Not one.

When I arrived, her husband opened the door. "Sorry, Maka's not in," he informed me. "You're welcome to wait though. She should be home soon."

I especially wanted to see her, so I decided to wait. By the time she arrived home, it was 3.30 pm. The shadows were lengthening as dusk slowly faded in. I needed to leave promptly if I was to make the hour-long walk home before curfew. They invited me to stay the night, and I readily agreed. We talked for hours about the Bible, Jesus, and the power of forgiveness, a totally new concept to them. They'd grown up with blood revenge being the norm.

Before going to bed we watched the news, where it was announced that all aid agencies were pulling out of Chechnya as a response to the murder of the six Red Cross workers. And Yeltsin declared that as the Chechen fighters hadn't surrendered, he was going to wipe Grozny off the face of the earth. And here I was, a sitting duck, in the centre of Grozny.

Suddenly a power cut engulfed us in smothering darkness. The only light was the faintest slither of moonlight peeking through a gap in the curtains. My soul also felt smothered by the darkness of the situation, as if I were drowning in pure terror. It was almost too overwhelming for me.

"I'm the only foreigner left in the country. And the place where I'm sitting soon won't exist."

Chills went up my spine. I started praying: "O Lord, please don't let the fighting start tonight. If it starts tonight, when I'm staying downtown, I would be right in the centre of it. I also would not be with the people I would choose to be with during a bombing campaign – my close believing friends who I can pray with. Lord, please, not tonight."

Maka and her husband retired to the other room, and I dropped wearily on their sofa, feeling as if a lead weight was lodged in the pit of my stomach.

Sleep eluded me. I tossed and turned for hours as a violent storm of fear and terror threatened to tear my soul apart.

Have you ever been in a situation like this, where you felt so terrified you were almost overwhelmed? It seems like unless a miracle happens, you're a goner. And it doesn't look like one is coming any time soon, as Jesus doesn't seem to be there for you.

That's more or less how I was feeling that night. And in Mark 4:35-41, the disciples were also having one of those moments.

They'd had an extremely busy day, helping their Master teach the crowds and heal the sick, and learning from Him as He went about His Father's business. Finally, as the crowds were heading home for the night and the last magnificent rays of sunshine reflected gloriously off the rapidly darkening Sea of Galilee, Jesus, worn out from the day's activities, stepped into the boat.

"Let's cross to the other side of the lake," He instructed them, yawning and reaching for a cushion. He proceeded to make Himself comfortable, then promptly fell into a deep sleep. Probably dreaming of sharing His heart with His Father in heaven as they walked along golden streets together, enjoying one another's company. Seemingly completely oblivious to what was happening on earth. Or maybe just completely at rest, because Jesus knew the outcome of this boat trip, and that all would be okay.

After He nodded off, a storm started brewing, which sometimes happens out of the blue on that Sea of Galilee. Some of his men were hardened professional fishermen. Their thick calloused hands had navigated their boats safely through countless storms. They could handle it. Knew exactly what to do. It was a piece of cake.

Thunder rumbled in the distance and lightning cracked up the increasingly ominous sky filled with angry black clouds. The wind started to howl, the rain to pound, as a furious squall whipped up. Suddenly, gigantic waves battered against the boat, almost swamping it. Gale-force winds knocked them down. This was a storm from the pit of hell. A thousand times worse than usual.

I'm sure you've been through your own personal storm from

hell, just as we all have. Even if it's under a completely different set of circumstances.

The furious panic of doing all you can to sort out the situation. Using your own hands, and then buckets to try and get the water out of the boat. Getting soaked to the skin as the icy water hits you in the face time and time again, freezing you to the bone and stinging like crazy. And in spite of all your best efforts, the water level in the boat is only rising higher and higher, until you're almost swimming in it. Holding on for dear life as the boat rocks so precariously, you're almost thrown overboard. Throwing up the contents of your stomach so many times, you feel like your insides are coming out. Finally realising there's nothing more you can do. It's futile to do anything.

Your life flashes in front of you as you say goodbye in your heart to your loved ones. You suspect this is it, this time.

But God.

Oh yes, God.

Jesus?

How could we have forgotten?

Where was Jesus? Fast asleep. Snoring loudly. How could He sleep right through this? "Jesus, You really picked a good time to take a nap!" you think.

His men frantically shook Him. "Wake up, Jesus, don't you care if we drown?"

"Jesus, don't you care?" It's a universal cry of the human heart. How many times have you asked Him this?

And how does He respond?

That night on the stormy sea, He got up and rebuked the wind and the waves, and they immediately calmed. Effortlessly.

It turns out He *does* care. Deeply. Enough to do something about the storm and turn the whole situation around.

And I desperately needed Him to calm my storm that night.

In the midst of the nauseating fear, I suddenly heard the Lord speaking into my heart: "Paula, my precious girl, you have a choice.

You can either dwell on the fear and 'fellowship' with it, or choose to fellowship with Me."

I remembered that I'd heard something similar from a missionary in Burundi, about how God helped her deal with her fear during the war there. I knew that if God could help her, He could help me too.

"Lord, I want to fellowship with You!" This was the cry of my heart.

Suddenly I was enveloped with a profound peace that penetrated the depths of my being. Jesus had calmed the storm, and all the fear and turmoil were gone. In one moment.

I felt exhilarated. Totally refreshed, as if I'd been on a long, relaxing holiday. I wanted to spin around and whoop up and down for joy.

"Lord, you're so good. I love you so much." I smiled at my Beloved.

"I love you, too, My precious girl. You're going to be okay. Even though the other agencies have pulled out, I'm calling you to serve Me here, and I'll be with you. You're safe with Me."

I eventually fell into a deep sleep, to the sounds of gunfire resounding close by. I marvelled, as Jacob did in Genesis 28:16: 'Surely the Lord is in this place, and I was not aware of it.'

How often we're unaware of God's presence because we're too focused on the storm. When we finally turn to look for Him, He opens our eyes to see that in fact He was right there all along. Closer than our very breath.

In the next couple of days, the crisis blew over, and full-scale war was averted, at least for the next three years or so.

Do you feel battered by storms raging around you? Is the cry of your heart to know deep peace which seems so elusive?

Jesus invites you to take your eyes off the rising waters and look to Him, the Calmer of storms. The One even the wind and waves obey. The Prince of Peace.

He, who calmed the storm 2,000 years ago, is the same, yesterday, today and forever (Hebrews 13:8), and is fully able to calm *your* storm today.

If you'll just turn to Him.

Chapter 17

ONE SUPERNATURAL WHITE CHRISTMAS

Some wish to live within a sound of a chapel bell,
I wish to run a rescue mission within a yard of hell.

C T STUDD, MISSIONARY TO
ASIA AND AFRICA (B 1860)[1]

Winter had truly set in. In most of Russia there was never a need to dream of a white Christmas; it's always a given. In southern Russia, however, because of a generally warmer climate, it's a bit hit-and-miss.

The winter of 1996–1997, however, was a true Russian winter in all its glory, one of the coldest in memory, with drifts of crisp, fresh snow carpeting the ruins of the city in a bridal-white, pristine blanket, giving it the air of a charming fairy-tale wonderland.

Mum was coming to join us for Christmas, and everyone was looking forward to seeing her again. Especially me.

This was her first trip inside Chechnya. Arriving in Grozny with Dasha in a taxi, she took in the scene, excited about what God was going to do.

"You know," Dasha told her, "there aren't many foreigners in Chechnya. They don't like to come here that often."

Mum, full of trust in the Lord and a tad naïve, turned to Dasha with a puzzled look on her face. Mulling it over, she asked, "But why don't foreigners want to come to Grozny?"

Dasha wondered how in the world to explain it without scaring her. Finally she said, "Well, it's because they can get killed."

"Oh," replied Mum, completely unfazed. "I see."

The whole church, around fifteen of us, gathered at Mila's house on New Year's Eve to celebrate and pray together.

The feast, spread out Asian-style on a tablecloth on the floor, consisted of all the goodies everyone had brought: salads, chicken, fruit compote, jam, cake, and biscuits. We allowed our creative juices to flow, as we transformed the children's faces with the face paints we'd been given, into wild animals, silly clowns, and exotic flowers. Amid eruptions of laughter, we played games together, then sat down on the floor to dine in style.

As the New Year came in, we thanked God for the old year and blessed the new one.

Persistent knocking, just after midnight, brought us abruptly back down to earth out of our lovely prayer time.

"It's after curfew; it must be soldiers," I instantly thought.

"Maybe it's just a *zachistka* – a house search," someone reassured us.

Sure enough, Chechen soldiers shouted through the door: "Open up, now!"

Mila sighed with a resigned look. "They're going to break the door down anyway if I don't open it." Fed up with soldiers breaking the door down, she opened it; at least now she wouldn't have to fork out the money to repair it.

We were greeted by the sight of two machine guns pointing at us as two young Chechen fighters stepped into the house.

Mum took one look at them and suggested brightly, "Let's offer them a nice cup of tea," as if they were English plumbers who'd popped in to mend our toilet.

"Mum," I whispered, "it's best not to speak English now. And I think it would be a good idea to pray."

"Oh," she replied, and we prayed under our breath.

Fortunately the fighters hadn't heard us speaking English; they were too busy scanning the room, surprised to see such a crowd.

"We're looking for Hadizhat and her baby who've been reported missing. Her husband advised us she might be here."

Hadizhat had recently become a believer and had promised to come, but for some reason she hadn't made it to the celebration.

"No, actually, they're not here."

Farida suddenly recognised one of the soldiers. "Zelimkhan – you're Zelimkhan, aren't you? Imagine that! We attended school number four together. Do you remember me? I'm Farida."

Astonishingly, he remembered, and they started chatting in Chechen. After a while, the soldiers apologised for disturbing us, and left. We rejoiced at God's goodness in rescuing us again. This time by somehow arranging in His providence for the fighter trying to break down our door to be an acquaintance. How on earth does He manage to pull these things off so often! Isn't He just so amazing?

Hadizhat and her baby showed up safely the following day, much to everyone's relief. Her inebriated husband had chased her with a sharp metal object, and she had hidden with her baby in the basement for the night.

If I close my eyes, I can still vividly picture Russian Christmas Eve, 6 January 1997, a clear and frosty night. As big stars shone over the silent neighbourhood, and the glistening moon cast silvery shadows on the snow-powdered apple trees in Mila's garden, Dasha, Mum, and I had a glorious time of prayer, asking God to reveal Himself to the precious people around us through dreams and visions.

Christmas morning dawned, a wonderful, expectant winter morning. After a delightful Christmas service, we headed home, full of bright-eyed wonder, singing festive songs.

Our joy overflowed even on the bus as we sang carols, and Hava boldly shared the true Christmas message. Normally it would be madness to be so open, especially with a Chechen fighter on the bus. But God gave us favour on that heavenly Christmas Day, and the people listened attentively.

As we stepped off the bus, a middle-aged lady got off behind us. "Do you have a Bible?" she asked, without waiting for our answer. More words flowed excitedly from her mouth: "My neighbour popped round this morning saying she saw a vision last night. She woke up in the middle of the night to see a man in white standing by her bed. She wasn't sure who he was. Mind you, neither would I, if I had a man in white show up in my room! Would you? So she asked him, 'Who are you?' And you'll never guess what he replied. He said he was the angel – gosh, what was his name again? Oh yes – Gabriel. Gabriel, that's it. And he said he'd been sent by God to bring her some good news. Can you imagine that? An angel sent to bring her good news. 'Find some believers in Jesus,' he told her, 'and find a Bible.' And what else was it? Oh yes: 'On a certain page of the Bible, you'll find the answer to the most important question in your life.'"

She continued, barely taking a breath: "My neighbour doesn't know who Gabriel is, but knows that he was definitely an angel sent from God. In the morning, she rushed over to my house to tell me. And then – imagine what a coincidence – I bumped into you guys on the bus! Do you have a Bible you could give me for her?"

"Of course," Hava responded, joyfully giving away her own Bible.

We walked away with a fresh spring in our step, rejoicing at God's wonders in our midst, and amazed at how He answered our prayers so quickly.

For Reflection and Application

Have you ever asked God to reveal Himself to people through dreams and visions? Have you personally heard testimonies of this happening?

I encourage you to pray for this right now. You never know who may have a visitation today as a result of your prayer. Pray for the Lord to send dreams and visions to any region or people group He lays on your heart.

Chapter 18

CORPORATE PRAYER AND FASTING

*The prayer of a righteous person
is powerful and effective.*

JAMES 5:16

The destiny of nations has been changed through corporate prayer and fasting. Nations going in one direction can be turned around. Completely. Both in the Bible, and in history.

A great example is found in the book of Esther. We think we have it bad sometimes, but poor Queen Esther was having more than a bad hair day. In fact, it was probably the most serious thing she'd ever have to face. Or anyone would, for that matter. Her people, the Jewish people, were threatened with being wiped off the face of the earth, and she was the only person who could possibly make a difference.

And she knew it. She'd been placed in the palace for such a time as this. But she needed divine favour. And courage. And wisdom to play her cards right.

She and her friends fasted for three days. Without food or water. God answered their plea, and Esther was able to successfully petition her husband, the king, on behalf of her people to have the right to defend themselves. God turned the situation completely around, and the Jewish people were saved from annihilation.

In 2 Chronicles 20, Judah's King Jehoshaphat was also having a particularly bad morning. Three armies had surrounded his nation to make war against them. He did what anyone in their right mind would do under the circumstances: proclaim a fast to inquire of the Lord. The whole nation – from grown-ups to the tiniest little ones – took part in the fast. The Lord answered, giving them a unique strategy: to praise and worship their way to victory.

As they worshipped, the Lord sent an ambush against the enemy armies. Without having to lift a finger to fight, the enemy were completely defeated. Dead bodies littered the fields as far as the eye could see. And the enormous amount of plunder left behind took them three days to collect. Three glorious days rejoicing in God's goodness.

Other examples from history are found in Derek Prince's book *Shaping History through Prayer and Fasting*[1]. His book introduced me to this idea initially and gave me the faith to believe for it in my own life.

Once, in 1997, a coup was prevented from happening right in front of my eyes. I believe the only logical explanation was the fasting and prayers of the corporate body of Christ in the region.

It all started during the summer of 1997, when Mum sent me a tape from Mike Bickle calling people to a forty-day fast. I felt God was asking us to join them, and so I shared the tape with Dasha. The Lord put a burden on Dasha's heart, and in turn, she invited all the churches in the Caucasus to join us.

We planned the forty-day fast to cry out for revival in the Caucasus, and for peace in Chechnya. To start the fast off with a bang, we held a prayer conference in the mountains. It's good we didn't know how much of a bang it was going to be!

The battle was intense right from the beginning. For days there were massive downpours of rain, and the rivers were overflowing their banks. Just reaching the conference was almost impossible, involving wading up to our waists through an icy cold river just to reach the camp. When we arrived, we found that not only was it an unheated summer camp, it was also damp, dingy, and drab.

But God was with us, and the fellowship was sweet – the most important things in life. What more do you really need to be happy?

Representatives from eleven different cities had joined us, excited and expectant of what God was going to do.

That first afternoon, the delegates who arrived early collected mushrooms for our last meal together before the long fast.

Before dinner, I taught the first session on intercession. At that time, I knew virtually nothing about intercession. I still don't know much more now. However, I'd pulled a few thoughts together to share with them. Unfortunately, as is often the case in foreign countries, to them I was the famous anointed foreigner, so the three cooks were in a hurry to prepare the dinner so they could hear the teaching. They sorted through the mushrooms quickly. Too quickly.

The meeting went well. After enjoying our last supper of fried mushrooms and chips, we wrapped ourselves in all the clothes we'd brought with us, plus our towels, in an attempt to keep warm. We crawled into the freezing dormitory with its not-so-welcoming sagging wire beds.

In the middle of the night, I woke up feeling overwhelmed with sickness. Queasy to the point of throwing up. Horrendous pain in my stomach. "O Lord, I think I'm going to throw up," I thought.

I tried to get out of bed in the dark but the mattress was sagging so much, I kept falling back into it. Finally with all my strength I flung myself out of bed and realised how light-headed I was.

"I think I'm going to pass out. Jesus, help me."

I stumbled past my sleeping roommates and stepped outside. On other nights, it had been almost pitch-black outside. There were no villages or roads nearby with lights; we were literally in the middle of nowhere. On one occasion, in such inky blackness, I'd almost fallen down the hole in the outhouse.

That night, thankfully, the moon provided a little light. I practically crawled to the outhouse, where I simultaneously threw up and had diarrhoea. When I felt a bit better, I headed back to bed. After lying down for a few minutes, I felt nauseous again. I headed outside and this time didn't make it to the toilet but found some grass nearby.

All night, I violently threw up until I was so exhausted, I could hardly move. My insides seemed to be coming out. I felt like a tube of toothpaste completely squeezed out until absolutely nothing was left.

"O God, I think I'm going to die."

A few times, I noticed other delegates out there who seemed to have the same problem. However, we all felt too poorly to talk to each other.

It suddenly dawned on me: "It's mushroom poisoning! Satan wants to take us out. Most of the key intercessors from all over the Caucasus are here."

A boldness from heaven rose up in my spirit as I took responsibility as a leader. I declared out loud: "You spirit of death, I command you to leave me and the others in the name of Jesus. I speak life into myself and all the delegates at the conference. I forbid you from taking any of us out."

With God's help, I made it through the night.

In the morning, we found out that half of the delegates had been unwell during the night. And it was indeed a case of mushroom poisoning.

The cooks had accidentally cooked some poisonous mushrooms along with the edible ones. Apparently, this type of Russian mushroom is so poisonous, people have died after eating it.

Half of the conference could have died. But that day, God healed us. Every one of us.

The fast turned out to be significant. More significant than we realised at the time. History was changed as we stood in the gap for our precious Caucasus region.

The situation in Chechnya was highly unstable when we arrived home. Rumours of war and coups had been making the rounds for weeks.

Less than a month earlier, we'd celebrated Chechnya's independence day on 6 September 1997, much to the chagrin of Russia, as they didn't recognise Chechnya as an independent country.

Thousands celebrated on the streets of Grozny in a massive street party, while guns and tanks fired wildly into the air. People queued up to pose for photos with famous Chechen fighters. Larisa and I climbed up onto a tank and had our photo taken with some fighters.

At one point, as we turned a corner, we almost jumped out of our skin, as a tank fired into the air right behind us, and something whizzed seemingly just over our heads. We turned to see who was shooting at us and were relieved to see it was just soldiers letting their hair down – not anyone actually trying to kill us! But I still prayed the bullets didn't land on anyone's head.

In the square, we recognised Raduyev, a thin young Chechen leader with dark glasses and an excessively long black beard, surrounded by bodyguards. He was heading in our direction. I pulled out my camera and tried to take a photo. One of the bodyguards fired some warning shots in the air to warn me off. I handed the camera to Larisa, hoping she'd manage to sneak in a shot. As she tried, the bodyguard started shooting all around her feet. We got the message and put the camera away!

When we arrived home, we popped into Malika's house. The news was on, and to our surprise, we saw that it was the day of Princess Diana's funeral. I was shocked, as I hadn't known. In those days, I still rarely heard news from the UK. I felt gutted for Diana's children and so wished I could be in the UK at that time. On so many occasions I'd missed historical events in Britain. Instead I'd been part of historical events in the country I'd chosen to call home. Such was missionary life.

Malika remarked sadly, "So many thousands of people weeping over the death of one young lady in the UK, and no one notices or even cares about the death of thousands of our young ladies here in Chechnya."

Unfortunately, so true.

We were also perturbed to hear that Mother Teresa had died the previous day.

About a month after the mushroom incident, we were in the middle of this forty-day season of prayer and fasting. We woke up to hear Aunty Asya warning us, "They cautioned us on the radio this morning not to go out. There's going to be a *perevarot* – a coup. Don't go out, girls."

I'd organised a day-long prayer meeting that day for Chechnya and had invited believers in Jesus from all denominations to join us.

Nothing was going to stop me reaching that prayer meeting. I was the one who'd invited everyone to come, and I knew I had to be there.

The streets were completely deserted. Not a soul in sight. The bus was running, but it was uncannily empty.

"I suppose everyone sane is at home sitting it out. No one else will probably brave the streets to come to the prayer meeting. But You'll be there, Lord, so it will be worth it anyway."

As we wound our way to the central square, we suddenly heard lots of noise and commotion and came upon hundreds of armed men having what was known as a *meeteeng*[2] – a large political gathering. One of the rebel leaders, Basayev, was attempting to take over the government. A burden to pray for peace rose up in me.

"What a perfect day You've chosen, Lord, for us to pray and fast together!"

A few brave souls ventured out that day for our prayer meeting. As well as from our lovely church, representatives from the Orthodox Church, the Pentecostal Church, and another Charismatic house group also came. We wept together on our knees, crying out for our nation for about five hours, as we experienced His presence tangibly and undeniably.

"*Stranno* – how strange – it's still awfully quiet out there," I noticed, as we finished praying.

On the way home, the streets were deserted. A woman approached us and asked if we knew what was happening.

"*Niet* – no, we don't, we were wondering ourselves."

As we drove past the square where the crowds had been gathered, it was deserted. Completely. The evening news reported that for some unexplainable reason the coup had been unsuccessful.

"Maybe a tea party had seemed like a better option. Thank You, Jesus!"

The Lord faithfully answered our prayers and prevented more bloodshed. The fervent effective prayer of a righteous man avails much (James 5:16), especially when brothers and sisters of various denominations pray and fast together in unity.

In June of 2000 I felt God calling us to do another corporate fast for Chechnya. A number of believers from our church did a three-week Daniel fast, where we ate only fruit and vegetables. This was followed by an Esther fast – three days without food or water – praying for peace in Chechnya. We joined with friends in Israel and Kosovo also doing an Esther fast and crying out for peace in their nations.

Once again, it was an amazing time. I was in Grozny for the end of the Daniel fast with a small group of believers. During the Esther fast, we spent most of the day praying together.

God's hand of protection was evident during the fast, answering our prayers in a tangible way. The first day of the Esther fast, we prayed together at a friend's house. On arriving home, weak and exhausted from the combination of not eating or drinking anything and the extreme heat and humidity, we went to take a nap, and promptly dropped off. I awoke suddenly, finding myself in the air, then landing back heavily onto the bed. What on earth had happened?

Stunned, Larisa and I both looked at each other and dashed into the living room.

It turned out that a minibus full of explosives had blown up just across the road from our house. Militants had targeted a passing Russian convoy of soldiers, tanks, and trucks. Our whole building shook from the force of the explosion.

We peeked out of the living room window and saw mounds of black smoke rising. Suddenly a burst of gunfire reverberated through the courtyard, breaking the eerie silence. One soldier seemed to be shooting directly at us.

"Quickly, girls!" Aunty Asya hollered. "Get away from the window and into the corridor. Now!" She beckoned us to join her. We sheltered in the corridor between apartments until the shooting stopped. It turned out that the Russian soldiers left alive started shooting randomly in every direction at anything moving and at all the houses in the neighbourhood.

Later we found out that all who'd been at our prayer meeting had arrived home safely just before the explosion and ensuing shootout.

Many others were not so fortunate, however. Besides the soldiers killed and wounded, other victims had been innocent bystanders, students coming home from the university, and ladies selling goods by the side of the road. Our neighbour's boys, who had nothing to do with the explosion but had foolishly gone out onto the street to see the action, were rounded up by soldiers and disappeared. One of them had just been bought back by his parents after being arrested a few months previously.

During this time, the Russian army killed one of the rebel leaders, Barayev. A man known for his cruelty, Barayev had been involved in the murder of many, including the beheading of the four foreign engineers in 1999. After he was killed, his parents wanted to take his body home to be buried, but the Chechen people were so fed up with violence and lawlessness that the local villagers refused to let his body be brought into the village for burial.

Many of Larisa's neighbours noticed a difference in the atmosphere during the fast. "You should spend your whole time fasting!" they quipped.

During that trip, I met with new believers. People were becoming believers in different cities and villages all around us. Larisa and I had the privilege of visiting them, listening as they shared their hearts, rejoicing with them over testimonies of God's work in their midst, and praying and studying the Scriptures together. What an encouragement they were to us too, as we shared together. Their quiet, simple faith was an inspiration in the midst of the darkness.

These believers were cut off from the outside world. Living without electricity, TV, newspapers, or telephone lines. All they'd known for the last seven years was violence and lawlessness. Day in and day out. Many had never met believers from outside. Or ever seen a foreigner who wasn't a fighter. Not once in their lives. So you can imagine what an encouragement it was for them to meet us and to hear that believers around the world were praying for them. Not only praying, but some were even fasting with them for their country. Their faces beamed. The corners of their eyes moistened. They were so grateful to know they weren't alone. Or forgotten.

For Reflection and Application

Are there any areas of your life that are seemingly hopeless? Have you ever tried fasting from food or from something else important to you – like TV, the internet, chocolate, or coffee – in order to ask God for a breakthrough in that area of seeming hopelessness?

Has God given you a burden for any particular region of the world where believers in Jesus are persecuted? If so, as well as praying for them, you could contact a mission working in those areas, like Open Doors, and send a letter to let believers there know they're not alone. Don't underestimate the difference one letter or prayer can make in someone's life.

Chapter 19

REFUGEES, TINY AND ANCIENT

A father to the fatherless, a defender of widows,
is God in his holy dwelling.
God sets the lonely in families.

PSALM 68:5-6

Jesus has a special place in His heart for refugees. Especially for the little ones.

After all, don't forget He's got personal experience. He knows only too well what it's like. Growing up hearing stories of His family's miraculous escape in the dead of night. Stealing away in the nick of time. With just the clothes on their back and their lives. Living in Egypt as a political refugee.

We saw Jesus, the suffering refugee child, in the eyes of the darling children in the urban refugee camp. And they saw Jesus, the King of love, in our eyes as we showered them with love.

Rows of metal huts, converted into living accommodation, with a tiny bedroom, living room, and kitchen, housed families whose homes were destroyed in the war. Shared public outhouses were situated just outside the camp. Teenage girls and women were constantly carrying buckets from the water pumps not too far from the camp and hunting for wood to make fires for warmth and cooking.

Soon after Dasha introduced me to the camp, we paid for gas to be put into the huts, making their lives much easier.

Kheda, a medium-built, stocky widow with four children, had experienced her fair share of tragedies. Her husband was killed on his way home from work. A few days later, their home was bombed and their possessions burned. Escaping with only the clothes on their backs, they were given a hut in this camp.

Kheda was extremely strict in the way she brought up her children, desperate to prove to her husband's family that she was a good mother. She didn't want to lose her dearest children to her in-laws as happened too frequently to Chechen widows.

Kheda hadn't met Jesus yet, but she enjoyed hosting meetings in her hut, allowing the children to come to our meetings and have books about Jesus. She always made sure the books were well hidden in case a family member came over. We'd bought a sewing machine and material for her to start a small business, and she and her daughter enjoyed sewing and selling the clothes to make a bit of an income for themselves.

Kheda's four children, two boys and two girls, were between six and eleven years old when we first met. Kheda's daughter Rosa – tall, skinny, and bright-eyed, and bursting with creativity and passion – was always eager to read us the poems she so painstakingly and lovingly wrote. She also loved to read the Bible.

One day when we popped in, her lovely, innocent face beamed with delight. "I've written a poem for Jesus," she said. "Would you like to hear it?"

"How wonderful!" I responded, thrilled. "Yes, please."

The poem was so touching, both Larisa and I were in tears. It was all about how she loved Jesus, what He had done for her, and how she would love Him until her dying day.

When we first shared the gospel with Kheda's family, her eldest son, Alan, wasn't convinced. Not in the least. He was determined to discover the truth for himself. Whatever it was.

"That's a bunch of fairy stories!" he exclaimed, his astute brown eyes smirking at us. "I'm going to test out your theory."

We'd mentioned to him that if you pray and believe with

your whole heart, then you can move mountains (Mark 11:23). His daily trek to school took him past one of the many rubbish dumps accumulating in Grozny over the past few years since the war started.

"I'm going to test their stupid theory and prove them wrong," Alan thought. "How could this Jesus move a mountain of rubbish when no one has bothered to take away any rubbish for months?"

"In the name of Jesus Christ, if you are God, as these believers in Jesus have been telling me, get rid of this rubbish," he commanded, pointing at the rubbish dump.

On the way home from school, to his amazement an elderly lady was sweeping up the rubbish and taking it away. He excitedly ran back to the camp, declaring to anyone who would listen: "Jesus *is* alive and answers prayer!"

Alan told everyone how Jesus had answered his prayer.

A few months later, he fell off a swing, banged his head, and suffered a concussion. When the other believers in the camp laid hands on him and prayed, he was healed, the pain in his head instantly disappearing.

Another dear friend in the refugee camp, Hadizhat, was also a war widow with two sons and a daughter. An educated, elegant, self-sufficient businesswoman, she hated being seen as needy. When her daughter Liza had suffered a serious heart problem, Dasha had prayed with Hadizhat, and Liza was completely healed. Hadizhat went around telling everyone, "Liza's heart is completely healed. Jesus did it!" She still insisted, however, that she was a Muslim. A Muslim who believed Jesus answered prayers! This seems to be a common thing these days with more and more Muslims around the world finding that Jesus is answering their prayers, hallelujah!

She was always pleased to see us, as we were to see her.

Hadizhat wasn't in the camp for long. She soon managed to get her shop up and running. With the income, she started restoring a bombed-out flat in a high-rise apartment building. When one room was completed – with a new roof, walls, and doors – they left the refugee camp and moved into their new home. The fact that the one room had a shining new toilet in the centre of it didn't bother them too much. This was not a problem if it was just female guests or children, as we would hold up a sheet and just go for it.

If we had male guests, however, this turned out to be a major problem. In Chechen culture, it is shameful to talk about such delicate matters in front of people of the opposite sex; only married couples are allowed to do that. So typically the man would quietly tell his wife, who would whisper to Hadizhat, and then we would all discreetly leave the room. Once, when I was staying the night at Hadizhat's, a visiting missionary named Steve was also staying there. He needed to use the toilet before going to bed, but there was a curfew, and as far as we knew there weren't any outhouses nearby. Steve discreetly indicated to me that he needed to use the toilet, I whispered to Hadizhat, and we all left the room and waited in the corridor for Steve to finish his business.

Our trips to the refugee camp would usually involve bringing food, eating and drinking tea, playing with the children, reading the Bible together, and praying for anyone who wanted it. On the children's birthdays we would come with a cake, balloons, and presents. The mothers would always be so grateful: "If it wasn't for you, we wouldn't have been able to do anything special for our kids. Thank you so much."

The children would often plead with us to stay the night in their little huts.

One time, Larisa and I sneaked into the refugee camp and hurried toward Kheda's hut, hoping no one would see us.

We were exhausted after a busy day, longing for a cup of *chai* and a sit-down before we did anything else.

"Lord, I'm feeling a bit faint," I prayed.

A girl rushed over. "I've been waiting for you to come," she announced excitedly. "*Poshlite, devochki* – let's go to this hut here."

She pointed to a dilapidated hut we'd not been to before. She explained: "There's a little boy who lives there with his mother. The family situation is tragic. Really tragic. The father is long gone. And the mother, may Allah bless her, has a drinking problem. The poor lad has been affected badly by the bombing. He's never talked or walked in his life. The doctors diagnosed him with cerebral – what was it called again? Oh yes, cerebral palsy. I know you can help. Please, girls. Let's go, and you can pray for him."

"Oh no, Lord, not now," I complained to the Lord. "I just feel so ill. I could do with sitting down, putting up my feet, and having tea first. And You give us this! You could've waited until we were feeling better, instead of giving us something so complicated. A headache to pray for would have been a lot easier!"

We stepped cautiously into a dark, bare, filthy hut. As our eyes became accustomed to the dark, we could barely make out the impoverished young mother as she acknowledged us and waved us toward a bed where her three-year-old son was asleep. Larisa and I laid our hands on him and prayed for him. I felt absolutely nothing as I prayed – except of course my faintness and my desire for a cup of tea. I'd practically no faith anything would happen. Sure enough, nothing observable happened as we prayed, so after a few minutes we left.

The next time we arrived at the refugee camp, we saw a young girl making a beeline for us, and realised it was the boy's mother.

"He's walking and running," she exclaimed joyfully. "The day after you prayed, he got up and started walking. He's also starting to speak. *Spasibo bolshoe* – thank you so much for praying for him."

God is so faithful to work! Even when we don't feel up to it. He loves to heal, completely independently of our feelings or our faith levels. Isn't that just amazing?

We often visited a refugee camp in a village near Mila's house, where a government building had been turned into accommodation for families made homeless by the fighting. Each family had their own small room, sharing a kitchen and bathroom. Basic but adequate.

Farida, our friend from church, and her toddler Nadia lived here. A mousey-haired young widow with a serious speech impediment, Farida struggled to communicate clearly. Having grown up in an orphanage, her lifelong dream had been to have a family of her own. Just before the war started, she was finally living in her fairytale world. Life seemed cut out for her: she had a warm, cozy home and an adoring husband, and was expecting their first child.

Then her world shattered. In one moment. Bombs started to fall from the sky, and the shock caused her to go into labour. On the way to hospital, her dear husband was shot by a sniper. He died in her arms. She crawled into a nearby basement, and in agony and alone, gave birth to her daughter. When she'd recovered enough to realise she needed to cut the umbilical cord she looked around to see what she could use. There was nothing to use. Literally nothing. And no one to help her. She ingeniously cut it with her teeth. Nadia's large and unsightly belly button was a long-term reminder of the tragedy surrounding her birth.

The bombing finally subsided enough to emerge from where they were sheltering. She headed home, only to find it gone; replaced by a hole in the ground, a pile of rubble and a few burned possessions.

Dasha and Larisa found her in the refugee camp when they were giving out aid. Farida was thrilled to hear about Jesus. Her whole countenance lit up as she accepted Him into her life. After prayer, her speech impediment improved significantly.

"I'm so grateful to the Lord that He loves me and found me," she declared, eyes blazing with newfound hope. "Jesus and my daughter are all I have left in the world, but that is enough."

Eleven-month-old Emin was another dear Chechen refugee who was rushed to the local hospital, diagnosed with meningitis. He was in a coma for three weeks. "There's no hope for him," said the doctors, and the relatives started discussing his funeral. As we held his tiny, limp, contorted body, praying for a miracle, I had little faith for anything.

God performed a miracle once again. And this in spite of our lack of faith. The day after we prayed for him, he came out of his coma. Over the next couple of weeks, he recovered astonishingly quickly.

God was in the business of healing the mothers as well. One young mother had a lump on her breast for a whole year and was about to go to the cancer ward for tests and treatment. As we prayed for her, she felt heat going through her body. The lump had disappeared. Hallelujah!

When we were handing out food parcels and praying for people in another refugee camp, we met an interesting refugee family with five generations living together. In one hut we first met a sprightly looking granny, probably in her sixties. Then her grandchildren appeared with their mother. Granny then introduced me to her ninety-year-old dad. He was in surprisingly good shape for his age.

But then I was astonished when she proudly introduced me to her own granny, the 117-year-old matriarch of the family, who'd been born in 1880. She even showed me her birth certificate. In those days they didn't put the day or month, just the year. So she had no idea when her birthday was. Just her birth year.

This 117-year-old great-great-grandma had lived through the revolution as well as five wars: the Civil War, First and Second World Wars, the Ingush War of the 1990s and this Chechen War. Her husband had died in his forties, leaving her to bring up her seven children alone. War had caused her to flee her home and lose everything. Not just once but three times. She still looked like a spring chicken – well, at least not a day past ninety – was remarkably full of beans, cheerful, and (surprisingly) in her right mind. She was so grateful for the food parcel.

God's heart is big enough to fit everyone in, from the tiniest to the most ancient. And even the very ancient are still children in God's eyes. Treasured, loved, and cherished by their proud Daddy. And it's never too late to find that out. To be celebrated by Him.

Let Him pour His love upon you now. You're His beloved son or daughter. A chip off the old block. No matter how old you are. Or what you've been through. Allow Him to love you, heal you, and be all that you need.

For when Jesus is all that you've got left, you realise He's all that you need. But you don't need to get to that place of desperation to realise that. You can understand it now. He's the most precious and important person you will ever have the privilege of meeting. He truly is. Get to know Him and find out that truth, just as Farida and so many of the others have.

Chapter 20

PEACE IN THE MIDST OF DANGER

I have told you these things, so that in me you may have peace.
In this world you will have trouble.
But take heart! I have overcome the world.

JOHN 16:33

"*Otkroyte bistro* – open up quickly."

Our afternoon *chai* was rudely interrupted by loud banging. Aunty Asya headed to the door and returned ashen-faced, eyes wide with fright, barely noticing that her headscarf had slipped out of place, revealing her still surprisingly dark-brown hair with only small patches of grey. "It's *huligani* – hooligans."

"O Lord, please help us," Larisa and I cried out simultaneously.

Thud. Bang. Thump.

We made out from the different voices that at least five soldiers were at the door, pounding it with the back of their machine guns.

"If you don't open up, we'll break down the door," one of them threatened menacingly.

"I recognise that voice – that's Julia's husband!" Larisa shuddered at the revelation.

Our fifteen-year-old neighbour, Julia, had two grubby, malnourished children; she gave birth to the first at thirteen. Larisa had helped her numerous times with clothes, food, medicine, and babysitting.

"You know what we're going to do to you when we open the

door. Ha, ha, ha." Their evil laughter made the hairs on the back of my neck stand up.

"Go away, *huligani*. We're not opening the door!" Aunty Asya shook uncontrollably. Memories of her husband being stabbed and left for dead still haunted her.

Another familiar voice made my heart miss a beat: "We know you've got an empty apartment next-door. We're going to take it."

"Oh no, Julia's there too," I whispered, deeply disappointed.

"She's betrayed us," Larisa mouthed, dumbfounded. "Telling them we have no men living with us, and an empty apartment next-door. How could she, after all we've done for her?"

Poor Larisa shouted almost hysterically through the door. "The apartment next-door is occupied. Leave us alone!"

Suddenly I was flooded with the most perfect peace. "Lord, if You don't come through for us, we're as good as dead," I prayed. "But I know You'll come through for us." I almost chuckled. "However will You get us out of this one?"

The banging continued for a while, then suddenly stopped. One minute pounding, the next minute gone. No reason. No explanation. God had pulled off another miraculous deliverance on our behalf.

I spent the evening comforting Larisa and Aunty Asya, who both needed *valeryanka* – a Russian tranquiliser – to calm their nerves.

It was an undeniably dangerous time to be in Chechnya, not just because of bombs or bullets, but because of widespread lawlessness.

Groups of armed men 'policed' the streets. They looked for empty apartments to steal. Unofficially carrying out a policy of 'ethnic cleansing,' they got rid of Russians still left in the city. They eliminated so-called Russian collaborators, including nurses who worked in Russian hospitals, administrators, and so forth. Russian civilian families disappeared or were murdered just because somebody fancied their apartment.

By 1998, kidnapping in and around Chechnya became more frequent – the easiest way to make big money in a land with practically zero job prospects and where wages were sometimes unpaid for years.

Russian soldiers kidnapped Chechens, demanding ransom. If the family paid quickly, they sometimes received the person back alive. If not, only the body could be returned. And that wasn't even a given.

Chechens kidnapped Russians and used them: men for work, women as sex slaves. Chechen men kidnapped girls, forcing them to be their wives. Foreigners were particularly vulnerable, bringing big money. Kidnappings and killings for religious reasons and blood revenge were all too common.

The violence in the air was pervasive, hanging over everyone's heads like a smothering blanket, attempting to suffocate the life out of you. It was a battle every day not to be consumed by it.

A string of people I knew were kidnapped. Fellow missionaries, neighbours, friends. First, a neighbour from the eighth floor stepped out of our apartment building, only to be grabbed by masked men and pushed into a moving car. She worked in a bank, and after a few months, when a hefty ransom was paid, she was released.

One time I'd been planning on going back to Larisa's house, but had felt an urgency to stay the night at Mila's. The following day, when I arrived back at Larisa's, Aunty Asya came to the door looking quite shaken: "Thank Allah, you didn't come home last night, Polochka. Zelim and Mogamed, who live across the street, came asking for you and refused to leave, putting their guns over their laps and sitting on the sofa for hours. I didn't know what to do with them. Finally they got fed up waiting and left. I think you should go away for a few days until things calm down."

I was so thankful the Lord had warned me, and that I hadn't gone home that night. I had some lunch, then headed off to Mila's for a few days.

Next were a Swedish couple, Daniel and Paulina Brolin, part of the YWAM team I was involved with. I'd been concerned that they could get kidnapped when I met them: their graceful, blonde

Scandinavian features made them stand out as foreigners and as yet they didn't speak much Russian.

When they were kidnapped, it shocked me to the core. During the long five and a half months they were held, I became much more jumpy. As I walked around Grozny and Makhachkala, I often wondered where they were and if they were being held in a basement, perhaps underneath the very place I was walking. I often prayed they weren't being raped or beaten. Every time I heard a car coming up behind me, especially in the dark, my palms started to sweat.

"Is it armed gunmen coming to kidnap me?" I thought.

I decided to always carry in my handbag my Bible, a toothbrush, toothpaste, and clean underwear. Necessities I would need if I got kidnapped. I figured I could manage with those things, if nothing else. I never left the house without them for the next few years. Not once.

The good news of the Brolin's release came to us on 24 June 1998 while I was in Makhachkala. Here is what I wrote in my diary:

> Jesus, I'm so excited I can't sleep. Thank You for answering our prayers and for releasing Daniel and Paulina. It's the best news possible. I really want to see them and talk about it, but it will probably be the last thing they want to do. I'm imagining how happy their mums will be to see them, what a reunion, yay Lord!…
>
> Funny, they probably knew in the West before we did. It turns out that Swedish journalists phoned the church office at 2.00 pm to ask details and Dima said, "I didn't even know they'd been released!" Then journalists phoned from Moscow too.
>
> I found out around 8.15 pm when Naida came and told me that her mum had heard it on the radio. I was so pleased but couldn't 100% believe it. We tried to phone the office but our phone wasn't working and finally the last item on

the nine o'clock news was of their release. I jumped up and down for joy and kissed the kids. I then ran round to Sveta and Genna's to tell them and then we drove to the office where I sent a couple of emails...and left a message for Mum.

Thank You Jesus for Your goodness and faithfulness, for answering our prayers and that they're alive and well and FREE!! And that they were hostages for only five and a half months.

The Lord graciously ministered to me about my fear, and on 1 September 1998, I wrote:

Thank You, dear Papa, for ministering to me in my fear of being kidnapped here and showing me that I'm in the safety of Your hand and You've also got the whole world fitted onto that hand. You're so big and I'm so small and I'm in your hand, being held so close to your heart. Even though I walk through the valley of the shadow of death, You are with me, Your rod and staff they comfort me. You prepare a table before me in the presence of my enemies.

I purposely never informed anyone where I was going, in case the phone was tapped or the email read, and a kidnap could be planned. One September, however, I had a wake-up call when I travelled by myself from Krasnodar to Dagestan. My friends in Krasnodar knew I was going to Dagestan, but no one in Dagestan was expecting me.

Relaxing on a night bus, I chatted late into the night with a Russian refugee from Baku, relating stories from our lives. I shared about Jesus with her. In the early hours of the morning, we arrived at the Russia-Dagestan border, and a border guard I recognised climbed onto the bus to check passports.

"Hi Paula. You're coming with me," he announced, motioning

with his gun for me to come off the bus. Knowing better than to argue, I followed meekly.

"I want to get to know you better, Paula," he said. "You made an impression on me when you crossed the border a couple of months ago." Continuing, he explained, "I don't have many opportunities to chat with foreigners."

As the other guard looked through the passports, we stood by the bus chatting. "Oh, by the way, my name's Sergei," he introduced himself. "What are you doing here, Paula?"

"I'm a believer, and I've come to tell people about Jesus, that He loves them and wants to give them a new life."

"Oh, you're a Baptist, are you?" he interrupted me.

Russians assume anyone who isn't Orthodox is Baptist.

"No, I'm just a believer who loves Jesus," I answered.

"Do you want some *chai*?" he asked, changing the subject.

"Okay," I assented, even though having tea alone with an armed guard was the last thing I wanted to do. Not only did he probably not just have *chai* on his mind, but the bus could leave without me. The gun in his hand dispelled all arguments.

He turned to his friend, "Keep an eye on the bus, and when it's about to leave, call me."

The bus usually stayed at that border for at least an hour, and sometimes longer, while passports and bags were checked.

Sergei led me into what must have been the guards' common room and put on the kettle for tea. A good sign. But I was still nervous about being alone with him in the middle of the night. I took the opportunity to talk to him a lot about Jesus. As I talked, he asked me the usual questions Russians ask: "Why don't you cross yourselves the way we do? Why don't you have icons in your churches?"

I was happy to tell him the good news of the gospel and that God was touching and healing people's lives today.

"But have you actually seen any real miracles?" he asked, intrigued.

"Well, yes, I have actually. The best miracle I've seen is God healing my mum from mental illness. When she was a teenager, she was so ill that she didn't know who she was and spent time in a mental hospital. Now God has healed her, and she works as a nurse in a mental hospital."

Changing the subject, he queried, "Aren't you afraid to travel alone to Dagestan? You know it's downright unstable, and it's likely that war could soon start."

"No, I'm not afraid. I'm okay because I know God's looking after me. He'll be with me no matter what, and that gives me peace."

"I wish it was always so simple," I thought, trying to stay in that place of peace.

Offering me a sandwich, he asked, "Do you want a normal slice or the crust?"

"The crust, please," I replied.

"Did you know that the crust is what Russian teenage girls ask for when their breasts are developing?"

I didn't answer. "Lord, please let that bus go soon," I sent up a quick prayer.

As soon as I'd finished praying, the other soldier popped his head around the door. "Your bus is leaving."

That was one of the quickest answers to prayer, and also the quickest I'd known a bus to leave that border. I didn't even have time to drink my *chai*.

"Thank You, Jesus!"

Sergei escorted me back to the bus. I thought the lady sitting next to me would notice I'd been gone, but she was fast asleep when I climbed back on. The guard could have taken me off the bus, and I could have disappeared with no one ever noticing.

I felt disquieted that it would have been at least two weeks before anyone would even know I was missing, maybe longer. I thought that even worse than being kidnapped would be being kidnapped and nobody even noticing you were gone, and therefore nobody looking for you.

After that, I made sure I let people know when I was coming, and I warned them to raise the alarm if I didn't show up.

One time, however, this worked against me. I'd let Dasha know I was coming out of Chechnya on a certain date, and we agreed to meet in a village in Russia. Somehow we mixed the dates up. I thought we'd agreed to the week after. Really I did. She was sure it was a week earlier and waited for me. I didn't show up. Communications in those days with people in Chechnya was challenging, as phone signals were still blocked, and there was no internet access.

Assuming I'd been kidnapped, Dasha sent out a prayer request asking people to pray for me. People all over the world fell to their knees, praying for me for strength and for deliverance. Somehow the news reached my cousin, Gina, who was waitressing and living in Los Angeles at the time.

Going into work the next day, she divulged the news to her friends: "My cousin's missing in Chechnya. She's possibly in a basement with Chechen rebels."

One of her friends asked, surprised, "What's she doing in a basement with Chechen rebels?"

Before Gina could utter a word, he blurted out the answer obvious to his Hollywood way of thinking, "Oh, she must be enjoying herself with those gorgeous hunky rebels!"

Gina replied, "No, no, that's not it. You don't know my cousin, Paula. She's like a nun!"

We laughed so much when Gina related the story to me. It would never have crossed my mind that anyone would have thought that. We can so easily come to the completely wrong conclusion if we assume things based on our own culture and worldview.

With the whole world thinking I'd been kidnapped, Dasha decided to take the bull by the horns and come to Chechnya to look for me. When she arrived at Larisa's house, she found me blissfully unaware, merrily sipping tea with my friends.

Chapter 21

JOY IN THE MIDST OF PERSECUTION

I have found truly jubilant Christians
only in the Bible,
in the Underground Church,
and in prison.

RICHARD WURMBRAND[1]

Sometimes joy comes in the most unlikely of places. In the most desperate of situations. Unexpectedly and out of the blue. Almost knocking us off our feet as it wells up inside of us, bubbling over. Giving us the strength to love against the odds, to endure hardship as a good soldier (2 Timothy 2:3) and to willingly lay down our lives. All because we know we are His – and because we've read the last page of the book and know how it ends.

In fact, the whole last book of the Bible, Revelation, was written to strengthen persecuted believers by giving them a glimpse of the glorious future that awaited them.

In the past, Revelation had always scared me as I shuddered to think about what was to come. A bit like the book of Lamentations had taken on a completely different light when reading it in Chechnya, I now also found such comfort reading Revelation. I realised that even though bad things were going to happen, we were on the winning side, and there would be justice in the end.

I started to see martyrdom in a completely different light. What a privilege it would be to be among those under the altar who'd been martyred. To lay your life down for Jesus and to be given a white robe (Revelation 6:9-11).

Jesus, for the joy set before Him, endured the cross (Hebrews 12:2). Joy gave Him the strength and courage to face unthinkable pain and suffering. The joy of knowing He was a beloved son. Of bringing delight to His Father through obedience. The delightful anticipation of being reconciled with us, His children, for eternity.

Joy comes from the simple things in life: goofing around and laughing with family and friends; going out of your way to help someone in need; holding a loved one tight as you're reunited after a long absence; looking up and suddenly being overwhelmed by the beauty of a sunset, glorious in all its hues of pinks and blues.

But the joy I experienced in Chechnya was much deeper. Living with the reality that today could be your last day on earth strips away the frills, bringing a clarity in a way nothing else can. And I clearly saw that the deepest joy, the joy that gives us the strength to go on, comes during the darkest moments of suffering. When there's no earthly reason for joy, it bubbles up from somewhere deep within and overwhelms us. It's the joy of knowing our Father in heaven; of knowing our sins are forgiven; of knowing He's with us in reality, and He's got us covered – in all circumstances, come what may.

And it's the joy of knowing that when this earthly life is over, we'll be welcomed into heaven by family and friends, we'll receive our crown, and we'll hear the words, 'Well done, good and faithful servant!...come and share your master's happiness!' (Matthew 25:21).

It makes all our momentary troubles here in this world seem so worth it (2 Corinthians 4:17) in light of an eternity of delights and pleasures with Him.

Friends who'd narrowly escaped being martyred testified to this profound joy gracing them as they faced their potential murderers.

One of these was Maria, a twenty-three-year-old Russian girl from our church family. During an intense period of fighting, she'd been concerned about her grandparents on the other side of town, and so set off to visit them. She'd not quite realised how bad the fighting was, and suddenly found herself on the Chechen front-line. Soldiers captured her, and when they'd ascertained she was Russian, informed her they would kill her. As the soldier pointed the gun at her head, she pleaded, "Could I please pray before I die?"

"Who will you pray to?" he queried. Being a Muslim, he feared Allah.

She responded, "To the true living God who is above all others." This was one of the ways Muslims described Allah in Chechnya.

The soldier agreed, and she burst out exuberantly in tongues. Suddenly she felt a gentle touch on her shoulder, reassurance that the Holy Spirit was, indeed, with her. Joy and peace welled up within her, and she almost laughed out loud.

The soldier became edgy. With shaking hands he blurted out, "Shut up and prepare to die."

Suddenly she heard a commotion. Other soldiers scuttled in. "Get out of here," the fighter ordered Maria brusquely.

Hurrying away, she thanked God for saving her life.

It reminded me of the story of Stephen in Acts 7:54-56, who as he was being condemned to death, saw the heavens opened and experienced the glory of God. His face shone like an angel. Heaven was more visible to Stephen at that moment than the horrors on earth surrounding him:

> When the members of the Sanhedrin heard this, they were furious and gnashed their teeth at him. But Stephen, full of the Holy Spirit, looked up to heaven and saw the glory of God, and Jesus standing at the right hand of God. "Look," he said, "I see heaven open and the Son of Man standing at the right hand of God."

Another friend was working in a village sharing the good news about Jesus. Some Islamic fundamentalists pushed him into a car, took him to a deserted place, and beat him up. He was blindfolded and thrown to the floor onto his knees. He realised they were about to behead him; they were feeling for the bones in his neck.

"Renounce Jesus, or we'll kill you now," a gruff heavily accented voice threatened him. Suddenly he was enveloped with incredible joy and light. The excitement of laying down his life for his Jesus was all he could think about. What a privilege!

He didn't think about the pain. Or dying. Or leaving his wife a widow and his young daughter fatherless. All he could see was Jesus.

"I'll never stop serving my Jesus, who gave up everything, including His life, for me," he exclaimed blissfully and confidently.

Suddenly a car drove up from the Mosque. He heard someone shout, "Stop. Don't kill him." An argument ensued, going back and forth as to whether or not to kill him. In the end, he was roughly picked up and driven somewhere. He must have passed out because the next thing he knew, he woke up abruptly as he felt the coldness of sea water stinging his open wounds. The pain of being roughed up as the men tried to wash the blood stains off him. Then blackness enveloped him again until he woke up the next day in his bed, his whole body throbbing with pain. His sweet wife's young face lit up, so relieved her beloved husband had woken up.

"What happened?" he asked her, confused.

"I don't know," she replied, lovingly stroking his hair. "I found you unconscious on the road outside the house, and I brought you home."

Suddenly it all came flooding back, and he wept as he realised how close he'd been to being martyred. To never again see his lovely wife's face. Or to hold his baby daughter again. Well, at least not this side of eternity.

But at the moment when he'd nearly been martyred, his heart had been filled with grace, complete peace, and joy.

Chapter 22

A FIGHTER TOUCHED BY GOD'S LOVE

But now, for the first time, I see you are a man like me.
I thought of your hand-grenades, of your bayonet, of your rifle;
now I see your wife and your face and our fellowship.
Forgive me, comrade. We always see it too late.
Why do they never tell us that you are poor devils like us,
that your mothers are just as anxious as ours,
and that we have the same fear of death,
and the same dying, and the same agony –
forgive me, comrade; how could you be my enemy?

ERICH MARIA REMARQUE[1]

In early 1997, I was greatly refreshed and encouraged at a Catch the Fire conference I attended in the UK. I found out the team were planning to hold a conference in Moscow.

"Wow, you're coming to Russia. I'd love to host a conference in my area," I exclaimed to the plump middle-aged American evangelist. The next day he found me, his kind face lighting up: "I somehow feel it's right to send you a team. You know, I don't normally work with people I don't know, but I sense the Lord's giving me the go-ahead. We have a number of teams going to different parts of Russia to do conferences after the one in Moscow. Until yesterday, there was still one team with nowhere to go. I told the Lord that if by last night He didn't find anywhere for them to go, I'd have to cancel the team. That was when you came up to me."

I was amazed again at God's timing.

A succession of miracles, one after another, allowed the conference to happen in spite of fierce obstacles.

First of all, Dasha and I had a battle to leave Grozny. We'd found out that the train was leaving at 2.30 pm. At 2.00 pm we'd come to the station only to find that the train had already left. At the time, Chechnya had decided to adopt an hour time difference with Moscow, but the train was running on Moscow time, so it had left at 1.30 pm Chechen time. This time difference seemed to only bring chaos and confusion in its wake, and I was relieved when they decided to go back to normal Moscow time.

That was the last train that day, and we were on a tight schedule as we had to reach Moscow in time to meet the team coming in from the UK. The train travels excruciatingly slowly as it winds its way throughout different towns and villages in Chechnya before heading toward Moscow. We decided to try and reach Ishurskaya, the last village in Chechnya before hitting the border with the Stavropol region of Russia, in time to catch the train when it arrived there. We managed to catch a *marshrutka* – a minibus – and when we arrived in Ishurskaya, it was 5.30 pm and the shadows were just beginning to lengthen. The train wasn't due until 8.00 pm.

"What are we going to do for two and a half hours?" we wondered.

We walked to the station and found it crowded with Chechen soldiers; there were hardly any civilians in sight. The prospect of spending hours in their company was not tempting in the slightest. So we decided to go for a wander around the village.

We strolled across a field, watching a farmer leading his cows home for the night. Villagers started looking at us suspiciously, so we decided to head to the main road. To our dismay, as soon as we approached the road, a car pulled up filled with men carrying guns, leering and laughing and trying to force us into their car. As soon as we'd rid ourselves of them, another car stopped. The same thing happened. Then a third one.

"Aren't there any normal people driving in cars around here?" I thought.

Dasha did a great job of persuading them we weren't going with them, but we soon realised this wasn't the best plan. We decided it was better to be with the soldiers at the station.

As soon as we arrived at the station, we tried to buy a ticket, but the office was closed. We stepped outside and found a quiet spot near a bush. Trying to blend in, we took a seat on a bench.

Unfortunately, we'd been spotted. Four soldiers immediately came up to us, pulled a bench up right in front of us, our knees almost touching theirs, and plonked themselves down on it. They laid their machine guns down across their knees and said, "We want to get to know you. Tell us about yourselves."

I looked nervously at Dasha. She took a deep breath, and after introducing us, started to tell them the story of how she'd come to know Jesus. Suddenly the presence of the Lord descended on us all in such power. The guys sat there meekly, hanging on every word, mouths open, completely speechless. I was almost overwhelmed.

After recounting her story in detail, Dasha then shared the gospel message with them. One of them, a short, skinny lad with a pale face, was in tears by the end of it. He thanked her and said he was so glad to hear this amazing story about God. He then proceeded to relate his life story to us, how he'd had a difficult start in life, and how he didn't really want to be out there fighting, being only eighteen, but he felt he had no choice. He was thrilled at the offer of prayer and was tangibly touched as we prayed for him.

In front of my eyes, God showed me that these hardened fighters, who'd seemed menacing and threatening before, were only young men caught in a conflict not of their own making, who needed love just as much as anyone else. It reminded me of the apostle Paul, who was there holding the coats, approving of the stoning of Stephen, only later to become a pillar of the early church and a father of the faith.

Suddenly in the middle of our sweet fellowship, the train made an abrupt entrance. I was surprised it was already 8.00 pm. Time had flown past. Our new friends saw us onto the train. As we had no tickets, the conductor didn't want to let us on, saying sternly, "Sorry, the train's full up. No seats for you."

Our new little buddy raised himself up to his full stature, gun resting on his arm for maximum effect, and insisted firmly, "These are our friends, and you *will* find a place for them on this train!"

"Oh, alright then," she acceded, reluctantly. "They can sleep in my compartment."

The soldiers escorted us onto the train as if we were royalty, putting our bags up safely into the overhead compartment and making sure we were okay.

"You look after our friends, okay," he ordered the conductor as he stepped off the train. They all stood proudly by the window waving us goodbye as the train jerked forward, beginning its two-day journey to Moscow.

Again, we were so amazed at God's love. He loved those young soldiers so much that He went to all the trouble to arrange for us to bump into them at the station. He goes to such lengths to reach His lost sons and daughters. He's an incredible Father. The best in fact!

Train travel in Russia was an experience in itself and often took days. The Trans-Siberian Railway's Moscow-to-Vladivostok route takes seven long days to make its 6,152-mile journey. The journey often became part of people's vacations in and of itself. On my many train journeys across Russia, I enjoyed the chance to catch up on sleep, pray, read, write, and get to know the people in the carriage with me. I often had the opportunity to share the gospel and pray with them.

We mostly travelled third class, as we did on this occasion. Third class, known as *platskart*, consisted of an open-plan dormitory car with fifty-four bunks per coach, arranged in bays of four on one side of the aisle and bays of two along the coach wall. At each end of the corridor was a toilet with a sink and running water. They weren't always the cleanest. Russians didn't like to sit down on public toilet seats and often stood on them and squatted. With the train in motion, this often meant that many people missed the toilet bowl. Conductors were supposed to keep the toilets clean but didn't always do their job. The waste flushed straight out onto the tracks, so doors to the toilets were locked when we approached stations and big cities, then reopened when we were back out in the countryside.

At the front of the compartment was the bedroom and office of the two conductors who looked after each compartment. This was where we were sleeping on this occasion. Opposite this was a big *samovar*[2] providing a free flow of welcome boiling water for endless cups of tea. In each bay there were two tables, usually filled with food. People boarded the train with food for the length of the trip, usually enough for themselves and to share with fellow booth-mates. Lifelong friendships were made, and I heard that some even found soul-mates and spouses around the table, as passengers shared life-stories, deepest secrets, roast chicken, salted fish, pickled cucumbers, beer, and vodka. Followed of course by weak black tea with sweets, biscuits, or sometimes homemade jams that *babushkas* would pull out from large bags overflowing with food they were bringing to give to relatives.

We settled down to enjoy the journey, rejoicing once again at God's goodness to us. The conductor, following her orders well, looked after us splendidly, and we truly travelled in style.

Meanwhile the team of twenty in the UK was having great trouble obtaining their visas. My mum made five unsuccessful trips to the Russian Embassy in London. Another team member tried also, to no avail. Finally, the day before leaving, a third person travelled to London, and the visas were granted. Amazingly in one day.

The conference in Moscow was powerful. Many met with God in a tangible way and were touched and healed. On the evening it finished, Dasha and I joined the visiting English team and headed out for a thirty-two-hour train journey. We boarded the train with difficulty, loaded to overflowing with luggage: clothes, shoes, and blankets I'd bought at the local flea market, along with a myriad of suitcases filled with clothes and shoes donated from the UK.

Most trains from Moscow to the Northern Caucasus travelled though the Ukraine. This had been no problem before the breakup of the Soviet Union, because the Ukraine and Russia had been one country. In my first couple of years in Russia, you could freely cross the border with no problems. But now you needed a visa. We'd purposefully bought tickets for a train avoiding the Ukraine, as we didn't have transit visas. "You'll be fine," assured the lady at the ticket counter, smiling as she handed us our tickets. "It's not going through the Ukraine."

After settling everyone down in the three different compartments where our team was scattered, I wearily lay down on my bunk and the soothing, rocking motions promptly caused me to drop off into a deep sleep. I woke up suddenly as the train lurched forward before grinding to a complete halt. I glanced out of the window. Everything looked suspiciously like a border – the Ukrainian border.

"It can't be! She promised us it wouldn't go through the Ukraine," I thought.

But lo and behold, it was the border.

"Bummer, how could she lie to us and sell us tickets through the Ukraine?"

Dasha and I rushed around all the compartments encouraging everyone to pray. As we prayed, Dasha saw legions of angels surrounding the train, and God filled us with faith. He'd got us this far. We knew He would somehow get us the rest of the way.

A guard ordered one of our groups off the train. When we saw our motley group stepping down onto the platform, we directed them to get back on the train.

Explaining to the guards that we'd made a mistake, we asked them to please make an exception for us. I knew it would be a miracle if they did; I didn't know of anyone who'd been allowed through since the law had changed. Four people had been sent back to Moscow the day before, and two others who were sent back had to pay $120 for three-day transit visas.

A hefty-looking guard phoned his boss on his walkie talkie.

We heard in reply: "Go ahead and give transit visas to them all."

"What, all twenty of them?" he asked, stunned.

"Yes, all twenty of them." Then he added, "And don't charge them anything!"

The guards were noticeably surprised by their boss's decision.

One turned to the other and said, "On whose authority is this?"

"Jesus'," Dasha boldly exclaimed before anyone could answer.

Then one of the guards took me into his office and asked, "Do you have any money?"

"Bummer," I thought, "if God doesn't intervene, this could be expensive!"

"How much do you want?" I queried.

With a confused look he answered, "Niet – no, I didn't mean that. I mean do you have any English coins. I collect foreign coins."

"Oh, I see," I replied, somewhat taken aback. I fetched him a few odd English coins.

In the end, we received twenty visas for a few English pennies! It didn't break the bank this time.

After that, we had wonderful opportunities to witness to many passengers who wondered why the train was being held up. Especially one old beggar called Anton, who invited Jesus into his life.

Churches from all over the Northern Caucasus came to the conference. A significant breakthrough occurred when estranged pastors asked for forgiveness and washed each other's feet.

Our church family came from Chechnya. It was a great joy for them to be able to worship openly and to fellowship with other believers. One time I remember vividly worshipping God with many of my dear friends on the stage, waving flags for the whole world to see. We so revelled in the freedom of being able to worship publicly and without fear of being killed or arrested.

We saw a number of physical healings. After prayer, one teenage girl sobbed on the floor, then started laughing. The following day she announced that her heart, liver, and lungs had been healed! Yay, God!

The most dramatic physical healing took place during one of the evening meetings. That morning, the allocated speaker felt he was to swap sessions with John, another member of the team. God had already given John a message about Mephibosheth, the lame grandson of King Saul (2 Samuel 9), to share that evening.

No one knew a crippled boy was going to be brought to the meeting that night. Except God, that is. And fifteen-year-old Igor and his devoted mother.

A month previously, Igor's hips had been crushed when he'd been run over by a car. Walking was excruciatingly painful for him. His mother, full of faith, had brought him on a long bus journey from another city in Russia, knowing God would heal her precious son.

After sharing from the Word, John invited those with leg problems to come forward for prayer. Igor and others responded and our team prayed for them.

I laid my hands on Igor's hips and commanded healing. We then helped him to stand and take baby steps before finally encouraging him to walk unaided. He walked back and forth, tentatively at first. Testing to see. Was there any more pain? No, he didn't think so. No, none at all. Hallelujah! He was completely healed. You could see it written all over his glowing young face.

The tent erupted in praise as both mother and son burst into tears of relief and joy. At the end of the meeting, they left – Igor with a spring in his step, pain-free for the first time in weeks, and his mother triumphantly carrying his crutches.

The next night, his mother was back, face still radiant, with a fantastic report: "Igor has been walking and leaping and praising God all day (Acts 3:8). He couldn't come back to the meeting tonight. He's the eldest of my fifteen children. He's babysitting so that the babysitter from last night could come to the meeting tonight!"

Chapter 23

GOD WORKS IN MYSTERIOUS WAYS

"For my thoughts are not your thoughts,
neither are your ways my ways," declares the Lord.
"As the heavens are higher than the earth,
so are my ways higher than your ways
and my thoughts than your thoughts."

ISAIAH 55:8-9

On the way home from the wonderful conference, Alexei, a young lad from our church who sometimes led the worship, vanished from the train. He seemed to just disappear into thin air without a trace. We suspected he'd been arrested by police or border guards, but no one had seen or heard anything. But as God loves to work in mysterious ways, He ended up turning the situation around in a way only He can do, for His glory.

A small-built and pale-skinned Russian boy with short brown hair, Alexei lived with his mother, grandmother, and sister, and had no male relatives. His mother had a drinking problem, and his grandmother was quite frail. In a male-dominated society like Chechnya, you need men in your family or among your contacts to fight for you. As Alexei had neither, we found it extremely difficult to find out any information about his whereabouts.

Larisa and I tried as hard as we could, phoning every police station in the area to no avail.

But thank God, our most important contact in high places, the Lord Almighty, was working in the background!

My friend Pastor Valera from Vladikavkaz came to the rescue. He phoned the local prisons, and I was taken aback when I heard him saying he was a lawyer (even though he wasn't!). But he knew the ropes there, and this enabled us to find out that Alexei was in prison.

Apparently, Alexei had been arrested by soldiers on the train after a concealed weapon had been discovered under his clothes. This didn't sound like the Alexei I knew and loved, so I was shocked.

Valera managed to speak to the judge personally and asked, "When's the trial going to be?"

The judge replied, "Whenever you want, really. Or if you wish, we don't have to bother with a trial at all. I can just have a personal meeting with the defendant's family."

He was obviously waiting for a bribe. Feeling we should put our trust in God and not give a bribe, we asked for a trial. I decided not to go to the trial because if they found out I was a foreigner, they could have easily seen dollar signs and been tempted to ask for a substantial bribe.

The trial took place a few days later, and Larisa stood in as the 'public defender' or advocate.

When the judge saw Larisa's Bible, he asked, "What's that book you have with you?"

"It's an Injil[1]," Larisa answered.

"Why on earth are you reading the Injil?" he asked, surprised.

"It's the Almighty's holy book, and there's lots of wisdom in it," Larisa boldly proclaimed.

He looked up intently. "Can I have a look at it?"

Larisa passed it to him, and it opened at Proverbs chapter 3, where her bookmark happened to be. The judge sat in silence reading, probably these words from verse 30: 'Do not accuse anyone for no reason – when they have done you no harm.'

After hearing the various petitions, the judge declared, "We've decided to fine and release Alexei on the condition he keeps himself out of trouble for the next year. The fine will be seventeen million roubles" – about three thousand dollars[2].

"I'm sorry, but we don't have that kind of money," Larisa informed the judge.

"Well, how much do you have?"

"Actually I have two hundred dollars. Will that do?"

That two hundred dollars had just been given to us by our friend Kevin, a tall, thin church leader in his fifties from the UK who'd come out to help us with our summer camp. His mother had given it to him before he left, saying, "Use it in Russia to help someone in need." As Larisa was leaving, Kevin felt an urgency to give the money to her to use for a person in need.

Alexei turned out to be that person!

"Alright then," the judge agreed, happily taking the two hundred dollars and immediately releasing Alexei.

Alexei later explained what had happened. "I took a kitchen knife to the conference."

"What?" exclaimed Larisa, dumbfounded. "*Zachem* – why on earth would you do that?"

"Well, you know, in case I needed to defend myself or my sister. Or you guys." He looked at us, from one to the other. "You never know what's going to happen. And I also – well, I thought it would be cool to carry a knife, like a real fighter!"

"Alexei!!!" Larisa groaned exasperated, "you silly boy!!!"

After we both recovered from the shock of what he'd just said, I asked, "How on earth did the soldiers know you were carrying a knife?"

"You won't believe it even if I tell you. I had it hidden under my clothes, and – well, I was walking between compartments when the train suddenly lurched forward and I lost my balance. A soldier standing in front of me reached out his hands to steady me and felt something hidden. He then did a search and found it."

The kitchen knife had been concealed under his clothes the whole time, and we'd been blissfully unaware of it. The soldier arrested Alexei immediately for having a concealed weapon and took him to the police station. Alexei spent three months in prison.

Both Larisa and I were surprised that Alexei had chosen to carry a weapon. I personally had decided years before not to carry one; I knew I couldn't hurt or harm anyone. I'd entrusted my life and destiny into God's capable hands. I knew He'd protect me and, if necessary, fight for me, His precious daughter, in a much better way than I ever could have imagined. And if the worst came to the worst and I died, I would go straight into His presence anyway, so that was also not a bad option!

Most believers in my circle of friends had the same opinion. Alexei was the first believer I knew to carry a weapon. And in the end, it cost him a lot.

Conditions in Russian prisons at that time were pretty grim. Horrendous overcrowding, with often forty people in a cell designed to hold only twenty, meant that inmates took turns sleeping. The food was measly, consisting mostly of watery soup, porridge, and bread. Inmates relied on family members to bring food parcels, which were shared with fellow cellmates. Abuse and violence were rampant. Tuberculosis and other illnesses were commonplace. When we found out Alexei was in prison, all we could do was pray and trust God.

God faithfully answered our prayers for Alexei, and his time in prison turned out to be a blessing in disguise.

Having no Bible when he arrived, he prayed God would provide one. He noticed one of his cellmates was using a New Testament to roll up cigarettes. The guy gladly gave it to him when Alexei asked, and Alexei pored over it. He was able to share the gospel with the men in his overcrowded cell. One Jehovah's Witness invited Jesus into his life and was filled with the Holy Spirit.

Another cellmate happened to be a policeman who'd been arrested for hooliganism. Due to his contacts in high places, this policeman was treated like a king and fed scrumptious meals three times a day. Really taking a liking to Alexei, whom he affectionately called 'Father Alexei[3]," he shared all of his leftovers with him; Alexei even put on weight during his incarceration! And thanks to his new friend no one dared to lay a finger on him the whole three months.

When Larisa and I were searching for Alexei, we travelled to Vladikavkaz with his grandmother. There her life was changed forever as she met Jesus and was filled with the Holy Spirit at Valera's church.

A couple of days later, we had a divine appointment with a girl we met on the street, and she also became a believer in Jesus. The next day we prayed for her deliverance, and she was delivered of tormenting demons oppressing her for years. She immediately immersed herself into the life of the local church.

Just like for Joseph in the Bible, God turned a seemingly hopeless situation around for our good (Romans 8:28): 'You intended to harm me, but God intended it for good to accomplish what is now being done, the saving of many lives' (Genesis 50:20).

Chapter 24

MONEY RAINING DOWN FROM HEAVEN

I have but one candle of life to burn,
and I would rather burn it out
in a land filled with darkness
than in a land flooded with light.

JOHN KEITH FALCONER[1]

We lived by faith. As God's workers, we asked Him to show us what He wanted us to do, and then we would do it, knowing He would provide. God is a good and just employer. In fact He's the best you could ever ask for!

Money didn't usually rain down from heaven; God used people to give generously in both money and kind. Provision nearly always arrived at exactly the right time; only occasionally did it come early. It was never late by God's standards, even if it sometimes seemed delayed by our timetable; lack of provision usually meant God had other plans, and our job was to find out what they were.

While writing this chapter, I'd been waiting for my support to arrive, and it was already days late. I'd written to the British charity supporting me to ask when the money was coming. Just after writing the paragraph above, I received an email from them: "No money has come in for you this month."

Here I was again writing down conclusions I'd come to, and God was testing me a second time. A lack of finances meant I had to find out what God was trying to say to me through this.

God's timing and way of doing things really make me chuckle sometimes!

We were planning our summer camp in 1998, and I needed to go to Dagestan, via Grozny, to put down the deposit for the base and to buy food and supplies. Nothing came in until just before I was due to pay, a couple of weeks before the camp, when the Lord provided exactly the sum we needed – about two thousand dollars. In those days, the banks weren't hugely trustworthy, so I was often forced to travel with ridiculously large amounts of money. On this occasion I also needed to take another two thousand dollars as a down payment for a house we were buying for a refugee family.

Rumours predicted that war was imminent, possibly starting up again on 19 July. I decided to go to Vladikavkaz first, as it broke up the journey and meant that I didn't have to be up all night on various buses, plus I wanted to spend a couple of days catching up with Valera and family. If everything was okay, I planned to head back to Grozny on Monday 21 July. I arrived in Vladikavkaz with the four thousand dollars in my pocket.

Everything was still peaceful in Grozny, but it looked like war might break out between Ossetia and Ingushetia.

"Oh no, I'm on the wrong side of the border. If war breaks out, I'd much rather be at home in Grozny than stuck here in Vladikavkaz," I thought.

On the news, I saw there'd already been three days of *meeteengs* (demonstrations) on the streets, as thousands and thousands of Ossetian and Ingush men decided whether they would go to war. I still felt I needed to try and go to Grozny. I hoped the *meeteengs* would break up, or in the very least, that we wouldn't drive past them.

So at the crack of dawn on the Monday morning as planned, I climbed onto the bus.

That beautiful summer morning, with rays of sunshine cheering up the open dusty fields of Ossetia, I was happily worshipping Jesus in my head and praying for the region. Suddenly in the usually deserted fields, we came upon the *meeteeng* after all. We drove past thousands of armed civilians preparing for war.

All the borders were closed.

"Not again!" This seemed to happen to me too often. Way too often.

"Lord, I find myself in need of another miracle. The kind You're good at pulling off." I glanced upward, smiling. I wondered how He would get me through the border this time.

"Apparently they've gathered in response to some of their men being kidnapped by their Ingush neighbours[2]," I overheard someone explaining to their fellow passenger.

We ended up waiting by the side of the road for what seemed like hours. I had a lovely, long conversation with Zara, a sweet elderly lady sitting next to me on the bus, and ended up sharing my meal and the gospel with her as we waited.

I was greatly relieved when they finally opened the border and we made it safely into Ingushetia. "Now we'll be safe," I thought.

To my dismay, thousands and thousands of Ingush men had also gathered to discuss how to respond to events of the previous week, when three Ossetians had shot at a bus and killed a number of Ingush, and also blowing one girl's legs to pieces.

I couldn't wait to get to Chechnya. "Lord, help me to get out of Ingushetia before a conflict starts," I prayed.

As we crossed the Chechen border, I was shocked to see – for the third time that day – a massing of warriors. Hundreds of armed Chechen soldiers with tanks and weapons poised and ready to cross[3]. "Oh no, not here too!"

The bus came to a grinding halt, and a gruff Chechen soldier climbed on, yelling, "Everyone off – now! With all your things and documents. We're going to do a search." This was the last thing I needed.

Today was especially bad timing; not only was I British, but I had the four thousand dollars in my pocket, a great 'gift' for any soldier who would choose to search me.

We stumbled off the bus carrying our worldly possessions with us: clothes, bags crammed with jams or pickled cucumbers or tomatoes, crates of goods for sale, and one live squawking chicken. I helped my new friend Zara carry her two heavy checkered bags, the cheap Chinese sort you buy at the market, stuffed with supplies for her daughter.

Surrounding us on both sides of the road were ominous signs reading, 'Landmines – be careful.'

Suddenly the driver became nervous and shouted, "I'm going home; anyone want to join me?"

Before I had time to even think, I'd jumped onto the bus along with about five others just before the driver banged the door shut. Putting the bus into reverse, he screeched out of there as fast as possible. We were unceremoniously tossed around like rag dolls, holding on for dear life as we struggled to sit down, greatly relieved to have cleared out of there before any shooting started.

As we hurtled away, I struggled to adjust my headscarf which in all the motion had slipped off my head. Through the window I caught a glimpse of my elderly friend Zara, who we'd sadly left behind. Waiting by the side of the road – alone in a crowd of dust, conflict, and chaos, vulnerable and disorientated, her headscarf disheveled – she clung to her two bags for dear life.

"Lord, please bring Zara to Yourself. And help her and the others we've left behind get safely to their destination."

I was awakened out of my prayers by a lady near me drawing a deep sigh of relief and saying, "Thank God, I got out of there before they checked passports. I thought I was a goner. I'm Ossetian."

"Whatever are you doing going through Ingushetia and Chechnya?" someone queried.

"It was cheaper and quicker than going all the way around them," she explained.

"You're not the only one relieved they didn't check passports," I said, divulging one of my secrets, "I'm English!"

With that I gained the undivided attention of the whole bus;

none of them had ever met a foreigner before, and couldn't believe a foreigner was travelling by herself through Chechnya. Thank God, they had no idea about my other secret – the four thousand dollars in my pocket!

I shared my testimony with my captive audience as they leaned forward on the edge of their seats, straining to hear above the sputtering and spitting of the overworked, weary engine. The lady behind me was extremely interested, and I gave her a Bible and invited her to come to the camp.

Finally we made it safely back to Vladikavkaz. I returned to Valera's, where they were more than surprised to see me. On the news we saw that no wars had started that day after all, but tensions remained high, and conflict could erupt at any minute.

That evening, I spent time with the Lord asking Him if I should try and go again. At the time I was studying the book of Jeremiah. I opened my Bible and it fell open in Jeremiah 39:18: 'I will save you; you will not fall by the sword but will escape with your life, because you trust in me, declares the Lord.'

The words jumped off the page and stirred something deep in my spirit. But I still needed more confirmation. I turned a few pages and my eyes fell onto Jeremiah 45:5: 'Should you then seek great things for yourself? Do not seek them. For I will bring disaster on all people, declares the Lord, but wherever you go I will let you escape with your life.'

I could feel the sweetness, warmth, and strength soaking down into my very bones, enveloping me completely. A realisation, a knowing that all would be okay. That I was in God's hands, and He would protect me throughout my time in Chechnya.

After that, even though fearful thoughts sometimes came in dangerous situations, I had a deep confidence that I'd escape with my life.

I decided to risk travelling to Dagestan again the following day, but to leave behind the two thousand dollars (donated to buy the house), just in case. You never knew what might happen on journeys around the Caucasus. I could always pick up the money another time.

I considered telling Valera about the money but figured it would be too much of a temptation if he knew. Better to hide it. As I regularly stayed there, I always left a plastic bag with a few personal items on top of their huge Narnia-like wardrobe in their spare bedroom. Hiding the money in the bag, I put it back safely in its place.

While I was gone, Valera was praying for provision for a specific large need he had. His young sons, one of whom had been raised from the dead after our camp, were playing cheerily in the spare room and climbed inquisitively onto a chair and up the wardrobe. Finding the bag, one of them grabbed it, ripping it as he hurled it at his brother. Their worn-out grandmother came into the room and scolded them; as she leant on the tall, wooden wardrobe, hundred dollar bills floated down past her head onto the floor.

"God has answered our prayers!" she exclaimed excitedly, stooping down to pick them up. "Come and look, money is raining down from heaven."

"Oh my goodness," said Valera, as he came into the room to see money literally falling from heaven.

"I hope this isn't the work of the Mafia!"

On closer look, however, he was relieved to see that it was coming out of my bag.

"Why didn't Paula let me know?" he wondered, mulling things over in his head.

"Oh, well, thank you, Lord, for this answer to prayer. If she can leave a big sum of money here and not tell me, then I can borrow it without asking her!"

When I arrived, they recounted to me the story about God's provision raining down from heaven. Of course, I would have been happier if he'd asked me to borrow it, as I would have loaned it to him anyway. But God had answered his prayer, and eventually, I did get the two thousand dollars back, just in time to pay for the house.

For Reflection and Application

Do you need a financial breakthrough? Can you remember times in the past when God has been faithful to provide for you? Thank Him for those times and that He hasn't changed. He is the same yesterday, today and forever (Hebrews 13:8). Ask Him for a supernatural gift of faith to believe for His provision in your area of need in whatever way He chooses to give it to you.

Chapter 25

CONFLICT AND CELEBRATION

Be still, and know that I am God;
I will be exalted among the nations,
I will be exalted in the earth.

PSALM 46:10

Our annual seaside summer camps were always faith ventures since the guests couldn't afford to pay for their passage let alone accommodation and food.

That fateful camp in the summer of 1998 (described in the first chapter when the Chechen bandits ordered me to stop playing the guitar) was held in a three-story building that was basic. Probably too basic. But as usual, when running on tight budgets, we made the best of it.

There was no running water except one tap on the street. At one time there had been running water, as the building was designed for it, but obviously not for years. By carrying buckets from the tap in the yard, we were able to supply all three floors with water.

The toilets and bidets on every floor were disgusting, a real challenge to keep clean. They looked like they hadn't been cleaned in months. Outhouses would have been much more practical and sanitary.

The basement kitchen and corridor were in the worst state. A burst pipe somewhere had obviously flooded, giving us water but not in the right place or the way we wanted it. Everything was damp, musty, and dingy. Murky water dripped down the walls in the kitchen and dining room. The bathroom and some of the corridor were flooded up to ankle level. As if this wasn't bad enough, someone with an upset stomach had missed the toilet and relieved themselves in the bidet.

When we rented the camp, they hadn't informed us that electricity was scarce during the day. Our cook, Mama Lena – a short, cheery local believer with two young children – had to do most of the cooking at night. It sometimes took her five hours to prepare soup on the two rings on our newly bought electric camping stove.

On the plus side, the base was only a two-minute walk from the sea. For many war-weary refugees, this was the first time they'd ever seen the sea. Most hadn't had a holiday in years; some had never had one at all.

At the beginning of the camp, I'd gathered the leaders together. We discussed the cleaning rota, as there was a lot to do to clean up the place. Handing out jobs, I asked, "Who's brave enough to clean the toilet in the basement?" I hoped for a willing volunteer.

Unbeknownst to me, my friend Kevin from England who'd given the $200 to help release Alexei from prison had already slipped out unnoticed and cleaned the toilet.

"We don't need to clean the toilet," Luba observed. "Kevin's already done it." She pointed at him edging his way sheepishly back into the room.

After that, Kevin instantly became the camp hero. It was so counterculture for an older man, our guest, a minister even, to take on such a belittling job, and it really opened people's hearts to receive the message he had to share with them from the Bible. He was a great example of a laid-down, humble leader, the kind Jesus taught us to be (Matthew 20:25-28).

Kevin later recalled that it was the worst toilet he'd ever seen in his entire life. Though it was the only flushing men's toilet in the entire building, after his first glimpse he preferred to relieve himself among the sand dunes.

No light, either natural or electric, meant you couldn't see how bad it really was. In the two inches of water covering the floor, things appeared to be moving. Frogs – slimy, jumping, croaking frogs. And mosquitoes – the kind especially thirsty for English blood! You couldn't see them, but you sure could hear them buzzing … and of course feel them when they bit.

A few brick stepping stones in the water helped you reach the toilet if you dared to risk venturing in that far. Which others had obviously not managed, leaving piles of evidence on the floor and in the bidet. Lovely jubbly!

Kevin had prayed desperately: "Lord, let someone notice the problem and arrange to have it cleaned."

"Why not you?" The thought came back as God convicted him he needed to be an answer to his own prayer. We need to be careful how we pray, don't we!

It wasn't until after the campers arrived that he finally gave in. He found some old rags and a broken cooking pan to use as a shovel, put on surgical gloves from his first-aid kit, and set to work.

Later, when the caretaker found out, he was absolutely thrilled and insisted on introducing Kevin to his friends – the Chechen guys with the expensive car. Those same guys who later barged into the meeting and commanded me to stop playing.

At that point, Kevin had already picked up on the fact that they weren't good news. So when they offered to take him out and show him the local mountains, he politely explained he was there to serve the campers and unfortunately much too busy to take up their 'kind' offer. They accepted his apology and wished him well. Knowing with hindsight what happened to the two doctors recently kidnapped there, he has often wondered how different his life might have been if he hadn't cleaned that toilet. God works in mysterious ways!

The last evening of our camps was always a time of celebration. After worship, we put on a special concert, and all were invited to take part.

That celebration in 1998 was particularly memorable. The children enthusiastically sang songs they'd learned. I can still picture the tiniest little ones doing actions as they sang about being a little lamb in God's sheepfold. They recited poems and performed a skit about Noah's Ark. Adults and children danced together as we sang a mixture of Chechen, Russian, and Jewish songs.

As always, the evening ended with the *Leizginka* – a traditional Chechen dance depicting an eagle leading a swan in an enchanting rhythmic flow. Couples take turns dancing the *Leizginka* in the middle of a circle. Only a beat and a couple of dancers are needed for this dance (a man as the eagle, a woman as the swan). At every possible opportunity Chechens enjoy the *Leizginka*: at weddings, at parties, to welcome guests or at the start and end of the school year.

Once, when a market was being bombed, I saw a young man and woman defiantly dancing the *Leizginka*. With heads held high they declared to the world they were proud to live as Chechens, and if necessary, to die as Chechens.

It was during this concert at our camp that the group of enraged Chechens came looking for the base director, to avenge the perceived humiliation of the previous night.

"He's not here at the moment," they were informed. "He'll be back later."

The men found out where his living quarters were and found his wife, Patya, and his tiny stepchildren there. After forcing their way into the room, they ripped her dress and, as one of them tried to climb on top of her, she suddenly started to foam at the mouth. The shock of the assault had caused her to have an epileptic seizure.

Perturbed, they ran out of the room without harming her further.

After that, they walked straight into our meeting while we were worshipping.

"Where is that Avar[1] dude?" they asked some of the guests.

People shook their heads, "We don't know."

Some of our team members were Avars, as was the base director.

But no one was giving anything away. The Avars and the Chechens weren't the greatest friends even at the best of times.

That summer evening in Dagestan, I didn't hear the fighters asking for Avar people, but I could see they'd come looking for trouble. That's when they threatened me, screaming at me to stop playing the guitar, before apologising and running out of the room.

The moment the men had entered, Luba ran to the base director's room, knocking on his door to see if we could find some help. There was no reply. After a minute or so, Luba tentatively opened the door and found Patya fitting on the bed. She hurried to call the camp nurse and together they attended to and prayed for Patya, who slowly came around.

Later on she remembered why her dress was ripped. When her husband returned home, she recounted what had happened.

"They won't get away with that," he said, "hurting you and bringing shame on our family. I'm going to find them and avenge what they did to you."

He headed out to look for them, found one of the bandits, and beat him up. The cycle of revenge continued.

After our guests had gone to bed, Lipa ran to find us.

Struggling to catch her breath, she anxiously implored, "Girls, come quickly. Please hurry. I saw a group of Chechen lads gathered on the stairs. I think it's the same gang. I heard them, in Chechen, discussing our musical equipment. They were wondering if we were still there. I think they're planning to steal our equipment."

We called some of the men from our team to help us carry all the equipment to a bedroom for safekeeping.

As the camp slumbered uneasily in the early hours of the morning, Luba and I got ready for bed and headed downstairs to use our 'bathroom,' the lone outside tap. We went in twos after dark for safety reasons.

Suddenly, out of the corner of my eye, I saw a silvery shadow swaying in the moonlight, the silhouette of a man holding a *kinzhal* – a large knife.

"Luba, stop," I whispered, pointing. "Look over there. At the bottom of the stairs. The men are still there."

Frozen to the spot and barely making a sound, we prayed quietly as we strained to hear their conversation:

"Yes, Abdur, we need to go to that other base tonight."

"What, now? Maybe tomorrow."

"Are you kidding? You need to avenge those freaks tonight. Get them back for what they did to us."

"Yeah, let's show them what we're made of."

We couldn't stand there much longer waiting for them to go. Beside myself with tiredness, I was almost asleep standing up, way too tired to listen or to even be afraid anymore. Turning to Luba, I carefully mouthed my words: "Let's walk past them. Slowly and quietly. God will hide us."

We tiptoed past them on the other side of the stairwell and somehow they didn't notice us. On our way back from the 'bathroom,' we mercifully discovered they'd gone.

For Reflection and Application

Is there something you're praying for in which you sense God may be asking you to be the answer to your own prayer? If so, ask Him to guide you in what He wants you to do about it.

Chapter 26

TRANSFORMED
BY LOVE

The only currency that will heal every culture is ceaseless love.
To be a minister, we must walk like Jesus, talk like Jesus,
and be like Jesus for a broken and dying world

HEIDI BAKER[1]

One elegant lady from the refugee camp had a cute curly-haired baby boy with pleading brown eyes. Her husband had no time for her or her little one, as she was the least important of his three wives.[2] He was always busy with the other wives and families.

Her dark green eyes were moist as she thanked us: "This week I've felt as if I was in paradise. I'll remember it for the rest of my life." After a sigh of happiness, she added, "I've never been in such a wonderful atmosphere where people just loved me, accepting me for who I am and not expecting anything in return."

Some young lads in the camp were a real handful, especially one who turned out to be a Chechen fighter, normally hanging out around the central market with his machine gun. Another camper, a lawyer associated with the Sharia (Muslim) law courts, changed during the week from being extremely argumentative to thoughtfully listening to what we had to say.

Lipa's two younger sons – Mogamed, now seven, and Zelim, nine – were hugely excited to be at the camp. So unspoilt, they enjoyed every moment.

The previous year, I'd brought toys with me from the UK, and

Mogamed had received a little wooden car with a string to pull it along. It was his only toy, and he was thrilled. He took it everywhere with him.

One afternoon, I found him distraught, weeping in his mama's arms.

"What happened?" I asked.

Lipa explained: "He's lost his car. I think someone's stolen it."

"We can't have that," I declared. Boldness rose up in me at the injustice of it, and at the pain of little Mogamed. He'd had so little happiness in his short life and had been through so much. "Let's ask Jesus to bring it back. I know He'll find it for you. Jesus, thank You that You know where Mogamed's car is. We ask You to bring it back, in Jesus' name. Amen."

I knew God would do a miracle and somehow bring the car back. That evening, Olya came in with a little wooden car looking suspiciously similar to Mogamed's.

"I saw it on the beach, and I thought it looks like your car, Mogamed. Is it yours, sweetie?"

"Yes, it is." Little Mogamed's face beamed as he sheepishly took it from Olya. He was thrilled beyond measure as he played with his car and treasured it. God was looking out for His precious son.

One of the guests brought her new kitten to the camp – her pride and joy and consolation. Really playful, the kitten was always trying to escape. And this poor lady certainly needed all the consolation she could get. She'd recently lost her father and then her husband. The Lord met her in a very special way during the week as she let the pain out and received His love in the deepest part of her being. And her kitten brought a lot of laughs, especially from Mogamed, as they frolicked together.

Twenty years later – now grown up and a father himself – Mogamed thanked me for all we did for him: "All of my happy childhood memories are with you guys." Hearing words like those make all the years of hardship so worth it.

A contentious older lady, Galya, heavy built with short black hair, almost caused a fight in my small group at the start of the week when she shouted, "That talk was awful, you guys are fanatics!" By the end of the week she sobbed as God's touch seeped into the depths of her being, melting down the walls she'd built around her.

Before she left, she thanked me profusely, her eyes filled with wonder: "Spasibo bolshoe – Thank you so much, Polochka – I've enjoyed the fellowship, and you've given me a chance to think about the spiritual things of life and to hear about the Christian faith."

Galya became a believer a little while later and softened considerably. She shared her faith with her neighbours. Two of them, a blind elderly lady and a mentally-ill teenage lad, soon ended up with nowhere to go after their houses had been bombed and their relatives had died. Galya took them in and lovingly looked after them both, and we started a home group in her house. Our Father God transformed Galya with His love – and she, in turn, passed on His love to others.

What an unfathomable privilege that God would choose us, in the midst of our own brokenness, to be His body, hands and feet here on earth. Oh the joy of being vessels for His love to flow through as He woos His precious lambs gently to Himself and heals them from the inside out. One touch of His love - even sometimes through our far-from-perfect hands - transforms everything. None of us would ever be the same again. Hallelujah! What a glorious Saviour we serve.

Chapter 27

THE EVENTFUL JOURNEY HOME

Though an army besiege me,
my heart will not fear;
though war break out against me,
even then I will be confident.

PSALM 27:3

The next morning the guests headed home. Even this was not without a miracle.

The coach we hired didn't arrive so the guests were forced to wait with packed bags for hours by the side of the road. Transporting forty people to Grozny from a base in the middle of nowhere on the shores of the Caspian Sea was challenging for a number of reasons, one of them being that coaches with Dagestani license plates weren't willing to go to Grozny. Especially without advance warning.

"Lord, please send us a coach soon."

Shortly afterward, a posh new coach with soft seats suddenly appeared. It was an Ikarus, the pride of Soviet transportation.

I asked, "You couldn't by any chance take forty people to Grozny, could you?"

"Well, yes, as a matter of fact we're heading for Grozny to pick up some tourists coming here. We'd rather not take an empty bus. Yes, we'll take them."

We agreed on a reasonable price, since they were going to Grozny anyway. "We'll just have lunch first," one of the two drivers remarked, "and then we'll be on our way."

Our gang climbed onto the coach, excited to have the soft comfortable seats and legroom to enjoy. Some had never been on such a 'luxury' coach before.

We normally hired the cheapest possible coaches to transport guests, but this time, the Lord had graciously upgraded us to 'business class' so His children could ride home in style!

With everyone seated and ready to go, the drivers proceeded to fry eggs on a makeshift stove inside the coach. With fascination, we watched them prepare and enjoy their hearty lunch.

Emotions were mixed as we waved the guests goodbye. Some were pleased to be going home. Many of them had been concerned for relatives, animals, and houses left behind in the war zone. A number of the ladies wiped away tears from their eyes. They were grateful for the fun they'd had and for all that God had done in their lives, yet sad to leave new friends and this beautiful place of rest and refuge.

I stayed in Makhachkala for a few days to finish off business and get some rest before heading home to Grozny. Maksim begged to be allowed to stay behind with me in Dagestan. Having been deprived most of his life, he was thoroughly enjoying all his new experiences, just like a little boy on Christmas morning. At the camp, swimming in the sea was a first for him. With surprise he noted, "Paula, it's really weird, but the water tastes salty!"

My friend Larisa was celebrating her birthday on the following Tuesday, with a party in the evening. I promised her I would come home to Grozny in time for the party. And I'd promised Mila that I would bring her son home safely.

That Tuesday morning, I sat in the church office in Makhachkala sending emails. We were planning to leave for Grozny in the next hour or so.

Suddenly Zina, the pastor's wife, scrambled into the office: "Something serious is going on out there. We need to pray. I've never seen anything like it." She reported that women in the yard had warned her that the main square was cordoned off, and trucks in the centre of town were rounding up all able-bodied lads to fight the Wahhabists, the Islamic fundamentalists.

Then Zina's husband, Pastor Artur[1] burst in with the news: "Basayev is on his way from Grozny. They announced he's already taken the police checkpoint at Khasavyurt, and that the tanks are on their way." Basayev, a young Chechen freedom fighter, had a track record for committing horrendous atrocities. Khasavyurt was on the same route we were meant to be taking.

One of the office staff phoned his brother working in the government, who advised, "The situation is extremely serious. Everyone should stay at home and avoid going out at all."

At that, we all fell on our knees and cried out for peace, for the fear of the Lord to fall on those wanting to fight, and for mercy for Dagestan.

By then it was 1.00 pm and our bus was leaving in twenty-five minutes.

Someone put into words what everyone was thinking: "You can't go, it's too dangerous."

"Yes," added another, "sit it out for one more day and see what happens. It would be stupid to go."

I was inclined to agree but decided to go into the other room and ask the Lord. In situations like this, it's often difficult to hear God's voice clearly because the voice of fear shouts much louder.

Fear was telling me, "If you make a mistake, you could not only get yourself killed, but also Maksim, Sveta, and Genna." Our friends Sveta and Genna planned to drive us to the bus station.

I fell to my knees and prayed. Suddenly the recent words of my friend Julia Davison in England came into my head: "Don't listen to other people or fear but go for it." This encouraged me that I should go, despite what other people had said.

I had to get Maksim home to his mother.

I'd promised to be there for Larisa's party.

If a war started, I would rather be at home than trapped behind enemy lines.

However, because I didn't want to be proud or presumptuous, I asked the Lord for more confirmation.

I opened my Bible and was surprised to read, 'I have determined to do this city harm and not good, declares the Lord. It will be given into the hands of the king of Babylon, and he will destroy it with fire' (Jeremiah 21:10).

I asked, "Which city, Lord?" But I didn't receive a clear answer.

Then the Bible fell open at Proverbs 3:5: 'Trust in the Lord with all your heart, and lean not on your own understanding.' Those words 'lean not on your own understanding' jumped off the page. We didn't know what was going on in reality, but God knew the whole situation. In my spirit I knew we had to try to leave. He'd promised to direct our path, so we just needed to trust Him. And if it wasn't right, He would close the door.

By this time it was already 1.15 pm. The only bus for Grozny left in ten minutes. It would be impossible to get there in time.

I prayed and felt that if the bus was still there, it was a sign we were meant to leave.

Zina looked extremely concerned as she prayed over me, "May the Lord protect you."

We bade a quick farewell and sped off.

Around the city, everything seemed normal. I suddenly remembered I needed to change money to buy bus tickets. "Wonderful timing, Paula," I thought.

We stopped at an exchange place and were strangely able to change money straight away.

As we raced into the bus station I glanced at my watch – 1.35 pm, ten minutes after the bus should have left. Amazingly our bus was running late and just leaving. We were obviously meant to go. Genna flagged it down and asked the driver to take us. He kindly pulled the bus up alongside the car and we climbed in, dragging our luggage behind us, which included a recently donated keyboard.

"Perfect time to take a keyboard into Chechnya!"

The bus was not a posh Ikarus like the one that appeared to take our guests home, but a Passik, a small bus with hard seats. Filled with too many people as usual, it shook and made an ominous noise as we set off on our way.

I soon realised why the bus was determined to try and reach Chechnya that day. The Chechen driver in a bus with Chechen licence plates and full of Chechen passengers was desperate to return to his country before the war between Dagestan and Chechnya started. I also preferred to be in my home in Chechnya if a war was commencing, and especially wanted to bring Maksim home safely to his mother.

Chapter 28

ETHNIC CONFLICT

I have but one candle of life to burn,
and I would rather burn it out
in a land filled with darkness
than in a land flooded with light.

JOHN KEITH FALCONER[1]

The road was lined with hundreds of men, apparently Dagestani civilians, armed with whatever weapons they could find – guns, knives, sticks, forks, axes – preparing to defend their country.

Maksim and I prayed under our breath as the magnitude of the situation hit us. We were on a Chechen bus driving through an 'army' of Dagestanis poised and ready to attack Chechens. Amazingly, the men paid absolutely no attention to us as we hurtled past them. We made it safely to Khasavyurt bus station and picked up more passengers.

Approaching the border, we could see complete chaos had erupted. Buses and cars were backed up for what seemed like miles. Clouds of dust and dirt and swarms of people spread out as far as the eye could see. The long narrow bridge marking the border had been blocked completely by two lorries parked side by side at right angles to the road. No one could go in either direction.

Dagestanis had obstructed the road when they'd heard Basayev and his tanks were on their way. Soldiers geared themselves up on the hillside with machine guns and bazookas pointing in the direction of Chechnya, ready to attack if any tanks rolled up.

Our driver shouted to everyone on the bus, "Who wants to go to Chechnya?"

Everyone, including us, replied in unison, "We do."

"Okay, let's go home," he cried out, suddenly manoeuvring the bus between people, buses, and cars. To everyone's surprise, we accelerated past tanks and soldiers. Lying through his teeth, he shouted at the border guards, "We're going back to Makhachkala!" – where we'd just come from.

My heart almost missed a beat.

"Lord, don't let any of the tanks or soldiers shoot at us when they realise where we're actually going."

The bus swerved off the road under the bridge into the fields below.

"And, Lord, please don't let the bus hit a land mine."

The bus, rickety on normal roads, now tossed us about uncontrollably, banging our legs on the seats in front and throwing us out of our seats onto other passengers. My headscarf kept sliding down my head and I struggled to keep in in place. It was hard at the best of times to stop it from slipping down. Having worn it for so long, I was now more or less used to adjusting it without a mirror, as Chechen ladies were so expert at doing. But with all this motion going on, it was a challenge to keep it on.

As we raced through fields and bushes, along a riverbank, and through potholes, ditches, and tree branches, boxes fell down from the luggage rack, and bottles and bags rolled around under our seats. I continued to pray fervently the bus wouldn't break down or get stuck in the mud in the middle of a minefield.

My body trembled inside from fear and shock, and my knees shook uncontrollably. As we flew over one particularly jerky bump, my knees knocked hard against Maksim's knees, and I realised he too was shaking. We looked at each other embarrassed, then burst out laughing. I noticed other people were telling jokes and laughing too.

One way of coping with war is by laughing, even if you're

shaking like a leaf inside. If you're going to die anyway, you may as well die laughing.

But this wasn't the day for us to die. God still had plans for our lives.

After driving through fields and along dirt roads for about an hour, we once again approached a bridge surrounded by soldiers.

"Thank God, we must be near Grozny by now."

As we got closer, I thought the bridge looked surprisingly familiar. To my horror, I realised it was the same bridge we'd driven under an hour earlier on the border. We'd come full circle!

The same soldiers stood poised, looking in our direction.

"Oops," said the driver, as he hastily turned the bus around and headed off in a different direction into the countryside.

I realised he had absolutely no idea where he was going.

We found ourselves driving once again past the thousands of armed Dagestani men having their *meeteeng,* who still paid no attention to us.

We soon ended up at the bus station again in Khasavyurt, where we picked up more desperate passengers relieved to go home to Grozny.

The driver headed the bus back out into the fields.

After another hour or so of careering wildly through the countryside, we eventually found ourselves back on a completely deserted dirt-track road. It was such a relief to finally see the familiar landmarks of the outskirts of Grozny.

When we arrived home, the streets were eerily quiet. I don't think I'd ever been so pleased to be home. And here everything seemed right with the world. It was hard to believe all those *meeteengs* were happening just a few miles away.

We reached Larisa's house in the early evening, in time to celebrate her birthday and reflect in amazement on the extraordinary ten days we'd experienced.

Chapter 29

THE LEAST OF THESE

We are contemplatives in action right in the heart of the world,
seeing and loving and serving Jesus twenty-four hours
in the distressing disguise of the poorest of the poor.

MOTHER TERESA OF CALCUTTA[1]

"Then the King will say to those on his right,
'Come, you who are blessed by my Father;
take your inheritance, the kingdom prepared for you
since the creation of the world.
For I was hungry and you gave me something to eat,
I was thirsty and you gave me something to drink,
I was a stranger and you invited me in,
I needed clothes and you clothed me,
I was sick and you looked after me,
I was in prison and you came to visit me."
"Then the righteous will answer him,
'Lord, when did we see you hungry and feed you,
or thirsty and give you something to drink?
When did we see you a stranger and invite you in,
or needing clothes and clothe you?
When did we see you sick or in prison and go to visit you?"
"The King will reply, 'Truly I tell you, whatever you did
for one of the least of these brothers and sisters of mine,
you did for me.'

MATTHEW 25:34-40

'The least of these'- the poorest of the poor, widows and orphans –
are very dear to God's heart.

Baba[2] Vika was a sweet, one-legged, bedridden *babushka*
whose house had been bombed and who'd lost all her relatives.
Neighbours found her and asked our church to help her. Taking us
through bombed-out ruins, we were led to the only room that still
had walls. The roof hadn't fared quite as well as the walls, and half
of it had caved in. Baba Vika's bed was in a part of the room where
there was still ceiling.

The glass had blown out of the window a long time before. Her
cat and chicken used the window like a revolving door, constantly
jumping in and out at will. Baba Vika, unable to walk, barely able to
see or hear, spent long days lying in her own excrement surrounded
by chicken poop. It was amazing she was still alive.

Her neighbours brought her food, but being disabled themselves,
they weren't able to do much else to help.

Her wrinkled face lit up every time she heard us coming in, and
she kept praying over and over for us in her Russian Orthodox way:
"Lord, *dai im zdorovye* – give them health."

When we undressed her to wash her, a stench of rotting flesh hit
us. An infected bed sore in her back was literally crawling with little
black maggots – wriggling and squirming grubs, eating her flesh.
Revolted, I quickly started to pick them out, one by one, until they
were all gone.

We tended to the wound and washed her and cleaned the room
as best as we could. She then heartily began eating the food we'd
brought for her.

Before we left, we prayed with her.

The next time we came, she was so grateful to see us again. We'd
arranged for a plastic sheet to be placed over the window to stop the
chicken coming in, but this hadn't happened yet. So unfortunately,
her room was once again full of chicken poop. After washing her
thoroughly again, we brought food out for her.

"Lovely," she said, "Have you brought me that sweet sausage again?"

"Sweet sausage?" I asked in surprise, "We didn't bring anything sweet, did we?"

Then it dawned on me, "Oh, the banana!"

Having never eaten a banana before, she'd thought it was a sausage!

Unfortunately we had no banana with us, but we made sure we brought one with us every time after that and we stopped by as often as we could.

Baba Vika was a true hero. Nobody would have blamed her in her circumstances for feeling sorry for herself or being angry or bitter for all she'd gone through. But I never saw a trace of complaint or self-pity in any bone of her body. Only joy and gratitude for the smallest things we did for her.

We were not sure that Baba Vika truly knew Jesus. One day when Mum was with us, she asked Baba Vika if she was sure she was going to heaven when she died. She wasn't sure so Mum had the privilege of leading Baba Vika in a prayer asking Jesus to forgive her for the wrong things she had done and to be her friend, her Lord and her Saviour.

Then Mum and Dasha felt led to pray for God to release Baba Vika and take her to be with Himself. Soon afterward, she passed from this world to the next and was welcomed into her eternal home by her friend Jesus. And with a fanfare, no doubt.

I was out of town when she died, but Larisa conducted a little funeral for her. It was a privilege to have been able to pour out God's love on one of His precious children. And as we looked after her, one of the least of these, we were looking after Jesus Himself.

For my first couple of weeks in Chechnya, I lived in a tenth-floor flat with a family whose children belonged to our church. One day their eldest daughter Ksusha introduced us to a group of orphans living by themselves a few floors below us – six children from different families who'd lost parents and homes.

Initially, too frightened to open the door to us, they wouldn't even talk to us through the door, only pretend no one was in. But seeing them charging in and out to fetch water gave the game away.

Orphaned children were especially vulnerable, as always. It was no surprise these poor children were so terrified. With no adults to protect them, many orphans disappeared, some sold into sexual slavery, others killed and their organs sold for transplants.

Finally the oldest girl, Nastya, who was fourteen, opened the door and allowed us to come in. I was taken aback by the state of the flat. Orange peels littered the floor. I noticed the paint on the walls had an unusual colour and pattern with dirty brown patches. No, wait – the pattern seemed to be moving.

"Yuck, it's cockroaches."

A large crawling, scuttling, scaling mass. I'd never seen so many cockroaches in one place. Never before or since.

The eldest boy of fifteen worked at the market, making and selling cassettes, and brought in a bit of money. The next two oldest were Nastya and her thirteen-year-old sister. The youngest was a six-year-old boy who'd hide whenever we came over. One day a piece of frozen chicken fell off a market stall; Dasha saw him grab it from the floor; running out of sight, he promptly wolfed it down, still raw and frozen.

We started to bring them food on a regular basis, and we celebrated Nastya's birthday.

I gave them a New Testament. The following week, we came back and Nastya surprised me: "I loved that book about Jesus you gave me," she exclaimed, her eyes burning with excitement, "I've read the whole thing from beginning to end."

We asked if she wanted to invite Jesus into her life to be her friend, and she eagerly agreed. We prayed with both Nastya and her younger sister to meet Jesus.

Shortly after this, as I knocked at their door, a little girl who lived nearby informed me, "They're not here anymore."

"What?" I asked, my heart missing a beat. "Where are they?"

"A nice American lady came and took them."

"Where to?" I asked incredulously.

"Er, I think, to a better life," she said.

"Oh no, how awful, they've been taken by the Mafia," I thought. I was gutted. I knew there couldn't possibly be any American women in Chechnya taking children to a better life. But God!

This happened in December 1996. I had no more news of them – thinking they were probably dead – until almost two years later.

In February 1998, the Lord laid it on my heart to go to Israel to celebrate the Feast of Tabernacles.

My friend Julie, from the USA, invited me to join her there. As soon as I arrived, I ended up translating[3] into a headset for the new Russian immigrants who'd come to the celebration and couldn't speak Hebrew or English. The doors had recently opened for Russian Jews to return to the land, and they were flooding there in droves.

Unknown to me, a trip to the Knesset was part of the conference we were attending; Prime Minister Benjamin Netanyahu addressed us, and I had the privilege of shaking his hand.

However, the main reason I'd come to Israel was yet to be revealed.

Both Julie and I were short on cash and had prayed for a cheap place to stay in Jerusalem. Before my arrival, Julie had visited a Messianic Jewish community on Shabbat and had chatted with an interesting lady named Sara.

The day before I arrived, she'd bumped unexpectedly into Sara again at the market.

"Both you and your friend are so welcome to stay with me. I have a house full of people," she remarked, "but you're welcome to sleep on my living room floor."

Taking her up on the offer, we arrived at Sara's home late. She'd already retired for the night, so we took removable padding off the sofa and armchair and made a makeshift mattress for ourselves on her living room tiled floor. The following morning, the seven o'clock news on the radio woke me up, news about Russia: demonstrations for the anniversary of the October Revolution. I walked toward the radio to hear the news more clearly, and came upon a lady in her fifties, sturdy and well-built, with a kind, open face, sitting by it listening to the news.

"Hi, you must be Paula," she introduced herself, "I'm Sara, welcome to my humble abode."

"Lovely to meet you. Thanks so much for putting us up, I so appreciate it. Did I hear the news mention something about Russia?" I asked. "The reason I'm so interested is that I'm a missionary in Russia."

"Where in Russia are you working?" she inquired.

"Chechnya," I replied.

"Wow," she exclaimed, her brown eyes sparkling with excitement, "I can't believe it. I was there in December 1996."

"I was there at the same time. How amazing!" I could hardly believe my ears. It's not often you get to meet people outside Russia who've been to Chechnya, so I was very interested. I sensed I would find a kindred spirit in her. "What were you doing there? Aid work of some kind?"

"Well yes, of a sort. I rescued children in danger."

"Wow, how wonderful!" I exclaimed, intrigued.

"I pretended to be in the Mafia," she continued, piquing my interest even more. "I've done it many times and paid large sums of money to buy the orphans back. After walking them through the mountains to safety, I found families for them to be adopted into."

Initially I didn't know what to make of it; not knowing this woman from Adam, what she was saying seemed too incredible for me to believe. The more we chatted, however, the more I realised she knew places and details she could have known only if she'd actually been there. It turned out we also knew some of the same people.

"I'm a holocaust survivor, that's why I've such a passion to save children," she recalled. A pained look clouded her face, highlighting the wrinkles on her forehead. "My whole family perished in Auschwitz. The Nazis allowed my pregnant mother to live while they experimented on her. After she gave birth to me, they killed her. A kind lady smuggled me out of the camp in a laundry basket and saved my life. I've spent my whole life trying to save other children in danger."

As she was talking, I remembered the six orphans who had disappeared. Maybe, just maybe, she knew something about what happened to them.

Taking a deep breath, I asked, "You don't happen to know anything about six orphans who were living in – – region of Grozny, do you?"

"Let me think," she answered, reflecting for a moment. "Were they living by themselves on – what was it, the seventh floor – near the central market?"

"Yes, and the eldest was a boy."

"And the next two were teenage girls, weren't they?"

"Yes, yes, they're the ones I've been so concerned about. Are they alive? Are they safe?" I questioned excitedly, barely able to wait for the answer.

"Yes, they're alive and safe. I took them. They're now living with families in northern Europe," she responded, eyes sparkling with contentment at the thought of having saved yet more imperilled children from certain death.

"What a relief! Thank you, Jesus!" I was so overjoyed, my eyes welled up with tears of happiness and relief.

The little neighbour girl had been right; a nice woman had taken the children to a better life. Of course, to most Chechens, any foreigner is an 'American.'

In answer to our prayers, God had rescued these precious children in a far more wonderful way than I could ever have imagined. Go, God!

With an exuberant smile lighting up her face, Sara added, "And I'm pleased to say, they're doing well under the circumstances, extremely well. Adjusting to life in a new country isn't easy. But they're happy to be alive and to be able to be children again."

I smiled as I thanked my Jesus for His goodness. I was blown away again by His ingenuity. How likely statistically would it be for us to meet up like that, without anyone organising it? No chance whatsoever. But God.

Our God, in all His grandeur, has such a wonderful way of pulling these things off so smoothly! Anyone would think He's Almighty. Which He is, indeed! Hallelujah! Don't you just love Him? I know I do.

Chapter 30

HE RIDES ACROSS THE HEAVENS TO HELP YOU

There is no one like the God of Jeshurun,
who rides across the heavens to help you
and on the clouds in his majesty.
The eternal God is your refuge,
and underneath are the everlasting arms.

DEUTERONOMY 33:26-27

Chechnya was becoming more and more dangerous for the Russians living there. We continued to cry out fervently for the Lord to provide a new home for our Russian friends in a safe place outside of Chechnya.

In the fullness of time the Lord showed us there is truly no one like Him as He rode across the heavens to answer our prayers in an unexpected, remarkable way, just as He loves to do!

One day in the autumn of 1996, Dasha invited me to a conference where a team of Americans were ministering. I desperately needed spiritual input, so I decided to go. One night after a powerful meeting where the Lord had spoken to me, I couldn't sleep, so I popped into the kitchen to pray and write in my diary. I could still feel the Lord's tangible presence.

I heard His voice clearly instructing me: "You need to go home, phone the local newspaper, and ask them to write an article about the work in Chechnya."

It would have never crossed my mind to do such a thing. Never before or after have I phoned a newspaper and asked them to write an article about my work. I treasured it in my heart, and prayed for confirmation about when I should go home.

In January of the following year, Mum phoned me: "Paula, the church has questions about you being under proper covering in Chechnya. You need to come home, talk with them, and get it sorted out."

This was the confirmation I needed. In mid-January, I travelled back to the UK.

"We're not happy about you being in Chechnya," my pastor Bill cautioned me. "We're worried about you being alone in a war zone. But we've also received an email from Russia, saying you're a loose cannon and not under the correct authority." Continuing, Bill added, "I want you to stay in Krasnodar and help the local church there run an Alpha course[1]."

I knew beyond a shadow of a doubt I was called to Chechnya; the last thing I wanted to do was to run an Alpha course in Krasnodar. I wrestled long and hard over what to do, until the Lord lovingly told me: "Trust me and be obedient to your leaders."

I let Bill know: "I'm willing to do whatever you think best."

On arriving in the UK, I'd decided to organise a twenty-four-hour sponsored 'famine' to raise money for relief in Chechnya. I encouraged everyone I knew to join us or give money. As the Lord had instructed me, I phoned the local paper and asked them if they wanted to do an article about our work. They agreed and entitled their article 'Paula Needs Support for Famine.'

When I saw the newspaper, I was shocked that my phone number was included at the end of the article. What if Chechen terrorists found out where I was and killed me?

My fears turned out to be totally unfounded.

The morning after the article came out, Mum was at our friend Pam's house in the very same living room where their house church had started when I was a small child. They were praying for provision, and suddenly Mum received a scripture, Isaiah 45:3: 'I will give you hidden treasures, riches stored in secret places, so that you may know that I am the Lord, the God of Israel, who summons you by name.'

Mum boldly declared, with Pam agreeing, that those finances needed to rehouse families would be released from the places where they were hidden. And Mum felt that they would come through a wealthy person we didn't yet know, who didn't actually believe in God.

I walked in to pick Mum up only to find her bursting with excitement. God had given her a word, and she knew an answer was coming. And soon. She was sure of it.

We headed home, and the moment we stepped through the front door, the phone rang.

To my surprise the man on the other end explained he'd read the newspaper article and was interested in finding out more. He invited me to come to his house and tell him and his family more about the work. I agreed saying I would bring my mum with me and we fixed a time.

His phone call was, in fact, the only one I received in response to the article. But it was the right one and the answer to our prayers.

It turned out that he was a neighbour, living in one of the big posh houses that Dasha had posed in front of for a picture when she'd visited us in the UK.

We arrived at the house to find that Paul and his wife, mother, and children were all waiting for us. After introducing ourselves and sitting down, I showed him pictures of our work.

Almost immediately he said, "I'm very interested in helping, and will give you one thousand pounds to start with."

Completely taken aback, I nearly fell off my chair. The kindness and generosity of this man, who I'd never met before, nearly blew me away. And offering such a large sum of money.

Trying to look as calm and dignified as possible, I smiled and responded sweetly, "That would be lovely!"

The next surprise came when he told his children, "Go and

get some of your best toys for Paula to take for the children in Chechnya, who have no toys and nothing to play with." His children immediately ran off, and soon came down the stairs with some lovely toys which greatly blessed the children of Chechnya. For most of these children, it was their first and only toy. You remember the story of Mogamed and the little wooden car that he so treasured. Well, that was one of those toys that I now held in my hands.

It turned out that the morning the article had come out, Paul had woken up thinking it was about time for him to do something to help others. Having lost everything in 1991, he'd worked his way up in seven years to become a millionaire. Not trusting charities or churches, he wanted to give the money to someone actually making a difference firsthand. With those thoughts in his mind, he opened the paper, and the words 'Paula needs support' jumped out. When he saw that I was a local, living down the road from him, and that I was actually on the ground helping the people myself, he was extremely interested.

Realising I needed to be up front with him, I took the bull by the horns: "Paul, I want to let you know that I'm a Christian, and as well as giving people aid, whenever I have the opportunity, I also tell them about the love of Jesus."

Looking at him to gauge his reaction, I added, "If that bothers you, then I don't want to take your money."

In fact, he didn't react at all.

"That's no problem," he said. "You can tell people what you like. Anyway, I don't believe in God."

"Mind you," he added after a bit of thought, "I'd probably believe in God if I lived in Chechnya!"

His wife nodded her head in agreement.

When Bill first heard about the money, he reiterated, "I still want you to do an Alpha course in Krasnodar."

I took Bill to meet this businessman, and they hit it off straightaway.

My new friend filled us in: "It's my aim to raise fifty thousand pounds for the work in Chechnya." Continuing, he notified Bill outright: "I'm suspicious of churches, and I'm not too sure about giving the money through your charity, Kingscare."

Still addressing Bill, he said, "If I raise fifty thousand pounds, can you promise me that it will all go to Paula and her work in Chechnya?"

Bill, of course, instantly replied, "Yes."

It was the strangest of situations – God speaking to my pastor through a businessman who didn't even believe in God. After that, there were no more questions about me going to Chechnya; everyone in the church was extremely excited about what God was doing.

I shared with Paul about the situation in Chechnya and what was on my heart for rehousing families.

"I'll try and raise fifty thousand pounds to help these families," he said hopefully. "I want to spend my money on something that would make a big difference in a few people's lives, rather than a small difference to a lot of people."

What an answer to prayer!

Soon afterward when back in Russia, something eye-opening happened, highlighting the urgency of helping our Russian families leave Chechnya before it was too late.

Our friend Karina was an attractive teenager, sweet and shy, who lived with her mother in a neighbourhood close to Mila's house. Her Armenian father had tragically died when Karina was only tiny so she'd been brought up by her Russian mother. Karina must have taken after her father in looks, looking typically Armenian with her thick, sooty-black abundant hair, tied up in a pony tail and her olive skin. Culturally, however, she identified much more with her Russian heritage. Although still in her teens, she already had a baby son. The baby's father was a Chechen lad who came and went as he pleased.

One day when her mother Masha was alone at home, their house was bombed and completely destroyed. Masha was found alive, hanging upside down holding on to a twisted stairwell in the corridor, shocked but not badly hurt. Neighbours took pity on them and let them live in an empty flat in the same building.

Karina met Jesus and became a believer, coming to our church with her little boy. She worked as a cleaner in a kindergarten to feed her family, but she didn't earn much; they were always hungry, and we fed them whenever we saw them.

One night when Dasha was in town, she stayed the night with Karina. In the middle of the night they heard knocking, and the colour drained from Karina's face.

Men were shouting through the door: "If you don't let us in, we'll break down the door."

Karina's mother, Masha, opened the door, and four Chechen fighters stormed into the room.

"We've come for you, Karina," they leered, "We're going to have a fun evening with you again."

Karina's whole body started to shake.

"You're not taking Karina," Dasha said boldly. "She doesn't want to go with you."

"Yes, she does, she loves it," said one of them, taking her by the arm.

"*Niet* – no – she doesn't. Tell them, Karina. Tell them, you don't want to go."

Karina was frozen to the spot, tongue-tied and shaking.

"Go on, tell them. Go on," Dasha encouraged her.

"*Niet* – no, I don't like it," she finally whispered, looking down at the floor.

"Well, we don't care, she's coming anyway, and so are you," they said to Dasha.

"Oh no, we're not," said Dasha firmly. "We're not going any-where."

"Oh yes, you're coming with us," they said. They started to describe in detail what they were planning to do to them. Dasha stood arguing with these armed fighters, and they were unable to do anything to them or take them away. After two excruciatingly long hours, Dasha suddenly looked them in the eyes with unusual authority and asked, "Do you believe in God?"

One of them said, "Yes."

Dasha declared, "I serve the Almighty God, and He's not going to let anything happen to His servant."

It was as if God Himself had stepped in. The fighters looked at each other and said, "Let's get out of here."

When they'd gone, Dasha asked Karina, "Has this happened before?"

Karina nodded. Looking down at the floor, her lip trembled as a single tear rolled down her flushed cheek. "They're my husband's friends. They often come at night. They take me away to where there's a large group of them, and they take turns – you know – abusing me all night. Then in the morning they drive me home. I never know when they're going to come."

"Why didn't you tell us before?"

"I guess, I was – ashamed. And also scared."

The following day, Dasha shared with me what had happened, and I determined that Karina was never going to sleep in that flat again. She stayed with us for a few days.

The men returned to Karina's flat a few days later; her mother realised it was them, and managed to escape through a window with her little grandson.

Shortly afterward, we travelled to the town where the conference was being held. While there, we found a house to rent for Karina and her son, and for Irina and baby Varya. Varya was malnourished and needed hospital treatment, so we felt it would be beneficial for her to stay in that town as well. We rented a house for them for six months. I hoped Paul's donation would come through soon so we could buy them houses and their whole families could then join them.

During this time, a couple of incidents reinforced my Father's love for me personally. A friend accidentally poured boiling black tea down my back as we sat around a campfire. The pain left immediately as my friends prayed for me. The next morning there weren't any signs of burns at all.

A few days later I was walking down the road when a *babushka* suddenly opened her gate, and her three dogs came running out. One of them saw me, barked viciously, and lurched forward to bite me. I wasn't particularly scared; it was as if I was in a dream, and I just stood still. The dog bit me, and when the *babushka* shouted, cursing it, it ran off. Feeling nothing, I looked down to see that the dog had bitten a large hole out of my tights but hadn't touched me at all. When I arrived home, I saw that I had only a couple of scratches on me.

I marvelled again at the goodness of God in reaching down to touch us in our point of need. He rides across the heavens to help us in every area of our lives. Both in the big things and the small ones.

Chapter 31

THE GIFT OF
A NEW HOME

Defend the weak and the fatherless;
uphold the cause of the poor and the oppressed.
Rescue the weak and the needy;
deliver them from the hand of the wicked.

PSALM 82:3-4

I flew to the UK for Christmas in 1997 and ended up being gone for four long months, the time it took me to get a visa to return. But God used the time and while I was there Paul generously donated the first twenty thousand pounds for the resettlement programme.

I arrived back in Russia in the middle of a terrible economic crisis, as well as a social and political crisis. Things were chaotic and in the middle of it all we were trying to find houses for various families including those of Karina and Mila's. We had no success in the spring or summer.

By the autumn of 1998 the economic crisis was at its height. The exchange rate was fluctuating unpredictably every day. One day you could get a mere 6.3 roubles to the dollar; the next morning it was a whopping twenty roubles. The following day eight. No one knew what to expect or which way it would go next. One morning we awoke and prices had gone up three times overnight.

Once, while standing in a long queue for train tickets, the tickets doubled in price by the time I reached the counter. Anyone with savings went crazy buying everything and anything so that their money didn't become worthless, as had happened in crises in the past. Everywhere people were panicking and buying up supplies, because they didn't know what tomorrow would bring. People bought television sets, sacks of flour and potatoes, anything in fact they could get their hands on to rid themselves of their rapidly devaluing banknotes. Soon there was nothing left in the shops.

On another occasion, I arrived in a village near Chechnya. The pastor and his family were so poor they'd been surviving on a diet of semolina made with water, along with pears from their garden. Going to the shop to buy them some food, I found only four items left on sale: vodka, bread, tinned fish, and vegetable oil.

In such a time of great confusion and desperation, people were living in fear of another famine or civil unrest. Many people couldn't afford to feed their families even before this present crisis, as salaries were low and people weren't paid for three to six months or even longer. Miners, who hadn't been paid for eight months, started striking all over Russia.

One form of protest was to stop trains from running by sitting on railway tracks. Teachers fed their families by collecting money from their pupils, and doctors by charging their patients. And while much of the population spent day after day not knowing where their next meal would come from, plush 'palaces' were being built in the streets of most cities by the small minority who gained from the crisis.

The divide between the rich and poor was growing, and the injustice was glaringly obvious.

During this time, I'd been sent the money for the resettlement programme in dollars. I needed to change it into roubles to buy the houses. This was easier said than done.

I would agree on the price of a house based on the amount I had in dollars and the exchange rate for that day. However, I then couldn't find anywhere to change the money as banks had no roubles to give me or were scared to change money as the rate was fluctuating so much. At other times the price I'd agreed one day might be only half that amount of money in roubles the next, or in some cases double the amount.

As a result, I was able to buy only a room in a hostel for Karina's family. However, Mila's family fared much better. She came with me to look for a house and we found a suitable two-bedroom house, changed the money for a good price and bought the house immediately. Mila set out for home, taking Irina and baby Varya with her, to collect the rest of the family and their things.

Unfortunately, soon after Mila returned home, word got out that they were selling up and moving. Armed bandits broke into the house and stole most of their things. When Mila and family finally arrived in their new town, we were all tremendously relieved and grateful they wouldn't have to return to the horrors of war.

The day we brought Masha, Karina's mother, to her new home was unforgettable. Her bones poked through her thin, ragged dress. Her inquisitive brown eyes, filled with wonder, peered out of her sunken face, glancing back and forth, astonished to see houses and streets where life continued as normal.

Turning to me, she cried out incredulously, "I'd no idea there were places left untouched by war. I thought the whole world had gone crazy. And everywhere had been destroyed."

This was the first time in her entire forty-plus years of life that she'd ever left Chechnya. She was like a little girl hungrily drinking in a newly discovered world.

She was thrilled when she saw their new home, a small room in a communal house, with a shared bathroom and kitchen. I'll never forget the joy and relief on her face as she leapt up and down, thanking the Lord for bringing them to a place of safety.

All in all over a five-year period, we had the privilege of rehousing the majority of the Russian families in our church.

Soon afterward more money came in unexpectedly to buy a home for one more needy Russian family. A good friend from Ellel,

Jean, came out to help us and, meeting Alexei's family, developed a real burden for them. She went home and kindly raised the money for them to be relocated as well.

I'd been hoping to rehouse some homeless Chechen families in the houses that some of our Russians had vacated, but for various reasons this proved to be impossible. In the end, we helped many Chechens rebuild their bombed and damaged houses. New roofs, walls, doors were refitted.

One Chechen family, we were friendly with, had barely escaped with their lives during the second war by walking across front lines carrying a white flag. When they returned to Grozny, we'd had the privilege of accompanying them as they'd returned to their house. Most of the house had been reduced to rubble; in fact only one wall was still standing.

The youngest boy, who was about ten, ran straight to where his room had been and shouted, bewildered, "Mum, where's my room gone?" Before she could answer, he cried out, "Mum, where are my things?" He kept asking, "Where's my bed, Mum? What's happened to my toys? Where are my clothes?" All his mother could do was shake her head and say, "Sorry, sweetie, it's gone. All gone."

He was becoming more and more frantic as he scrummaged through the rubble for his treasured possessions. Then suddenly, with shrieks of joy, he yelled: "Look, Mum, I've found my rucksack." It was intact, though the worst for wear. He held it up for us all to see.

But that wasn't the best thing. A squeal of delight made us all look his way again, as he held up a poster from his room which was still relatively undamaged, "Look, Mum, my poster is still here. Look!"

"That's so wonderful!" his mother and I both cried at once. Isn't it amazing that the smallest things can bring children such joy?

We were thrilled to help this family restore their house from the ashes to become a liveable family home again.

One elderly Chechen refugee was blessed with a new flat of

her own. After losing her home twice in her life – once during Stalin's deportation and then when her husband threw her out for becoming a believer – she was longingly scrutinising a poster of Irish cottages on my wall and choosing which cottage she'd like to live in. A young couple, who were volunteering at our summer camp, watched her doing this with great interest and compassion. They then went home, promptly sold their house and lovingly donated enough money for us to buy her a flat. Their kindness and generosity just bowled me over!

I was thrilled to see our heavenly Father going to such lengths to rescue His suffering children and deliver them from danger. Lavishing His love upon them in the form of a new home of their own in a safe place. Demonstrating in a practical way that they weren't second-class citizens but worthy of honour and highly esteemed. Well and truly treasured, beloved sons and daughters.

And isn't it so beautiful the way God moves the hearts of individuals to give extravagantly to help fellow humans in distress? He gives us the opportunity to share with Him in the joy of seeing lives changed forever. The excitement of planning, dreaming and then working hard to make it become a reality. The privilege of seeing the amazement and delight on people's faces as they realise their dreams have come true and their lives will never be the same again.

The joy and satisfaction experienced in those moments causes us to come alive in new ways. It is truly what we were made for. As Jesus so aptly put it: 'It is more blessed to give than to receive' (Acts 20:35).

What a privilege it is that we, mere flesh and blood, get to partner with the living God to fulfil His plans and purposes.

Paul mentioned a few months after he'd donated the money that his business was prospering more than ever before. He had been blessed as he blessed others: 'A generous person will prosper; whoever refreshes others will be refreshed' (Proverbs 11:25).

Both giving and receiving bring great joy. In the end I'm not sure who was more blessed, Paul and the others who gave, or those who received. All I know is that there was enough joy to go around. And more besides!

For Reflection and Application

Do you personally know anyone who is in need of something specific today? Could you be the answer to their prayers by meeting that need? Or helping them in another way? What a tremendous joy it is to give and to show someone in a practical way that they're loved and special.

Chapter 32

POST-TRAUMATIC STRESS DISORDER AND GROWTH

The Lord is close to the brokenhearted
and saves those who are crushed in spirit.

PSALM 34:18

Praise be to the God and Father of our Lord Jesus Christ,
the Father of compassion and the God of all comfort,
who comforts us in all our troubles,
so that we can comfort those in any trouble
with the comfort we ourselves receive from God.

2 CORINTHIANS 1:3-5

A loud clap of thunder echoing through the mountains woke me from a deep sleep. My heart nearly leapt out of my chest.

"Lord, they're bombing right overhead. Maybe tonight's the night I'm coming home," I thought.

Another rumble – and I realised it wasn't another bombing raid, but only a thunderstorm.

"I can't take much more of this, Lord." I was exhausted. I tried to go back to sleep, but sleep eluded me. My adrenaline levels were too high – Too many horrors – friends raped, children murdered, neighbours kidnapped.

My imagination was running wild: "They're bound to come for me next," I kept thinking.

Later on in the day, I went to the high-rise UN building where I received a distressing email. I excused myself to go out for fresh air and ended up gazing mesmerised at the ground ten storeys below, which seemed to be beckoning me. Something was calling me, daring me to jump – a jump that would end it all.

"Life's too painful; I just want to be with You, Lord."

A sweet voice broke into my consciousness: "What are you doing out there?" A friend, working in the building, put her arm round my shoulder. "Come in and have some tea," she said. I obediently followed her safely back into the building and away from the anguish and tormenting thoughts. Over a piping hot cup of sweet black tea and a biscuit, I started to feel more like myself again.

These thoughts of suicide scared me and alerted me to the fact that something was wrong. Terribly wrong. I needed help. I'd been traumatised by what I'd seen and worn down by the hardship and deprivation – the lack of so many things, including amenities, sufficient sleep, wholesome food, and most importantly, support needed to cope with all this stress and trauma. Added to this, unresolved traumas from childhood were resurfacing.

People somehow expect missionaries to be superhuman. To have no needs of their own. To always be there for them. But we do have needs. Very real needs.

Trying to live up to people's expectations had led me to overwork and to disregard my own needs for the sake of others.

I was suffering from symptoms of post-traumatic stress disorder (PTSD) but hadn't given myself time to realise.

PTSD is a psychological disorder first diagnosed by American psychiatrists treating veterans of the Vietnam War. It can develop after any traumatic event, especially after life-threatening incidents seriously disturbing to any human being, such as accidents, natural disasters, violence and abuse, rape, living through a war, or unexpectedly losing a home or possessions. PTSD can develop not only in those who experienced the trauma personally, but also in those who witnessed death, wounding, or physical violence against others. Secondary traumatisation can occur from hearing stories of atrocities.

Symptoms of PTSD, many of which I was experiencing, can include[1]:

1. *Flashbacks*
    Intrusive recollections of the event, which are unexpected and uncontrollable; they're like a broken videotape, playing again and again, and it's really hard to switch them off.

2. *Reliving the event*
    Out of the blue suddenly feeling in your body as if events that had happened in the past are happening right now. They can be set off by various triggers – a person's actions or words, an object, a smell, or a sound.

3. *Sleep disturbance and nightmares*
    Nights can often be very hard for people suffering from PTSD and I was no exception. I regularly couldn't sleep, or when I finally nodded off, graphic nightmares of loved ones and friends being blown to pieces or murdered caused me to wake up frightened and shaking. Only by clinging to Jesus could I manage to find some peace.

4. *Hyper-vigilance, over-alertness, or exaggerated startle response*
    Almost jumping out of your skin when someone taps you from behind or you hear a loud noise without warning.

5. *Generalised feeling of anxiety*
    Unable to relax, you can't put your finger on exactly why but there's always something to be anxious about.

6. *Feelings of shame and guilt*
    Many survivors struggle with 'survivor guilt,' tormented by the question of why they survived and others didn't. I myself battled with self-condemnation and often blamed myself for things happening around me even when it wasn't my fault.

7. *Emotional numbness*
    You lack a 'normal' emotional response to awful events
    which seem unreal. I remember one morning in Chechnya
    when Aunty Asya mentioned, "There's a dead body outside
    the window." We said, "Oh," without batting an eyelid, and
    carried on eating our breakfast as if this was totally normal.
    We were on emotional overload and couldn't take in any
    more pain.

8. *Outbursts of emotion*
    This can include grief over multiple losses, as well as anger.
    I often bottled up my emotions inside me while in Chechnya
    and so when back home in the UK and alone on a couple of
    occasions, I cried for hours for no apparent reason. Later I
    realised I was letting out pent-up emotions trapped inside
    of me.

    And I experienced anger especially when trying to explain
    to people back home what was going on in Chechnya. I was
    angry first because they seemed to have no clue what I was
    talking about, and second because they were living their nice
    little lives in their nice surroundings and didn't seem to want
    to do anything to help. Of course this was only my distorted
    perception as in actual fact many people really *did* care and
    gave generously to fund my work.

9. *Feelings of isolation and alienation from others*
    You feel like you're living on a different planet to 'normal
    people' who couldn't possibly understand what you've been
    through.

10. *Loss of energy and chronic tiredness*
    Waking up and going to bed exhausted. I found even a week's
    holiday didn't seem to get me over my tiredness.

11. *Despair and loss of hope for a good future*

12. *Inability to concentrate, poor memory*

Your mind is so full of worries that you can't concentrate, and you forget things you used to have no trouble remembering.

13. *Fears*

This is something I struggled a lot with after having so many friends and acquaintances kidnapped or killed. I can vividly picture the occasion when I was sleeping in a hotel room by myself in Vladikavkaz. Not feeling safe with just locking the door, I spent what seemed like forever manoeuvring the hefty oak cupboard up against the door. Then, to my surprise, I realised the door opened outward. I came up with the bright idea of tying a towel round the door handle and attaching the other end to the cupboard. Still not feeling safe, I perched my boots carefully on the door handle so they would make a noise to warn me if someone was coming in, and hopefully scare off the intruder. Finally, once I had my system satisfactorily in place, I breathed a sigh of relief. Shortly after flopping myself down on the bed, I heard knocking at the door. It was George, my colleague, staying in a room down the corridor. It must have seemed like forever before I finally managed to open the door a crack, as boots and towels fell to the floor. I was so embarrassed I could feel my toes curling! George tried not to look too surprised as he asked, "What time are we leaving in the morning?"

14. *Inability to recall, either partially or completely, some important aspects of the period of exposure to the stressor*

Everyone responds to trauma differently. An experience causing one person to suffer from PTSD may have no serious effects on another. Possible factors enabling a quicker recovery and protecting a person from PTSD include a stable upbringing, being able to process what you've been through, and a good support system.

Most people going through a traumatic event will suffer some of these symptoms in the first weeks. They should recover completely after a few months. This is a normal human reaction to a disturbing event. If you're still suffering from multiple symptoms six months after the trauma, you may be diagnosed with PTSD.

My symptoms of PTSD were well hidden except to the most discerning friends. To most people I was a successful missionary who had it all together. I hardly ever shared about how I really felt or what was going on inside. In fact, half the time I didn't even know what was going on myself. On top of that, I knew there were a lot of other people who needed help more than I did. I figured my problems weren't worth bothering anyone else with.

Many of my friends were suffering from PTSD and I realised I needed more training so I could help them. Through this desire to help others, God was about to bring me to a place where I could receive such training, and where I myself would also be healed in the process.

But, thankfully, PTSD is only one side of the coin. Psychologists have identified that people, who've experienced trauma, can go on to not only survive but also to experience 'Post-Traumatic Growth.' This can include finding fulfilment, developing as a person and finding inner strength.

As Nietzsche[2] stated: "What doesn't kill you makes you stronger."

Research suggests that between 30% and 70% of individuals who've experienced trauma report positive change and growth coming out of their traumatic experience[3]. There are three main benefits, all of which I experienced in my own journey, that research[4] has found:

- Feeling stronger and finding hidden abilities and strengths, changing the person's self-concept and giving them the confidence to face new challenges, eg If I can survive this, I can survive anything.
- Good relationships are strengthened, which is reflected in how people often speak of 'finding out who their true friends are' after experiencing a trauma.

- Priorities and philosophies change, eg learning to live for the moment and prioritising your loved ones.

Post-traumatic growth is not a direct result of the trauma itself but is connected to how the person struggles as a result of the trauma[5]. A number of things can help in this struggle (or wrestling) to come to terms with what has happened, including relationships where a person feels 'nurtured, liberated or validated' and experiencing 'genuine acceptance from others'[6]. Active, attentive and compassionate listening, by a friend, family member, spiritual leader or counsellor, brings healing and encourages post-traumatic growth.

The Lord was about to bring me to a place where I would find people who were able to listen attentively and compassionately, accept me for who I was and validate what I'd been through. With their help, I experienced a lot of post-traumatic growth: a much deeper appreciation of what Jesus went through on the cross for me and the depths of His kindness, a deeper inner strength, a greater humility, a fresh resilience, a more profound understand of the suffering of others and an even fiercer tenacity to bring hope and healing to the traumatised and broken.

For Reflection and Application

As you were reading this chapter, did it touch on anything inside you? Are you suffering from any of the symptoms I've described? If you suspect that you're suffering from PTSD and need help, ask the Lord if there's someone who can help you get through this. He will lead you to those who can help you, just as He did me.

Do you know someone who's recently been through a traumatic time, who could use a compassionate, listening ear? Could you make some time, in the next few days, to spend some quality time with them?

Chapter 33

THE ELLEL NETS TRAINING SCHOOL

Come to me, all you who are weary and burdened,
and I will give you rest.

MATTHEW 11:28

He heals the wounds of every shattered heart.

PSALM 147:3 (TPT)

I found out that Ellel Ministries was just about to start a six-month in-depth training school of healing, deliverance, discipleship and leadership called NETS (Nine Eleven Training School). NETS is based on Luke 9:11 where Jesus welcomed the people, taught them about the kingdom of God, and healed those who needed healing.

As soon as I heard about NETS, I knew I needed to go and study on it. I wasn't sure when would be a good time, however, or whether or not I could afford to be away from my work for such a long time.

Shortly after this, Mum told me that she was going to study on the NETS school.

One day during her time there, Mum missed me a lot and prayed, "Lord, I need my girl!" The following day, I went to the immigration office to have my visa renewed as I used to do at the time every three months. To my surprise, they refused to renew my visa and I was told I had to leave Russia within two days. I managed to catch a boat to Turkey, travel by bus to Istanbul, then fly back to the UK from there.

God had brought me to the UK in answer to Mum's prayer! Once again, I saw the Lord's heart in answering even the seemingly insignificant requests on our heart. He's interested in even the smallest of details.

Mum obtained permission for me to sleep in her room in the dormitory while I was there. I ended up staying in the UK for two weeks while I got a new visa, and then returned to Russia.

I found Ellel Pierrepont, where NETS was held, to be an amazing oasis of peace, safety and healing. I was struck by the beauty of this former boarding school, set in acres of lovely English countryside, majestic oak trees, bright green lawns, and a delightful river flowing through quaint bluebell woods.

The fellow students and staff were so kind, loving and accepting of Mum and me, and I could see that Mum was receiving a lot of healing. When it was time for me to return to Russia, I sobbed for a long time because of the love and security I was leaving behind. I decided to follow in Mum's footsteps and do the next NETS school – NETS 4.

As we drove up Pierrepont's long driveway to the impressive nineteenth-century country houses, I was excited about what God was going to do on my school. In the end, He did over and above my expectations. I thought I was going to learn how to help others, but God had me there in the first place to heal and refresh me! The love of the team, the amazing home-cooked meals, the life-changing teaching, the deep friendships with other students, and the fresh English country air all did me the world of good.

During the school there was a real emphasis on coming into a closer relationship with God and experiencing His love personally for ourselves. His presence was very close and real in the classroom as well as throughout the base. Anointed worship times led by Helen Burgess, with a voice like an angel, and her amazing team, ushered us morning by morning into the Father's presence to gaze upon His lovely face, pour out our love upon Him and, in turn receive His love, gentle embrace and healing. I had wonderful times alone with Him by the river in the morning just talking to Him and getting to know Him afresh. I so enjoyed the chance to just 'be', to not have others to care for and to receive my Father's love and healing.

Throughout the six months we were at Pierrepont, the Lord lavished His love upon us over and abundantly. He gently revealed to us things that were hindering our relationship with Him so that they could be dealt with.

One of many life-changing teachings was on the Father Heart of God taught by Ken Symington. Ken, with his delightful Northern Irish accent, was such a lovely, gentle man, the kind of father anyone would want, and he had such an anointing upon him to bring healing in this area. He taught us that one of the things that can affect our relationship with God is our relationship with our earthly father (or childhood caregivers or guardians). Generally speaking those whose earthly father was loving and kind find it much easier to see God also as loving and kind. If, however, our father was distant or abusive, we often struggle to get close to God. Negative childhood experiences from our authority figures can distort our view of Father God and what He is really like. We need to give all these negative emotions to God and ask Him to reveal to us what He is really like.

He truly is the best Father we could ever imagine and has a deep personal love for each one of His children. Religion has often portrayed Him as an angry old man with a big stick waiting to punish us for anything we do wrong. He so wants us to know that He is not like that at all. He is love (1 John 4:8), the purest, sweetest and deepest love we could ever experience in this life. No matter what we have done, we can come running into His arms and He will forgive us and embrace us. He longs to be in relationship with us and walk through this life with us. This truth really became a reality for me in a deeper way than ever before as Abba Father tenderly healed my heart in this area.

At the beginning of the school they taught us that man is

made up of three parts, just like God, with a body, a soul – mind, will and emotions – and a spirit (1 Thessalonians 5:23). Our ability to connect with God, creativity, intuition and conscience are all expressions of our spirits. When we are wounded in any way, by abuse, an accident or any trauma, all three areas of our being are affected. Medical doctors are concerned with making sure that our body is okay and recovers. But often our soul – with all its feelings, memories and thoughts – and are spirits are neglected.

When people fail to recover after an accident or traumatic situation, shock, trauma or other damage could be hidden away in their souls and spirits that needs to be dealt with.

I was privileged to meet Lynda, who was on the team at Pierrepont at the time. After suffering a serious fall on a mountain, she'd been left unable to work because of pain. When Peter Horrobin prayed for her at a conference for healing for her soul and spirit, she was completely healed and was able to go back to work and live a normal life. Her amazing story is found in her book, *Lynda: From Accident and Trauma to Healing and Wholeness*[1].

We were very privileged to have Peter Horrobin teaching us during the first week of the school. As he passionately shared the history and vision of Ellel Ministries and the many amazing things they'd seen over the years, I knew I was in the right place. I was so excited to be learning how to help the precious people I was working with. But little did I know that the Lord wanted to start with healing me first! And even during that first week through Peter's powerful teaching, the Lord gently began His work on my heart bringing up things that needed dealing with.

From the beginning we were encouraged to truly make Jesus Lord of every area of our lives. It is difficult for us in the modern world to fully comprehend what the word 'lord' means. A 'lord' was someone who was the boss, the master, chief, or ruler in his manor or area of influence. He was the person who had authority, control, or power over others. If a lord was bad, it could be a nightmare as all forms of abuse and neglect could take place. On the other hand, if a lord was good, people would gladly come under his lordship knowing that all their needs would be met and they would come under his protection.

Our Lord is the best Lord in the whole wide world and not only that, He is also the Lord of all lords! And He isn't just Lord, He is also a Good Shepherd (John 10:11). In Psalm 23 we read what a good shepherd does for His sheep: He meets all their needs and is always with them even in the darkest hour, guiding, protecting, comforting and restoring. When we give our lives to Him, we invite Him to be our Lord and Good Shepherd. We invite Him into our inner 'house' to clean it up, take charge and bring His wonderful order. But He is a true gentleman and waits for us to open the door for Him to have full access to every room, even the cobwebbed dark basement, so He can go in and clean up the mess.

In learning about the foundations of our faith we looked at the importance of repentance. The Greek word for repentance (*metanoia*) means having a complete change of mind. To repent means that we were heading in one direction away from God and now we have a 180 degree turn around and start walking towards Him instead. When we repent of those things that are still issues in our lives, it opens the door for the Lord to set us free.

Some people question the value of inner healing, arguing that everything has already been done at the cross. It is true that everything has already been done at the cross, but we need to specifically apply the finished work of the cross to areas of our lives where we are still not seeing the victory.

In the Old Testament, when the children of Israel were slaves in Egypt, God told them to take a young, unblemished male lamb (called the Passover lamb) and sacrifice it, putting its blood on the lintel and sides of the doorpost as a sign to protect them from the angel of death. Then in the morning they were to pass through the bloody threshold, almost like through a birth canal, leaving behind the old life of slavery and being 'born' into a new life of freedom (Ex. 12:21–23). Later on, Jesus - the perfect sinless man, fully human and yet also fully God - became that Passover lamb and shed His blood for us on the cross (1 Cor. 5:7).

So in the same way that the children of Israel applied the blood to their doorposts, we must take the blood of Jesus and in faith, apply it to those areas of our life where we still have issues and believe in its power to protect us, save us and lead us into a new life of freedom. Indeed it is through the blood of Jesus (and the word of our testimony) that we overcome Satan (Rev. 12:11).

Forgiveness is another key crucial to receiving healing. Jesus Himself taught us that if we want our Father in heaven to forgive us, we need to forgive those who hurt us (Matthew 6:15). Forgiveness involves acknowledging the pain of what has happened to us and choosing, even if we don't feel like it, to release the person who has hurt us into God's hands, letting go of any desire for justice or vengeance. Sometimes we can hold unforgiveness in our hearts towards God because He allowed something bad to happen to us (even though He hasn't actually done anything wrong). Or we may even hold unforgiveness against ourselves for something bad we've done or that has been done to us. If we refuse to forgive ourselves, God or others, bitterness can destroy us from the inside, causing physical sicknesses as well as emotional and spiritual problems (Hebrews 12:15). We heard testimonies of people who were healed of physical illnesses just as a result of forgiving someone who had hurt them in the past.

In the Ten Commandments the Lord tells us that the sin of the fathers will be visited onto the children to the third or fourth generation (Exodus 20:5). The actions of our forefathers can still affect us today. Just as physical sicknesses like diabetes can be hereditary, so can issues like alcoholism, anxiety etc. We need to forgive our ancestors for the consequences of any sins they committed that are still negatively affecting us and cut ourselves free through the blood of Jesus from ungodly generational lines.

Something that was completely new to me and seemed very strange when I heard it for the first time, was the teaching on soul ties. Soul ties are a spiritual connection between two people. They can form between anyone we are in a close relationship with, helping us to bond and connect with others. This is particularly important in families. New-born babies need to bond and form ties with their parents in order to survive and thrive. In marriage or any sexual relationship, a tie is formed in body, soul and spirit. In Genesis 2:24 it says that 'a man leaves his father and mother and is united to his wife, and they become one flesh.' Soul ties can also develop between close friends. In 1 Samuel 18:1, it tells us that David loved his friend Jonathan as his own soul.

Soul ties can become ungodly when they are formed through illicit sexual relationships, occult involvement, control, trauma or abuse of any kind. These ties can keep us connected not only to the person but also to any bad things that happened (or are still happening) in the relationship with this person. When ungodly soul ties are specifically broken, we can be free from that person and any influence they may still have over our lives.

I remember the first time I was actually praying for someone about this. We were on a church weekend conference and, a lady I was assigned to pray for, described her problem. It sounded like she had an ungodly soul tie that needed breaking. Even though I still wasn't totally convinced about it, I prayed to break the soul tie. We were both surprised when she suddenly lurched forward violently and then swayed back and forth for a few moments. Maybe there was something in this, after all! Afterward she thanked me profusely and said how free she felt. This really demonstrated to me that soul ties can actually have a powerful effect on our lives even if we aren't aware of it.

We learnt how to pray for people to be set free from demonic influence that may have come in because of any sin, trauma or abuse in their past that hadn't been dealt with. Often once a person had repented and forgiven those involved, the demonic influence would be easily broken.

I was amazed time and time again as we prayed for one another and others, applying these keys that we were learning, how we saw people set free and healed in front of our eyes.

Our NETS school was blessed with amazing speakers from all over the world, as well as having Jill Southern, the director of Pierrepont, as our main speaker. The authority with which she taught and ministered, her fun and her willingness to be real and open all made teaching sessions exciting and you never knew what to expect!

Jill taught us on the topic of emotional wholeness. I remember how she described vividly how children don't have the emotional maturity to cope with painful emotions and often stuff them into what she described as an 'emotional basement' hoping they'll just go away. Unfortunately these pent-up emotions don't just go away, but will fester and find ways of coming up, causing varying problems physically, emotionally and spiritually until they are dealt with. Jill was a very anointed speaker and as she spoke, I could feel emotions stirring deep inside me, presumably coming up from an 'emotional basement' that I hadn't even been aware of before.

The first step towards emotional wholeness is coming out of denial and into reality about the painful things that have happened in our lives: acknowledging these things and the ways in which they've affected us, to both ourselves and God. This is the key which opens the door to the 'emotional basement'. We then have to have the courage to face these festering emotions, which can seem unbearably painful, and find a legitimate way to release them.

There are many ways in which we can release these pent-up emotions so as not to harm ourselves or others. We can talk to God about how we feel and pour out our hearts to Him. David is a good example of this, as he poured out his heart honestly to God in many of the Psalms (Psalm 62:8). Talking to a friend or counsellor, someone we can trust, can also be an excellent help.

Writing down our experiences and thoughts in the form of a journal can be a great way to get in touch with our feelings. We can also ask God His thoughts on the matter and write down what we feel He is saying back to us. If we're still finding it difficult to get in touch with deeply buried emotions, we could imagine the person who's hurt us sitting in a chair opposite us and tell them how we feel or attempt to write our feelings down in an imaginary 'letter' to them, telling them how we feel about what they've done to us. If we write a 'letter', then burning it or ripping it up can be a powerful, symbolic way of letting those feelings go.

Sometimes physical actions can help us to release emotions by allowing our bodies to take an active part in it. It could be through exercise such as running, kicking a ball or playing squash. Or doing physical work, like sweeping or cleaning. Other physical actions, when done alone with God or a counsellor, can sometimes help us get in touch with long-buried emotions, for example punching or screaming into a pillow or tearing up newspaper. This can be a great release as long as we're not destroying property or hurting ourselves or others.

Creative arts such as painting, music, or making something with our hands can also be an effective way of releasing emotions and bringing healing.

We spent a lot of time on the school getting rid of negative pent-up emotions in the various ways described above, and a couple of days doing creative arts, which was very healing and releasing.

As the school went on, I realised that, not only did I definitely have an 'emotional basement,' but that it was totally jam-packed with painful emotions from different times in my life.

I grieved for the many painful things I'd experienced but had never really acknowledged in my life. I'd not been able to be carefree and enjoy my childhood as I should have been. I'd experienced things a child should never have to. I grieved for friends who I'd lost in Chechnya.

We spent quite a lot of time looking at the different types of abuse we face in life, how they affect us and how to minister healing into these sensitive areas. The Lord in His kindness had led me to NETS at just the right time. Listening to the teaching helped to bring my childhood sexual abuse back up to the surface. The anointing for healing in these deep areas was very strong and the Holy Spirit gave me the courage and strength to face it. He knew that being in such a safe place, I would finally be ready to acknowledge what had happened to me, to allow the heart-wrenching memories and emotions buried in a deep place to come to the surface and to have the courage to talk to someone about it for the first time in my life. I was so blessed by both fellow students and prayer ministers who patiently listened to me and held me as I sobbed, releasing the pain, trauma, shame, rejection and loss, and then gently prayed for me to receive God's comfort, love and healing.

I was blessed to develop close relationships with quite a few of my classmates but my closest friend was Kathy Klassen, a lovely Canadian pastor. We spent a lot of our free time together, talking and sharing. I thank the Lord for her compassion, gifting in the area of inner healing and friendship. She helped me tremendously as I worked through the pain that was coming up. It was such a relief to be getting free from those things and I knew I would never be the same again.

We also spent quite a lot of time learning about how to renew our minds. Most of the battle for freedom takes place in our minds. Proverbs 23:7 says that 'as a person thinks in his mind, so is he.' So our thoughts really determine who we are. 2 Cor 10:15 instructs us to 'take every thought captive.'

One of the ways we renew our minds is by using God's word to replace any lies we may be believing which lead to negative thoughts. Upsetting experiences in childhood can cause us to believe lies about ourselves, others, God or life in general. Jill explained that it was as if lies had been placed in our 'truth drawer' distorting our way of seeing things. Part of the healing process is allowing the Lord to show us the lies we've been believing, what happened to cause us to believe them in the first place and to receive His truth.

In the areas where we'd believed lies, Jill encouraged us to ask the Lord for a scripture with the truth in that area. Then we were to take that scripture, look at ourselves in the mirror and declare it over ourselves, three times a day, like medicine. At first, I felt really silly talking to myself in the mirror but I soon got used to it and have found this practice really life changing, allowing the Word to renew my mind.

Throughout our time at Pierrepont, the Lord ministered to us in a myriad of different ways. As we corporately worshipped Him, His sweet gentle presence embraced us and touched us in the depths of our being. During teaching sessions, the Lord brought life-changing truth and revelation to us and keys in how to live in freedom. Corporate ministry at the end of teaching sessions and personal ministry appointments provided space and time to tell our stories, let out our pain and receive prayer for healing and deliverance. The beautiful surroundings, opportunity to rest, wholesome meals, fun, laughter and friendship all brought refreshing and restoration. The rich fellowship we shared as we experienced the Lord's deep work in our lives led to life long friendships with a number of my fellow students and staff.

God brought deep healing to me in body, soul and spirit. It was so amazing to get rid of the pain, shame, trauma and lies I had buried deep inside of me and replace them with His truth, love and acceptance of me as His beloved daughter. Wow, what a relief! I left NETS feeling lighter and more healed than I'd ever imagined possible. Unresolved issues from my childhood, which I hadn't even been consciously aware of, had been healed. Only when they were gone did I notice how free I was. Yay, Jesus! I was well on the way to getting healed of PTSD.

I also had a new toolbox and keys to bring healing to my dear friends in Chechnya. Over the years since then I've used what I learned hundreds of times over in ministering healing and freedom to the traumatised and broken.

The Lord has graciously restored my soul. His deep, thorough work in me isn't finished yet. He who began a good work in me will be faithful to bring it to completion (Philippians 1:6). Sometimes when I think I'm totally healed in one area, He brings up things that still need working on. Only when my sojourn on this earth is over, and I look fully into the wonderful face of my beloved Jesus, will I finally be completely whole. But for now, I thank Him that I'm more whole than I ever dreamed possible in this life.

For Reflection and Application

Did anything in this chapter touch you? Are there areas that are hindering you in your walk with the Lord? Or where you are still not free? If so, ask the Lord to give you the courage to face these issues. If it is too difficult to do alone, ask Him to show you who to contact – a minister or friend – who can help you in this. If you feel you would like help from Ellel Ministries, the contact information is at the back of the book.

Left: Apartment block in Minutka badly damaged by the first war.

Right: With children from Chechnya.

Left: Filling buckets up at the local water pump.

Below: Newspaper article in 1997 asking for help for food for refugees.

Paula needs support for "famine"

by PAT FRANKLIN

A YOUNG Fleet woman is holding a "25 hour famine" to raise money for food for refugees in Chechnya, a republic which used to be part of Russia.

Paula (25), a former pupil at Farnborough Hill School, is working as an unpaid missionary in the town of Grozny and exists on the support of a few families from this area.

She says that although the war in Chechnya is over, the economy has collapsed and no one there has been paid for the last six months.

The only aid to the area comes from Baptist sources abroad and Paula helps distribute food and supplies when they come by lorry.

Paula is staying with her mother in Elvetham Road, Fleet. She went to Chechnya after graduating from Keele University with a degree in Russian and psychology.

She says that although the people she lives among have nothing, they are filled with joy when they become Christians.

Anyone wishing to join the one day fast or to help the work in Chechnya can contact Paula on 01252 620081.

Left: Central market in downtown Grozny after the first war.

Below: War wreckage in residential area of Grozny.

Left: A goat bought by Kingscare for a needy family.

Right: Enjoying a BBQ at one of the many makeshift 'cafes' springing up (with no walls, roof, tables or chairs) in downtown Grozny soon after the first war.

Right: The ruined home of Paula's friends from church. When the second war flared up, the family managed to flee in the nick of time, just before their home was bombed and completely destroyed.

Left: Celebrating New Year in a refugee camp.

Right: A Russian babushka in her hut in the refugee camp before being bought a new home with money donated by Paul.

Left: A family standing in front of their new home bought with money donated by Paul.

Left: NETS 4 morning worship with worship leader Helen Burgess (on guitar), and fellow students from left: Audrey Travis (who during classes always sat on front row with Paula), close friend Kathy Klassen and roommate Marianne Meier (on keyboard).

Right: During a NETS outreach on the streets in Guildford, UK, Paula sharing her testimony and the good news that God is in the business of restoring lives, hallelujah!

Above: NETS 4 graduates proudly displaying certificates during the Graduation Ceremony.

Left: With the NETS 4 school outreach team on the streets in Kiev doing action songs with local children.

Right: Paula sharing her testimony and the good news of God's love, on the streets in Kiev, with the NETS 4 team.

Left: George Dowdell with a child from Chechnya.

Right: Standing in front of the wall that protected her and George from bullets in downtown Grozny.

Left: Leading worship in the very same place and in the same blue dress the day after the Chechen fighters stormed into the room.

Right: Children heading for the beach at the summer camp.

Left: Ancient Caucasian towers in the mountains of Ingushetia.

Left: A military tent in the refugee camp housing a family or two.

Right: A teenage girl sells her wares at the tent refugee camp.

Left: A little boy in the refugee camp who was chopping wood when Paula came across him.

Right: Paula in the black coat registering a family to receive food parcels.

Left: Armed escort protecting the team as they distribute food parcels at the tent refugee camp.

Right: Chechen elder in typical Chechen hat at the tent refugee camp.

Left: Ladies queuing up for their daily soup ration from the Government.

Chapter 34

DON'T PASS US BY

If I have found favour in your eyes, my Lord,
Do not pass your servant by.

GENESIS 18:3

One of the NETS mission trips was to the capital of the Ukraine, Kiev, and I signed up to go.

There, I was able to meet up with Larisa, as well as ministering in a children's home and doing street evangelism. Larisa took a two-day train journey to meet me there. It was lovely to chat and pray with her. I also passed on money I'd raised for her to run a summer camp in my absence.

Unfortunately, the situation in Chechnya destabilised and all the borders closed, so the camp had to be cancelled. A few months later the second war started up.

After finishing NETS, the Lord led me to take some time out and I visited family and friends around the world. After a short trip in early 2000, I returned permanently to Russia in the summer of 2000, just in time to organise our annual summer camp. The situation in the Northern Caucasus was very unstable and we sensed that, instead of holding the camp as we usually did at the Caspian Sea, we should hold it at the Black Sea – a tedious twenty-four hour journey for the guests, but a much safer environment for all, far away from Islamic fundamentalists, ethnic tension, and explosions.

The border into Chechnya was constantly closing. A week before the camp, it closed again, and after much prayer on our part, it opened up the day before our campers were to leave and remained open until the day after they returned home. The camp dates turned out to be exactly right; one day earlier or later, and the people wouldn't have made it in or out of the city.

As I'd been away for a few months, I had to organise everything at the last minute.

The Black Sea terrain was vastly different from the flat, sandy coastline of the Caspian Sea. Winding hills awash in brilliant summer greens opened out onto the rugged Black Sea coastline. Alluringly steep, rocky inclines lead intrepid explorers to quaint stony beaches and bays; colourful pink, beige, and brown seashells, hidden between rocks, merrily dreaming of being collected by tiny hands; and of course the ever irresistible dark blue sea, almost black in its hue (hence its name), ready and waiting with all its charm to refresh and delight weary holiday-makers.

Just two weeks before the camp, Luba and I spent the best part of a day trekking through this hilly terrain looking for a base and getting completely drenched in a tropical rain shower. We eventually discovered the perfect place; to our surprise and relief, it was still available.

In the next few days, the Lord sent people from England to be on the team: my mum and friends from Ellel, Kay and Steve Anning. God opened the door for them to get visas and flights at extremely short notice and board the plane with five extra suitcases stuffed with presents, toys, and clothes, and not pay a penny in excess baggage. Throughout the week they ministered individually to all who wanted prayer and counselling.

The week brought a deep sense of joy, as always sprinkled with lots of fun and laughter, and with cleansing, releasing tears of healing. One lady exclaimed, "It's the best week I've had in the last eight years of my life."

The Father's love transformed lives.

I remember one particular meeting with the children. After sharing a story about Jesus, I became distinctly aware of His sweet, close presence.

"Close your eyes and talk to Jesus," I encouraged them all, "Jesus is here and I can feel Him. I think you can too."

My heart overflowed with love and peace, and I paused to drink it in. A gentle hush filled the room.

"Those who would like to invite Jesus into their lives, ask Him in. He's here. Right now."

Continuing, I expounded, "You can either invite Him to come in and be with you for the rest of your life. Or you can miss this moment, like so many others have done, and He will pass you by. The choice is yours. But He's here, and He's so longing to be your friend."

I felt such an urgency that I pleaded with Him out loud: "Jesus, don't pass us by. Please. We so need you and want you in our lives. You're the best friend we could ever have. We love you, Jesus. Come and meet with us."

I lingered a while in the beauty of the moment. When I finally opened my eyes, I saw that many of the children had received a profound touch from their heavenly Father. One girl, among believers in Jesus for the first time, had been overcome by the power of the Spirit and was leaning her head on her friend's shoulder with her eyes closed. Other children sat motionless in silence for a long time as they met with Jesus.

"If you'd like more prayer, you're welcome to come forward and we'll pray for you."

The majority of the room came forward. As we prayed, many fell to the floor under the power of the Holy Spirit. One little boy of about ten lay on the floor for half an hour in Jesus' presence. Their little faces were radiant as they shared what they'd seen and experienced.

I battled a chest infection the whole camp. I'd caught cold the day I'd got soaked, and this had turned into a nasty infection. My rasping cough became worse as the days went on. I was stretched to my limits: the only one leading worship, doing most of the teaching, translating, and organising. Once, while in the shower, I scared myself when I blacked out for a split second.

As we left the camp to go home, I coughed and coughed, my whole body racked with pain from every cough and movement. Halfway through the journey, as bright stars twinkled, casting silvery shadows over slumbering households, our hired bus driver stopped at an all-night chemist.

"Why have we made a stop here? Please, let's just keep going and get this journey over with," I cried inwardly.

The next thing I knew, the driver marched up to me, handed me some antibiotics[1], and said, "If you don't take these tablets and stop that awful hacking, I'll throw you off the bus." I obediently took the first tablet – as you do when directed to do so by a bus driver!

After seeing the guests home, we were due to fly out from Sochi, an eight-hour drive away. In the evening we went to catch the night bus only to find it was completely full. A taxi to Sochi was our only option if we wanted to make this flight. It was expensive by Russian standards but equivalent to the cost of a bus fare in the UK so we agreed to it.

By this time, I felt very ill, with a high temperature and shooting pains in my ribs and back every time I coughed or moved. I didn't know how I was going to make it through another all-night journey.

I'd promised to pick up a suitcase to take back for Christabel, my beautiful African friend, who'd relocated to England, so we had to make a detour via Krasnodar.

The Armenian taxi driver wasn't used to big cities and didn't know Krasnodar. After getting horrendously lost, we finally found the hostel, only to be informed, "There's no suitcase here of that description." We encouraged them to look everywhere, but sadly all Christabel's prized treasures from Russia had been stolen.

Being so short on time to make the flight, the taxi driver drove wildly to get us there. He couldn't find the slip road onto the motorway and turned up the wrong side of the three-lane motorway.

"Jesus, help, we're going to die!" I prayed desperately, seeing the headlights of oncoming motorway traffic speeding toward us.

God answered my prayer, and all the cars miraculously swerved out of our way before we managed to get off the motorway and find the right road. Somehow we made it to the airport in the nick of time.

By the time we arrived in England, Mum also had a chest infection, and the two of us lay in bed for a few days, too ill even to look after each other. When I eventually made it to the doctor, he let me know I'd had pneumonia, and it was good that I'd taken those antibiotics when I did. Apparently they'd caught the worst of the infection. Otherwise, he wouldn't like to guess what state I'd be in by now.

"Thank You, Lord, for the bus driver. He did me a great favour!"

You never know who the Lord is going to use just when you need it.

After a second course of antibiotics, rest, and wholesome food, I made a full recovery.

* In Russia you could buy most medicines without a prescription.

Chapter 35

TENT REFUGEE CAMP

You are the caller; you are the poor.
You are the stranger at my door.
You are the wanderer, the unfed.
You are the homeless with no bed.
You are the man driven insane,
You are the child crying in pain.
You are the other who comes to me.
If I open to another, You are born in me.

DAVID ADAM[1]

While I was still in the West, the Second Chechen War flared up with all guns blazing from August 1999 until February 2000.

Being so far away from friends and loved ones caused me to pray even more intensely for them. When I finally heard that Larisa and Aunty Asya were alive, I skipped up and down for joy and relief while in a friend's living room in Washington D.C. They'd escaped from Grozny a month after the bombing began and had made it safely to her younger sister's house just outside of Chechnya.

Those who'd survived both wars described the first war as a tea party in comparison with the second. Horrendous atrocities were committed on both sides. Weapons outlawed by the Geneva Convention – such as chlorine and vacuum bombs – were used, as well as an incredible number of Scud missiles.

Thousands of civilians fled Chechnya, many to neighbouring Ingushetia. It was estimated that over 300,000 people had been displaced from their homes since the fighting began in August 1999.

Approximately 174,000 were in Ingushetia. Of these, 120,000 were living in tents, railway carriages, barns, and empty warehouses; the other 54,000 had been taken into the homes of the local Ingush people. This effectively doubled the population in Ingushetia.

On my return to Russia, I was pleasantly surprised to discover Russian believers – who'd suffered at the hands of Chechen rebels – distributing food to starving Chechen refugees sheltering in refugee camps.

I'd planned to go straight back to Russia after NETS finished in the autumn of 1999, but God in His wisdom made it clear to me that I needed to take a break for at least six months. This meant that I completely missed the Second Chechen War. In January 2000 I made a short trip to Russia to visit the refugee camps and see how we could help.

While in the UK I'd raised money to bring relief to some of those refugees in Ingushetia. All-in-all we'd raised nine thousand dollars so we were able to distribute eight tonnes of food to around seven thousand refugees in one tent camp.

Zhenya and Nadya – refugees from Chechnya, ethnic Russians, and believers – were the first to inform me about the plight of refugees in the camps. A brave, determined young couple in their twenties who'd fled Chechnya after the first war, they were now living in Vladikavkaz.

They both dressed impeccably. Zhenya looked like most young Caucasus lads, clothed all in black with black pointed shoes, so shiny you could see your reflection in them. This was all the vogue at the time. Nadya was always adorned in the latest elegant designer dresses and skirts and stylish stiletto-heeled boots to match.

I'd met them through the Grozny Baptist Church, distributing food to the most needy. Zhenya and Nadya had experienced a lot of hardship in their young lives. When the first war started, Zhenya was away from home and Nadya and her tiny daughter, Anya sheltered with neighbours in a basement.

One day, Chechen rebels discovered them. Asking to see passports, they separated the Russians from the Chechens. All the Russians – a motley crew of old ladies, mothers, and children – were ordered to stand against a wall. One rebel started firing. Nadya and little Anya watched, horrified, as friends and neighbours were mown down one by one. As he reached Nadya, the last in line, who was holding Anya tightly to herself, he pointed the gun at them and pulled the trigger. Thankfully, there were no bullets left.

As he reached into his pocket to reload, a Chechen neighbour implored, "Stop. *Pozhalusta* – please – don't kill them. They're believers. Have mercy."

For what seemed like an eternity, he stood frozen with his gun pointing at the beautiful young mother in the prime of her life and her quivering toddler. Then, nodding his head at the neighbour, he scrambled out of the basement.

As soon as it calmed down enough, mother and daughter fled to Vladikavkaz and were extremely relieved to find Zhenya had also escaped and was alive and well. Local believers helped resettle them.

Zhenya and Nadya had a real burden to help those still suffering in Chechnya. They gathered a small team of Russian refugees from the Grozny Baptist Church. I brought in finances and a few helpers from time to time, and they organised the trucks, warehouse, packing, and government permission. Together we brought in as much aid as we could into one refugee camp.

The logistics involved in distributing aid in refugee camps can be complicated at the best of times. Conditions are dangerous and difficult. Locals are suspicious of foreigners. Corruption is rife, making it hard to obtain official permission and local help without paying exorbitant amounts of money. Desperate people aren't always appreciative of what you do. Many feel you owe them something, and they would be willing to kill you to get whatever it is you're offering.

During the first war, it had been relatively straightforward to send containers from the West and distribute them. Customs laws had now, however, become so complicated that it was just too costly, in terms of both time and finances, to get containers through customs.

The last container sent in 1999 with Christmas presents for children had taken months to get through customs; running from office to office, Zhenya and Nadya still ended up paying about two thousand dollars to get the container through.

It now seemed much more sensible to buy the food at the local market in Vladikavkaz, package it there, then truck it into Ingushetia. But getting aid from Ossetia to Chechens in Ingushetia was another challenge due to the animosity between the Ossetians and Ingush. Ossetians weren't particularly keen on Chechens either, as the Chechens where too similar to the Ingush in terms of religion, culture, and tradition.

However, we decided to give it a go on a frigid, cloudless morning in mid-January 2000, with the glorious snow-white mountains cheering us on as they sparkled like dignified ice sculptures.

Arriving at the local open-air wholesale market, we hit a mass of people and activity as far as the eye could see. The autonomous little market stalls were metal carcasses covered with plastic and tin sheeting, with wooden tables overflowing with food, clothes, and merchandise of all kinds.

Squeezed unceremoniously between hostile Muslim neighbours, Ossetia was an Orthodox republic. This was especially obvious by the appearance of the female stall-owners, who made up the majority of the workforce. Their sported short, styled haircuts, and a noticeable lack of headscarfs and trousers. In summer, ladies wore short skirts and dresses. These cultural differences always caught my eye, especially after coming back from Muslim republics, where women dressed so modestly, with long hair tied back in headscarves and full-length flowing dresses.

That wintry morning, as we made bulk purchases at the market, the shopkeepers wondered what on earth we were doing and asked us lots of questions: "Why are you buying so much food? Who's it for?"

"It's to help feed the poor," was all we answered, for security reasons. We didn't dare mention anything else.

My American friend, David Le Compte, who partnered with us on various projects, was with us. A fearless, adventure-loving aid worker in his late thirties, he pulled out his camera to film what we were doing. An old lady appeared, shouting angrily: "What do you think you're doing? Who are you? Put that camera away now."

Residents of the Northern Caucasus were generally extremely suspicious and nervous about publicity. These shopkeepers were concerned that we were the authorities checking up on them to get them into trouble.

As we loaded the truck, a freak windstorm swept through the market. Icy cold gusts, frenzied and determined, ripped off roofs, tossed empty boxes into the air like footballs, and spun electricity lines around precariously, crashing one chaotically down right in front of us. Everything was buffeting dangerously around us, so we hurried to finish. Sighing with relief when we made it to the warehouse, we unloaded the truck by the silvery light of the moon.

At the crack of dawn the following morning, we began packaging the eight tonnes of food into individual family food parcels designed to feed a family for a week. Larisa, Dasha, and Luba had come to help. We slaved away all day in the freezing unheated warehouse alongside volunteers from the Grozny Baptist Church, mostly ethnic Russian ladies in their forties who'd fled the fighting in Grozny.

Attractive young Anya was by far the youngest of them. Only thirteen years old, she was still a girl in a woman's body. Her drawn yet strikingly delicate face wore the look of a *babushka*, weary of life. When the war started, her father and sister had disappeared, and she had no idea if they were still alive. As a result of this terrible loss, her mother had a mental breakdown, and Anya and her grandmother spent the first war looking after her.

Only a few months previously, Chechen terrorists had stormed into the Baptist Church and kidnapped Anya. Her desperate mother pleaded, *"Niet, pozhalusta, niet* – no, please, no. Take me instead of my daughter." But to no avail. The dreadful, piercing scream uttered from her mother's lips, as Anya was pushed into a car and driven away in a cloud of dust, haunted the girl for a long time afterward. Her captors later cruelly informed Anya, "You'll never see her again. She's been killed."

During her captivity, Anya was horrifically tortured and abused. After being held for three months, she had managed to escape only a few weeks before we met her. She had no idea of the whereabouts of her family, or indeed if any of them had survived.

She worked hard all day alongside the rest of us, determined to make sure other children suffering in the camps had something to eat, a luxury she'd been deprived of, during much of her time in captivity.

As I stood there making food parcels with all these amazing people, each one with incredible stories of both suffering and deliverance, I marvelled at the goodness of the Lord in sending Russian refugees to pack up food for Chechens, the people their country was at war with.

Together we packed the food into plastic bags, making twelve hundred food packages. It soon became clear that packing so many in one day would be a challenge. We calculated that each bag would feed a family of five for about a week (costing only about a dollar to feed one person per day). In each bag we packed condensed milk, corned beef, tea, sugar, rice, buckwheat, and cooking oil. We wanted a treat for the little ones, so we managed to put in two lollipops per bag.

We opened and unpacked boxes, measured out food from sacks, packed food into plastic bags, then put bags into boxes. The work seemed to go on forever. Our feet and hands became like icicles, frozen to the bone. We stopped for only one food break the entire day, but we kept up our spirits by singing, praying, and laughing as we worked. We finished by loading the boxes onto a Russian military truck David had hired to take us to Ingushetia the next day.

Hiring a military escort or armed guards was a point of contention in Chechnya at the time. If we didn't take an escort, sometimes we weren't let across the border into Ingushetia or Chechnya. I didn't like having armed guards with me, not only was it expensive but it limited what you could do. Their beady eyes watched you and followed your every move. And sometimes it seemed to attract unnecessary attention. I preferred to put my life in God's hands and travel with only my 'spiritual' escort – the angels! I only travelled with a human escort when on a joint mission with others who wanted to hire one.

David always hired armed guards. Most of the time these guards were teenage lads, relatives of government ministers he was working with who didn't seem to have had any training. They were, however, making wonderful money – a whole month's wages in just two days of work.

On one occasion we popped into a café and all four guards promptly hung up their machine guns, along with their coats, and sat down to have lunch. David remarked: "Good job no one is coming to kidnap us at this precise moment or we'd really be in trouble!"

The guards got the message and quickly jumped up and picked up their guns. "Don't worry, lads, you can have some grub, just take it in turns. Two of you can guard us while the other two have their lunch." Everyone seemed happy with that plan.

One time my friend Nina Davidovich, the chairman of the Russian charity Druzhba, and I were working with David and were on our way to a refugee camp. Nina, a gifted, courageous Russian lady in her fifties, had worked tirelessly in the refugee camps and amongst other things had set up tent schools for the children. I enjoyed spending time with her and often spent the night at her place when I was passing through Ingushetia.

On this particular day, Nina and I were trying to get away from the guards so we could get into a shop without drawing attention to ourselves. We thought we'd managed to ditch our escort, when suddenly one of the guards noticed we'd slipped away and dashed up behind us. The guard caught the attention of two armed men near the shop who guessed we must be someone important with money. They approached us menacingly and Nina said, "Finally you've come for us. We've been waiting for you!"

That threw them off a bit and then they saw our three armed guards striding towards us. Realising they were now outnumbered, they must have decided it wasn't worth trying to kidnap us, so they made a quick getaway. Unfortunately, a few months later, Nina actually did get kidnapped and was eventually released after six long months in captivity.

On this particular occasion David had hired the military escort and armed guards for us to travel into Ingushetia the following morning. After loading the truck to capacity we fell into bed after 11.00 pm, exhausted but happy. Satisfied to know we were doing God's work. And making a difference in people's lives.

Chapter 36

AID DISTRIBUTION IN THE REFUGEE CAMPS

Religion that God our Father accepts as pure and faultless is this:
to look after orphans and widows in their distress.

JAMES 1:27

I was jolted awake by a discordant dawn chorus of yapping wild dogs and jarring cock-a-doodle-doos. I felt achy and stiff all over, as if I'd been run over by the aid truck instead of just packing it.

"It can't be morning already, I've only just fallen asleep," I thought.

Not feeling quite ready to rise and shine, I fell out of bed and hurriedly dressed. After gobbling down a simple breakfast, we were on the road by 7.00 am.

Two military jeeps, the worst for wear and unheated, accompanied the aid truck. Our armed guard, two Russian soldiers, were sober-faced and edgy. One of them barked, "Get in," opening the squeaky door for David and me. Zhenya was ordered into the jeep at the back.

A heavy silence descended on us. The chill in the atmosphere, worse than the lack of physical warmth, caused me to shiver, and I prayed under my breath.

The convoy came to a grinding halt. "Get out of the car," we were brusquely commanded. "Get into the one at the back."

Without questioning, we obeyed orders.

"The front jeep is just a decoy in case anyone wanted to kidnap you," the Ingush driver explained. "If we're ambushed, you'll be safe in this jeep." Soon the Russians headed back home.

"Are we going to get kidnapped, now that the Russians have left us?" I thought. Shuddering, I prayed even more intensely.

Our new driver, a young Ingush man named Mogamed, was relaxed and friendly once the Russians had left. "I'm so glad I was chosen to drive you. I haven't been on a humanitarian mission before." His comment and smile put us at ease.

Soon we reached the sprawling encampment, a sea of military green tents. One of the larger refugee camps, containing three hundred tents housing approximately twenty people each, it was awash with activity: small, ragged boys earnestly chopping firewood, children hauling buckets of water almost the same size as them, young girls tending small tables of wares, mischievous lads giggling as they held onto the backs of unsuspecting cars and slid along on the ice, women wearily queuing for their daily bucket of soup, and men desperately searching for what little firewood was left.

The harsh winter elements had done nothing for these government-supplied army tents, not designed to be permanent dwellings. Cast-iron stovepipes, allowing fumes from wood or gas stoves to escape, jutted out of the tops of the tents. Most tents had electricity, however, although it was sporadic.

Help from the international community had been very limited: the UN viewed the conflict as an internal dispute within the Russian Federation, so these Chechens were seen as "internally displaced persons" within their own country, and not refugees. This difference in terminology meant fewer resources were available to them. The political situation and lawlessness further complicated the matter.

On our pulling into the camp, expectant crowds gathered around the truck. Most of the refugees were Chechen woman and children who'd lost homes and the men in their lives. We met only one Russian in the camp, a young girl who seemed at ease among the Chechens.

With wide eyes, pleading for help, they implored us: "My children are hungry, please give us some food. And please give us the aid personally. Aid has come to the camp, but it hasn't made it into our hands."

"Don't worry, everyone will get some food." We reassured them, "We'll personally give out the food parcels. Please wait in your tents and fill in the form stating the number of people in your tent."

We had to be highly organised to stop riots, since the process of giving out twelve hundred food parcels took a good few hours.

As the bags were being distributed by the Russian team, we made friends with some of the refugees. We were introduced to a blind man in his fifties, led up to the truck by his daughter. He'd been blinded two months earlier by a cluster bomb. We had the joy of praying for him and seeing the Lord touch him.

At first, people were suspicious of us and our intentions. But as they saw we were giving out food parcels to every family personally, they softened toward us. Breathing a sigh of relief, they said, "Thank the Almighty, you've come. This is the first aid we've received since the war started in August."

Sometimes when we distributed food we took New Testaments, booklets or Bibles with us to give out to anyone who was interested. On one occasion, I'd been given a box of children's Bibles which I had with me in the truck. Hundreds of people milled round us, and someone asked, "Do you have any Bibles with you?"

"Yes, actually we do, let me get you one."

I made a big mistake which I never made again after that. I fetched the box out of the truck and gave the lady the children's Bible.

The crowd around me saw I'd given her something, and all wanted it too.

"Give me one."

"Hey, I want one too."

"It's not fair, let me have one."

A mass of hands started grabbing Bibles out of the box. Seeing that something was being given away, the mob increased; the more it increased, the more frantic everyone became, trying to snatch a Bible as it dawned on them there wouldn't be enough to go around. The throng pressed me so hard against the truck, I was almost unable to take a breath. I realised the only way out was to let go of the box; but with the heavy weight crushing me into the box, that was easier said than done.

With all the strength I could muster, and the Lord's help, I somehow managed to throw the box far enough away from me, then I squeezed under the truck and took a deep breath. The box fell into the surrounding people, then landed with a thud in the mud. The remaining Bibles were gone in a flash. The only thing left to tell the tale was a flattened, muddy, truly empty box.

People who have nothing become desperate for anything being given out, even if they're Muslims and it's Bibles that are being distributed. For many it was the only reading material they had. Even years later, some still had their Bibles hidden away in their homes.

The camp administration received us with open arms on that first trip. "Welcome to our camp. Let's give you a tour."

Our armed guards followed along.

"First, we're proud to show you our medical tent. The Chechen doctors and nurses working here are doing an amazing job. Under the circumstances, we're doing our best. But it's very challenging without the necessary equipment or medicine."

"What sort of illnesses are you mostly dealing with here?" we asked.

They filled us in: "The main complaints here are chest-related illnesses, including TB, aggravated by the bitterly cold living conditions, the exhaust fumes, and lack of nutrition. Those who are seriously ill are taken to the local Ingush hospital."

The next stop on our tour was the feeding station. "The government ration is a bucket of soup and a loaf of bread per tent," they explained. We watched a middle-aged lady cooking a large bowl of soup on an open fire, and queues of women with buckets awaiting their daily ration.

"It's insufficient, but keeps us alive," one refugee explained. "We supplement this food ration by selling anything of value we were able to salvage from our homes, or any jewellery we have left."

Later the administration took us to the outskirts of the camp to show us the water points and toilets – makeshift holes in the ground. Long queues of people, covered in mud, waited patiently to fill up buckets with clean water.

David took a step in the wrong place, and his foot slipped down a hole; before he knew it, he was up to his knees in brown gunge: "I hope it's mud!" he blurted out, laughing.

A helpful young girl with a bucket and cloth ran over, apologising and attempted to wipe the mud off his trousers. With no facilities for washing or bathing, this was the way they normally washed. In subzero temperatures, it was not only hard to keep yourself warm, it was virtually impossible to keep yourself clean.

After the tour, we were invited by a pretty teenage girl to see inside her tent and meet her mother. Unfortunately, our armed guards weren't happy about us going off alone, so Mogamed insisted on following us into the tent.

The sweet teenager introduced us to her mother and explained that the two of them had come here the previous week, after her father was killed. Stifling a sob as a tear trickled down her delicate pink cheeks, she composed herself quickly. "They were bombing everywhere in our town, Urs Marten. The house took a direct hit. We were lucky to get away with our lives." Those lovely innocent brown eyes had seen far too much in such a short life.

Pointing to a lady lying limply on a mat in the corner, she explained, "This is Asya. Her daughter and sister and niece also live in our tent."

Asya, probably still only in her forties, greeted me as best she could. I guessed she was suffering from an open form of TB; her sickly eyes bulged out of her sunken face, and she had a terrible hacking cough.

"Are you related?" I asked them.

"*Niet* – no. We just met when we were put into the tent together. There's a third family also living with us, but they're not here at the moment," the girl explained.

I prayed under my breath that Asya wouldn't infect all the people in her tent.

Anya, a middle-aged lady with a lined and worn face, also invited us into her home, a crowded tent teeming with children. "Come in and meet my family. These are some of my nine children." They greeted us shyly.

"My husband was killed two months ago in the fighting in our village, and we fled here. It's been so hard. My children are always hungry. We don't have enough clothes, especially winter boots or socks. The children take turns using shoes when they need to go out."

As she talked, Anya was cooking spaghetti. *Suhariki* – dried bread was drying on top of the stove. There was no other evidence of any food at all. I was glad she was receiving our food parcel. I suspected she was preparing to feed us with her last food. Anya was showing us true Chechen hospitality: you have to feed your guests, even if they say they're not hungry.

"Here, please, help yourselves," she invited us to the table.

"No, really, thanks, we're not hungry, we only just ate."

Not only wasn't I hungry, but knowing her children were famished, the last thing I fancied was eating in front of those hungry children. But it would be rude not to accept her hospitality.

"Come on now, please eat." She set the spaghetti in front of us.

We chomped on the spaghetti as the children sat around watching us. Two of the girls had their arms wrapped round each other. They didn't have much materially, but they certainly had each other.

As we were eating, a young girl with a baby on her hip and a dirty toddler clinging to her rugged skirt came into the tent.

"This is my eldest daughter. She's nineteen. She's a widow too. Her husband was killed soon after her dad was."

After eating, we offered to pray for the family who were quite happy to receive prayer.

As we came back to the truck, an attractive fresh-faced mother holding a little girl invited us to come to her home. Mogamed followed us there too. At the edge of the tents were old barns, converted into basic living accommodation. The smell assaulted my nostrils as I walked into the barn that had housed chickens. Inside were a number of makeshift 'rooms' with sheets and blankets hanging up, separating family dwellings. Her 'home' was at the end of the room. She insisted on giving us tea, as she recounted her woes to us. "My husband has been away on business for months." I couldn't imagine what business he could be doing so guessed he was probably away fighting. I didn't probe any further as Mohamed was listening.

Although he was an Ingush Muslim, he was wearing a federal[1] uniform so she couldn't be too open.

"It's so hard to feed my little ones," she said.

"How many do you have?" I asked.

"Eight. Six boys and two girls. My husband jokes that we have an army in the making. Or our own football team."

David wanted a photo of their 'football team,' so she lined up her six boys for their picture. Before taking it, she encouraged the children to shout their Muslim war cry: "Allahu Akhbar!"

Mogamed said nothing.

As we were preparing to leave, I asked, "I wonder if I could use your toilet please?"

Their outhouse was a little way from the barns. To my embarrassment, Mogamed insisted on accompanying me: "Don't want you being kidnapped from the toilet!"

He waited outside a little way from the door.

As we walked back to the truck, Mogamed looked intently at me, "You're a beautiful woman. I've been looking for a wife like you for a long time. Would you be my wife?"

A little taken aback, I replied, "Thank you for the compliment. I'm sure you will be a wonderful husband to somebody, but not to me."

"I promise, even if I do take another wife later, you will still be my first and most important wife. And I will only take two wives maximum." How could I resist such a tempting offer!

Chuckling to myself, I responded, "Really, that's very nice of you, but we have such different lives. I'm sure we wouldn't be good for each other."

"Do you want to get married?" he asked me.

"Well, yes, if God has a husband for me."

"What if I'm the husband Allah has for you?"

"*Niet* – no. I'm sure you're not," I replied firmly.

Continuing, I explained, "If God has a husband for me, he will be a believer who loves Jesus more than he loves me, and who's doing similar work to what I am doing."

I was relieved when we arrived back at the truck and it was time to leave.

As we drove away from the camp, we noticed a woman stumbling toward the camp with three small children in tow. The large checkered Chinese plastic bag she was dragging along probably contained all their worldly possessions. The dirt on their faces, their matted hair, and their weary eyes said it all.

We stopped the truck to talk to her. "Have you just come from Chechnya?"

"Yes, yes," she sighed. "We've been walking all day. The fighting was terrible, but somehow we made it through. Thank Allah. I heard there is refuge here."

The driver interrupted us nervously: "We have to leave; it's getting dark."

Not only was there a curfew in operation after dark, but it had started snowing again.

We wanted to do more for this dear lady, but all we could do was give her two food parcels and bless her. Then we jumped back into the jeep and drove back uneventfully to Vladikavkaz.

Chapter 37

CLOSE BRUSHES
WITH DEATH

For you, Lord, have delivered me from death...
that I may walk before the Lord in the land of the living.

PSALM 116:8-9

In 2001, we held our second camp at the Black Sea.

Our friend Kevin, the hero who'd cleaned that infamous dirty toilet, came out again to help, and as always his teaching was a much needed and appreciated blessing.

Another friend, Margaret, a short, sweet English grandmother from Ellel, also came out to help. As the camp nurse, she ministered medically and also prayed individually for all who wanted it.

Scorching temperatures sizzled to sixty-one degrees Celsius in the blazing sun, making the welcoming sea lovely and warm. Lots of fun was had by all. A supposedly 'healing' muddy bog was nearby, and we laughed until it hurt as we smeared mud all over ourselves, allowing it to dry on us and then washing it off in the deliciously warm water.

Although situated in a very beautiful area of the Black Sea among lush green palm trees, rolling hills, and enticing beaches, camp conditions were extremely basic. Dirty outhouses serving too many people were cleaned only once a day. Not enough sinks. No showers or hot running water. We heated up water in saucepans, kept in my chalet so they wouldn't go walk about.

Unfortunately, the sea water was also quite dirty, and this

combined with the lack of decent hygienic facilities meant that we battled with sickness and infection throughout the week.

Most of the team and some of the guests came down with something; the afflictions included cystitis, gastroenteritis, flu, chest infections, ear infections, and infected mosquito bites.

Karina's son was bitten by a dog as they waited for the bus to go to the camp, and the wound became infected.

Kevin came down with a chest infection but recovered quickly after prayer.

One particularly funny moment happened when Margaret was counselling a lady from Grozny. We'd lost all our interpreters: I was suffering from gastroenteritis, lying on a bed in the same room with a bucket next to me; the second interpreter had been forced to go home because of poor health; and the other interpreter's five-year-old son, at home with his dad, had come down with pneumonia, so she'd also had to leave the camp. A kind lady had stepped in to interpret, although her English wasn't brilliant, and she could hardly understand anything Margaret was saying.

Luba was also feeling poorly, lying on another bed in the room.

Consequently, Margaret was trying to counsel with two sick girls in the room laid out on beds, an interpreter who could hardly understand her, and people constantly walking in and out looking for saucepans – not a typical by-the-book British counselling session! But God still moved in power, and brought deep healing to the lady being ministered too. Thank the Lord He's not fussy about the way we do things; He just loves to come and touch us regardless of anything.

Two dramatic healings are forever etched into my memory.

Luba, the camp administrator, was ill in bed for most of the camp. From childhood she'd had serious back problems, which from time to time caused troubled breathing, severe pain, and extreme dizziness.

We'd called for the emergency doctor for her three times. The third time, the doctor decided that Luba needed to go to hospital.

The ambulance drove her for hours through the mountains, but the hospital sent her straight back without treating her, since she wasn't registered in that city. Altogether she drove in a claustrophobic ambulance in the sweltering heat for eight hours. She arrived back in a terrible state.

"If the sickness doesn't kill me," she remarked bitterly on arriving back, "then the hospital treatment, or lack of it, might!"

That night I had trouble sleeping. I suddenly felt such an urgency to pray. And not only to pray, but to pray out loud. I would never normally do this, as I wouldn't want to wake up the other four people sleeping in the room with me. I prayed forcefully out loud in tongues and rebuked the enemy.

The next morning I found out that just before I'd prayed out loud, Luba had seen a spirit of death come into the room. "I've come to take you," it told her.

Resignation and despair came over her as she realised she was dying and hadn't fulfilled her destiny. Just about to go with this demon, she heard me praying. Suddenly faith and indignation rose up within her. "Niet – no – I'm not coming with you," she declared boldly to the demon. "I bind you in the name of Jesus and choose life not death for myself."

Instantly, the demon was gone and Luba started to get better.

Kheda's son, Alan, who'd commanded the mountain of rubbish to be removed a few years previously, was by now a tall, lanky sixteen-year-old, dreaming of learning to swim. At the camp, he shared a dorm with Kevin. When Kevin found out Alan couldn't swim, he promised to teach him. "I'll give you my goggles if you learn to swim," he said.

Alan was thrilled at the prospect and determined to win those prized goggles.

One night Kevin awoke to see Alan sneaking into the room, seemingly drunk. He staggered onto his bed, threw up, then passed out. When Kevin examined him, however, he realised it was serious. He rushed to our hut seeking Margaret, the camp nurse and woke us up. "Something's terribly wrong with Alan. Come quickly, I thought he was drunk, but I'm not sure. He's in a bad way."

Dashing into the boys' dorm, I took one look at Alan and gasped. His eyes had rolled up into the back of his head, and he was turning blue.

"Jesus, You have to help us here, I can't have Kheda lose another family member, not after losing her husband so tragically," I prayed inwardly.

We prayed for him. No response. None at all. I was becoming desperate. Suddenly, gentle little Margaret spoke with an incredible authority that must have made all the demons in the area stand to attention: "I bind you, spirit of death, in the name of Jesus, and I speak life into you, Alan, right now."

Alan's eyes popped open as the words left her mouth. Looking straight at me and then at Margaret, he reassured us: "Don't worry, I'll be alright now."

With that, he turned over and went to sleep, as if nothing had happened.

"Amazing!" we whispered excitedly to each other. "But maybe we should stay a bit longer and make sure he's okay."

"There's no need, ladies," Kevin responded kindly, "I'll keep an eye on him."

In the morning, Alan was as bright as a button as he explained what had happened: "I was determined to get those goggles. I decided to go and practice my swimming. I waited until everyone had gone to bed and crept out and tried to go swimming in the sea. Suddenly out of nowhere this big wave came over me, dragging me under the water, and I couldn't seem to find the surface, swallowing loads of water. I nearly drowned. I was really petrified. I prayed and somehow got back onto the land. I lay on the beach for a while. I have no idea how I managed to crawl back to our dorm room."

He'd swallowed large amounts of sea water, some of which had accumulated in his lungs, causing him to stop breathing (known as 'secondary drowning'). But God had healed him.

In spite of all the difficulties, the Lord transformed lives during the camp. We headed home, refreshed and encouraged, ready to face the challenges ahead.

Chapter 38

CRITICAL INCIDENT DEBRIEFING AT LE RUCHER

The Lord is my shepherd; I shall not want.
He makes me to lie down in green pastures;
He leads me beside the still waters.
He restores my soul.

PSALM 23:1-3 (NKJV)

By 2001, a number of friends were concerned I was close to burnout. A close friend, Siny, and I were spending hours together coordinating fundraising efforts for the refugee camps and she noticed the signs.

"Paula," she said to me one day, "I really think you should go to Le Rucher. It's an amazing place, a ministry for missionaries and aid workers living in dangerous regions and war zones."

I'd only been to Ellel a few years previously and thought I was okay, so was reluctant to go. Anyway, I couldn't possibly spare the time.

Finally, after a couple of others also talked to me about it, I agreed to go on a critical incident-debriefing retreat, where they help guests process life-threatening or potentially life-threatening experiences occurring on the mission field.

Le Rucher was a completely different world from Chechnya. It was in a charming French village bordering Switzerland. The tranquility and beauty of the place struck me as we first drove through the village. I saw farmers carefully tending fields, an odd cow or two grazing contentedly, squawking geese and chickens wandering freely, elderly residents leisurely exercising enthusiastic dogs, intriguing woods, bright green meadows, and a lovely pond straddled by a pretty, wooden bridge. Looking closely, I could just make out the pond-skaters happily dancing to a merry frog-chorus among lilies and reeds. All this was surrounded by picturesque, glistening, snowcapped mountains on every side. Mountains just like in Vladikavkaz. But without the danger. No kidnappers. No checkpoints, soldiers, or landmines. What a relief!

We headed up the drive, my stomach churning with anticipation, as I drunk in the delightful, multi-coloured scene: quaint pink buildings with tasteful white windows; flowering plants in vibrant reds, purples, and blues, hanging gracefully out of baskets and window boxes; cherry trees white with full blossoms; and a well-kept, inviting green lawn.

Team members with friendly, open smiles warmly welcomed me. Their dogs, sweet and affectionate, also came up to say hello. I felt immediately at home.

The debriefing process at Le Rucher is based on the story in Luke 24:13-35 where Jesus appears to the two disciples on the road to Emmaus. It was the afternoon of Resurrection Day, and although these two disciples had heard the reports that Jesus had risen, they couldn't make head or tail of it.

Remember, these two disciples had witnessed Him beaten, ripped to pieces, and horrifically crucified. They'd seen the blood and heard the cries. Then watched His lifeless corpse, no longer resembling a human being, laid in a tomb. To them, Jesus was well and truly dead. A goner.

Talk about being the worst weekend of their lives. 'Disappointed' doesn't even come near to describing it. 'Traumatised' is more like it. Off-the-charts traumatised. You couldn't get more traumatised if you tried.

Their Master had been violently taken from them. The One they'd been following faithfully for three years. Their hope, their life, their purpose.

And it had all happened so suddenly, and in the most horrendous way imaginable. Images of His harrowing crucifixion flooded their consciousness, though they tried to push them away. Their faces were sad and gloomy as they quivered at the horror and seeming futility of it all.

They'd believed that Jesus was the long-awaited Messiah. The hope of Israel. The One sent to rescue them from Rome.

And now He was gone. Their dreams were dead. Everything was over. How could they ever believe or hope again?

They were so surprised when they realised this man hadn't heard the news. Was He the only one in Jerusalem who didn't know?

This kind stranger asked them what had happened. They shared with Him not only the details of the event but also their thoughts and their raw emotions. In this way, He listened to them as they wrestled with coming to terms with what had happened. They felt well and truly listened to and heard.

Jesus then explained to them from the Scriptures how this was all a fulfilment of what had been prophesied long ago.

When they arrived at their destination, Jesus didn't impose. He waited to be invited into the place they would be staying. He never forces Himself on anyone; He always waits to be invited. He's the perfect gentleman. He wants us to invite Him into those places of trauma in our lives, maybe places locked up long ago, but places where our wounds are still festering and need to be dealt with.

Finally, over dinner, when Jesus broke bread – they realised who He was.

"How could we not have recognised Him?" they kicked themselves as they looked at each other, overwhelmed by what had just transpired. "We should have guessed by the way our hearts burned within us."

In a similar way, the team at Le Rucher encouraged us to allow Jesus to debrief us.

First, we made a list of critical incidents – life-threatening or potentially life-threatening experiences that had happened personally to us or to others in front of us. I had over thirty critical incidents on my list from my time in Russia. "Wow," my counsellors exclaimed. "We've never met anyone with such a long list!"

I was surprised because I knew the list could have been so much longer. I'd only put on it traumatic things that had happened since I went to Russia in 1992.

Later I found out they hadn't been working at Le Rucher for that long so hadn't as yet debriefed that many people. But even so, their comment was a real eye-opener causing me to realise maybe I *had* been through more trauma than was usual, even though it'd all seemed so normal to me at the time!

The debriefing process involved sharing facts: what happened in the incident, and what we saw, felt, thought, experienced, etc. Then came the most important and heart-wrenching part: describing our thoughts, feelings, emotions, fears, and disappointments in as much gory detail as possible, to express as much of the pain as we could.

Next we compiled and read out a list of losses – primary losses of family or friends, or of possessions, health, or home; then secondary losses that were deeper and internal, such as loss of comfort, peace, hopes, dreams, etc.

Finally, on the last day, after physically nailing the list of our pain, trauma, and losses to a small wooden cross, the papers were burned, and we asked Jesus to exchange our pain for His peace and love. It was a powerful time of release, healing, and freedom, most of which I hadn't even realised I'd needed.

After I left Le Rucher, I stopped having graphic nightmares about war and people being killed. Most people who'd lived in Chechnya had nightmares, and it never even occurred to me they could stop. I thought it was one of those things you would just have to live with after going through a war. However, it turned out Jesus could heal me. And He did. Hallelujah!

At the end of the week, Siny and I were chatting with Erik, the founder and director of Le Rucher. Siny commented, "I think

Paula's on the verge of burnout, and needs more help than just this one trip."

Erik's response surprised me. "I totally agree," he said. "I want her to come again, and we will cover the cost." How amazing!

In the end for the next five years Le Rucher sponsored me to travel back for debriefing and rest twice a year. On most of these trips (apart from on that first occasion) I was privileged to have Erik and his wife, Jeltje, personally debrief me. They were a lovely middle-aged Dutch couple, and we soon became good friends. These trips became a lifeline for me, helping me to reflect on and evaluate the things happening in my life, as well as not to burn out.

For Reflection and Application

Does your heart burn within you sometimes when you talk about Jesus? That's because when we talk about Him, He often shows up to join in the conversation. Just as He did with the disciples on the road to Emmaus.

Can you feel your heart burning within you now? It's one of His ways of letting you know He's close by. He wants to fellowship with you. Why don't you stop reading now and just spend some time sharing your heart with the One who loves you more than you will ever know?

Chapter 39

REUNITED WITH FRIENDS AFTER THE SECOND WAR

The road to a friend's house is never long.

DANISH PROVERB[1]

Two are better than one, because they have
a good return for their labour;
If either of them falls down, one can help the other up.
But pity anyone who falls and has no one to help them up.

ECCLESIASTES 4:9-10

There is nothing on this earth more to be prized
than true friendship.

THOMAS AQUINAS[2]

The bus ground to a halt at what appeared, at first sight, to be a demolition site: heaps of rubble, twisted metal, and glass.

There was not one intact building anywhere in sight. No one on the bus moved; all were trying to find their bearings.

"Everyone off," shouted the driver impatiently. "We've arrived – *Vsyo.*"

"Where?" someone inquired, confused.

"It's Minutka roundabout, next to the bazaar," the driver exclaimed.

"O Allah, Allah!" cried one woman as she shook her head from side to side.

Stunned beyond belief, I couldn't take in what my eyes were seeing. I glanced around for the bazaar I knew well – *babushkas* selling homemade bread, rows and rows of busy market stalls, crowds rushing past each other. But as far as the eye could see, only debris, wreckage, craters, and ruins.

"Where's the market gone?" I wondered.

Turning round full circle, I tried to orient myself. Fellow passengers sobbed openly. An elderly man pointed to a parting in the road. "That's Minutka roundabout."

Casting my gaze in the direction he was pointing, I tried to focus. Minutka roundabout was in a lively part of town, on the main road into downtown, surrounded on all sides by four nine-storey blocks of flats full of activity. On the ground floor of the flats were appealing shops with extensive inviting windows. Nearby was the hustle and bustle of yards full of carefree children giggling and playing, *babushkas* sitting outside on benches idling away the day gossiping about the crowds coming and going, ladies selling sunflower seeds, and stray dogs and cats fighting each other.

I searched around again for the high-rises, but they'd all gone. Only one wall was still standing. A glossy poster of a model smiled eerily at me from the floral pink wall. I wondered what had happened to the little girl who used to sleep in that bedroom.

Surrounding me were broken shards of glass, ripped clothing and books, torn-out radiators and sinks, and burned-out shells of upside-down cars. No one and nothing was left here; life had been bombed into oblivion[3].

Looking in the direction of my friend Masha's house, I saw nothing but rubble.

Soon a bus came along that was going downtown. I hopped onto it, relieved to be out of there.

It was May of 2000, and I was returning to Grozny for the first time since the second war. On the way, we passed fields of brilliant scarlet poppies blowing brightly in the wind. The poppies reminded me of the Second World War. Too many people die in wars that have nothing to do with them. It's so tragic and such a waste of precious lives.

Wild yellow flowers reflecting the sunlight cheered me up a bit. As we approached Grozny, we saw blackened fields of dead and dried-up flowers. The lady next to me commented: "Last week it was raining, and I got covered in black spots. The ecology is really messed up."

Every now and then I heard a helicopter whirring overhead and saw columns of black smoke spiralling upward from distant villages barely visible on the horizon.

When I arrived downtown, I saw a lot more people than I'd imagined would have returned after the war. The streets teemed with people – buying and selling at the various bazaars, clearing away the rubbish and rebuilding. Mostly women. As is too often the case, the men destroy the place with their guns, bombs, and bullets, and leave the women to clear up and rebuild.

It was getting dark, and curfew started at 8.00 pm.

I asked the bus driver if this bus still went to a certain region.

A soldier overheard. "You can't stay there," he said. "It's forbidden. We're going to destroy all the buildings there."

I walked round the corner and away from his inquiring gaze, and took a taxi instead.

When we arrived at our flat, I was dazed by the trail of devastation. I made my way carefully to the front door, gingerly avoiding shards of shattered glass, twisted metal, protruding bits of concrete slabs, and pieces of broken furniture. Scattered intermittently between them were colourful bits of rag, once elegant suits and pretty dresses that frivolous teenagers showed off proudly. There were also burned, ripped-up pages of books, the remnants of treasured libraries. Homes, histories, and lives gone forever, decimated by a bloody war that the people neither wanted nor asked for.

"I hope there aren't any landmines lying around," I thought.

I made it safely to the front door, only to find it locked.

"Larisa! Is anyone at home? Larisa! Malika!" My voice echoed in the silence. A neighbour came to the window.

"Hi, I'm looking for Larisa. I was wondering how to get into the building?" I asked.

"Go round the other side. We're using the back door as an entrance."

I later found out that a bomb exploded on the ground floor, blowing up the stairs and the entrance on that side.

As I headed back through the rubble to reach the other side, I saw a book lying in the rubble. It looked like one of mine, and I picked it up. It was the autobiography of Kathryn Kuhlman in English, so it was definitely mine. How did it get there?

A welcoming face suddenly appeared round the door, beaming, displaying those wonderfully familiar gold teeth glistening in the sun! It was my dear friend Larisa. She ran excitedly to greet me and we ran into each other's arms. Larisa turned to the taxi driver, who'd been hanging around waiting to see if I got into the building safely.

"Thanks for bringing my sister, my best friend to me. Thanks so much."

It was such a relief to see her alive and well and to finally be back. Larisa was such a special friend, and I really felt at home with her and her mother. It was wonderful to be with them, even in the midst of a war zone.

Suddenly in the middle of the devastation, I realised the importance of friendship. You can make it through practically anything if you have friends. People who know you and love you just the way you are. Warts and all. Who you've laughed with and cried with. Shared your deepest secrets with. The good, the bad, and the ugly. Friends give you the strength to keep going and hope for a new day. That everything will be okay in the end. Regardless.

It's amazing how God puts people together. Value your friends today, for you never know what tomorrow will bring. Or even if there will be a tomorrow. Let them know they're loved and appreciated.

Apparently, intense fighting had taken place there in January.

A shell had exploded in Larisa's living room, blowing up the wall and many of the things in the room. The wardrobe was blown up, destroying or scattering its contents: tea sets, bed linen, books, family albums, and most of Maryam's childhood treasures. Some of my pictures and clothes were destroyed too. The sofa and chair were damaged. And some of our things were blown out of the house, which was why my book was out there.

A bomb had exploded on the ninth floor, which collapsed into the eighth floor. All the flats there were destroyed, and half of the seventh floor burned.

The flat of Larisa's sister, Malika, was badly damaged, but still had walls, roof, and floor pretty much intact. Our floor and the fifth floor had minor damage. The first and second floor flats all burned; the stairs almost collapsed. On the stairwell on the third floor, there was a chilling handwritten warning that wasn't there before: "Death comes in your sleep!"

There was now no gas, electricity, or running water there.

"Do you fancy a cup of *chai*?" Larisa asked.

"Yes, please – yes, that would be lovely."

I was really thirsty after the long tiring journey.

I had no idea how complicated it had become to have a cup of tea in Chechnya.

First we needed to fetch water. The nearest well was in the neighbouring yard. As Larisa and I went to fetch water, we heard the sound of machine gun fire close by. An ambulance full of Russian soldiers drove up. They ran out and started shooting at the building opposite.

"Do we have time to run, or should we throw ourselves to the floor?" This was the first thought running through my head. The next one followed rapidly: "Maybe we have time to finish filling our buckets so we can have tea!"

The shooting stopped quickly, and the soldiers ran into the building. Quickly filling our buckets, we hurried inside. Once inside, we prayed until things seemed to calm down. Later we found out that it was a fight between soldiers who were drunk. A woman and one of the soldiers were hurt in the crossfire.

A little later, Larisa and I took the full kettle to the fourth floor of the neighbouring house. The family there were kind enough to let us use their stove, as they had gas. One of the parents was Chechen, the other Ossetian – meaning they'd had their share of problems.

Larisa did most of her cooking here. Three times a day she lugged a saucepan full of ingredients and her kettle to their house, cooked the food and heated up the kettle, then carefully carried the hot pans and kettle home. This time we were just making *chai* so when we finally got home with our boiling water, we savoured every last drop of our *chai*.

Later I sat in Larisa's bedroom writing in my diary by the light of a candle on the windowsill. Larisa, her mother, and Malika were laughing in the kitchen. The window was covered over by plastic, obscuring the view. The glass had blown out when a Scud missile exploded too close.

Three cavernous craters around our house were a silent reminder of the war raging all around us. That is, if one could possibly forget.

Bright lights from burning oil wells lit up the horizon. The stillness of the evening was broken periodically by explosions and machine gun fire.

When Malika returned home from work, she took me around to show me how badly damaged her flat was. Despite the fact that everything remaining of value there had already been stolen, we found that somebody had climbed down from the eighth floor, cut through the plastic covering of the windows overlooking the balcony, and stolen a carpet. I shivered inside when I thought that somebody would do that in the daytime while we were there. It was pretty frightening to be the only people living in a nine-floor high-rise. But at least the front door locked, and that same day another family had returned home.

I found it hard to sleep.

It was freezing, there was no heat, and no glass in the windows.

I slept with three blankets as well as track-suit bottoms, a jumper, and my fleecy coat! It was worse than camping in the UK in the summer!

Larisa and I shared a rickety single bed because the sofa where I usually slept was too badly damaged. It was a good job we were both thin or I don't know how we would have managed! Explosions and shooting throughout the night intermittently shattered the silent night air.

The following morning we were determined to find news of friends from church, Peter and Tanya, who lived about an hour's walk away in the centre of town.

As we walked, I noticed my left leg was sore. I must have twisted it yesterday. It was too easy to twist your ankle just by going out of the house and trying to navigate your way safely through the potholes, rubbish and war wreckage.

Helicopters were circling so low overhead we could almost see the concentrated expression on the pilot's face. Watching intently for snipers or other suspicious-looking people on the ground. Hands on the trigger ready to take them out instantly.

"Lord, let them see we aren't snipers," I prayed.

Tanya and Peter were a Russian couple in their sixties. Opposites in many ways, they made a good match: she was plump, he was skinny as a rake; she was passionate and opinionated and loved to talk, he was quiet and unassuming. They took turns looking after each other. In the first war, their daughter was killed and her flat stolen by Chechen fighters. The grieving grandparents took in their orphaned grandson, and sent him to an aunt before the second war started.

Hardly any houses were left standing on their road so it took us a while to orientate ourselves. Finally when Peter popped his head out from behind two naked walls with a roof still half on, the remains of their kitchen, we realised we'd found the right house. He looked dreadful, pale and emaciated with a hacking cough, but was pleased to see us.

Once inside the kitchen, Tanya offered us herbal tea. "Peter collected the leaves. It's very good for the kidneys, and also for calming the nerves."

The people here were ingenious at using various herbs to treat their ailments. And astonishingly, sometimes they did seem to work better than Western medicine. With little access to doctors, or money to buy medicine, the local people were immensely resourceful with what they had.

We'd guessed they would probably have little food in the house, so we'd brought tea, sugar, and cake with us to enjoy together.

"This is where I sleep." Tanya invited us to sit down on the tattered sofa. "Peter sleeps on the floor next to me." She pointed to a tiny corner between the sofa and the kitchen cupboards.

"The rest of the house is gone. We didn't make it out of the city when the fighting got really intense. Or even to a basement for that matter. We just didn't have time. We spent most of the war at a neighbour's house. See that rubble over there."

She turned to the ruins of the neighbouring house visible through the window. "We were there when the bomb fell on our house. We sheltered there. When that house was hit, everything exploded into the air. Two doors flew through the air and landed on Peter's head. He bled for a whole month. I thought he would never stop bleeding. I kept dressing his wounds with all the sheets and towels I could find. Then washing them out and using them again. I couldn't take him to hospital, there was too much fighting going on. It's amazing he survived."

She turned to him. "Peter, dear, show them the wound." He obliged, showing us a nasty scar. It was amazing he was still alive – I thanked the Lord for sustaining him.

Larisa and I listened to her story, sometimes with a reassuring touch on her shoulder or arm, sometimes with a hug. Peter kept coming in and out but said nothing.

Before leaving, we prayed for them both: for healing from the traumas they'd been through, for God to comfort them and be especially real to them, for physical healing for them both.

"Thank you so much for coming, *devochki* – girls – it's always so good to see you. Thank you."

We seemed to have done so little; I wished we could have done more for them but we gave her a big hug as we left. I would have loved to whisk them away to a safe place where we could feed them up, and lavish the Father's love upon them.

Soon afterward, I was able to buy them a new home in a safe village. Tanya, Peter, and their grandson were reunited and able to start rebuilding their lives.

At breakfast the following morning – May 21, 2000 – we listened to the news on the radio: "The wife of British Prime Minister Tony Blair has given birth to a son and they've called him Leo." I didn't even know she was pregnant. Once again being so far from home, I'd missed out on important news from the UK. They also announced that Putin sent them a telegram to congratulate them.

"Let's go out for lunch and celebrate," Larisa said decidedly.

We thought it would be nice to take Aunty Asya to the 'café' in the central bazaar where Malika worked. We'd eaten there once before – it wasn't expensive, and when you didn't have gas at home, it was especially lovely. And having a meal there meant that Malika got to eat too; otherwise she was on her feet all day without a break.

The 'café' made me marvel at the amazing resourcefulness of Chechen entrepreneurs. Creating a business out of next to nothing. Almost out of thin air. The 'café' wasn't exactly what you'd call sophisticated. More like makeshift. And basic. In fact you couldn't get much more basic if you tried. No roof or intact building of any description. Only a couple of broken-down walls and bits of war wreckage scattered here and there. And two simple plastic tables and chairs placed in the middle of it all by the side of the road.

But what it lacked in comfort it more than made up for in atmosphere. Their menu consisted of two items: melt-in-the-mouth, freshly cooked Chechen pie, and sweet, black tea. And it was cooked on an open fire right in front of you.

Perfect on a gasless, it's-time-for-a-celebration type of afternoon.

Under an open heaven on yellow plastic chairs, amid a heap of debris and a panorama of bombed-out buildings as far as the eye could see, we had a delightful time, the four of us, munching on pie and sipping piping hot tea, celebrating little Leo's birth.

For Application and Reflection

Are there any friends you've lost touch with that you were reminded of as you were reading? Send them a message today to let them know how much you love and appreciate them and their friendship.

Chapter 40

GRATEFUL FOR SMALL MERCIES

I am not saying this because I am in need,
for I have learned to be content whatever the circumstances.
I know what it is to be in need,
and I know what it is to have plenty.
I have learned the secret of being content
in any and every situation, whether well fed or hungry,
whether living in plenty or in want.
I can do all this through him who gives me strength.

PHILIPPIANS 4:11-13

The next night the fighting was much worse. Throughout the night, from all quarters of the city, tanks and cannons were firing, as well as machine guns.

Sometimes it seemed close to the house. I could hear the shots whizzing past. Occasionally they lit up the whole sky. It was a strange light seen through the plastic sheeting over the window – fuzzy, distorted, pink, but still bright. It would have been pretty if it were only a fireworks display on Bonfire Night.

I wasn't scared until Larisa started shaking, which made the whole bed shake. Then I got nervous. Really nervous.

When the firing came closer, Larisa was praying out loud. I followed suit.

It seemed that if we fell asleep before the bombing and shelling started, we could sleep through it. But if we were awake when it started, it was harder to drop off, as fear and adrenaline kicked in so easily in the dark.

Eventually, we fell asleep, probably around three-ish. I slept soundly until 8:00 am.

At breakfast I remarked, "I'm glad it got quieter after three, so we could catch a few winks."

Aunty Asya looked surprised, "What? Didn't you hear it? The shooting carried on all night. It was actually pretty bad at daybreak. Just on the street below us. They were drunk – shouting and swearing and firing."

Amazingly, Larisa and I had slept right through it, even if it was terribly loud.

A kind neighbour popped in after breakfast to put glass in the windows. It wasn't the first time we'd needed his services, nor the last.

"It should be warmer tonight," Aunty Asya observed. I just hoped the glass wouldn't blow out again too soon.

We listened to the radio in the kitchen every hour or so to hear the news. Chechen President Mashadov had been on the news a few days earlier and had declared *jihad* again. He'd stated that they might start fighting again on the twentieth of the month.

"That's tomorrow," I commented to no one in particular. "We'll see."

I was worried that there would be a lot of shooting that night.

Later I dropped in to the neighbour's empty flat for some quiet time. Grabbing a chair, I slid myself carefully down onto the undamaged corner of the balcony. The other half of the balcony had a gaping hole in the middle with tangled metal and concrete dangling through it. Black smoke from burning oil wells curled apologetically on the distant horizon in a swirling melancholy dance.

The icy cold chill inside Larisa's flat had frozen me to the bone. I relaxed and enjoyed a few peaceful moments, talking to my Jesus as I warmed myself up in the lingering afternoon sunshine.

Our supper that night was scrumptious. It was the first time

I'd had potatoes in a week, and they were absolutely delicious. We each had the luxury of two whole potatoes, some salad, and a honey sandwich. A real feast! I savoured every mouthful of firm solid potato. It really made a change from watery soup.

Malika made an interesting comment at dinner: "It's such a relief there's no Sharia law anymore. I'm so thrilled my girls can dance again."

I could hardly believe my ears. Between the wars, when Chechnya was self-governed and Sharia law was in effect, she seemed to be so pleased. Back then she'd said, "It's so good we're returning to the laws of the Almighty and have Sharia law."

When the first public executions were announced in the main square, thousands crowded the streets to watch them and Malika took her daughter along. Aunty Asya watched it live on TV. Even though I was in the other room, I shuddered when I heard the burst of gunshots. Soon after, we opened the front door to Malika and her daughter both looking pale and shaken. They recovered over a cup of tea in our kitchen as they told us all about it. Even though it was so brutal, she asserted that it was good for the country.

And now she was saying exactly the opposite. It was amazing.

The following morning, we hopped on a couple of buses to visit Lipa's extended family in their village.

Lipa's sweet father, a respected village elder wearing a typical Chechen hat[1] welcomed us into his home where a mouth-watering spread, lovingly prepared, awaited us. Having heard so much about us, he wanted to express his appreciation for all we'd done for his family.

Lipa's father shared his home with his son and daughter-in-law who were a real comfort to him after his wife had passed away. They'd all become believers in Jesus after Lipa had shared the good news with them. They were thrilled we'd come, and joyfully gathered together to hear the word of God and have us pray for them. The Lord brought encouragement and healing as we shared together.

Later, Lipa took us on a guided tour of the house, showing us where they'd spent the best part of nine months in a basement being bombed. Where they'd prayed and interceded for Chechnya for hours and hours. I realised I really knew nothing about prayer, compared to prayer warriors like Lipa.

As in most of Chechnya, there was no running water in the house. Lipa's teenage sister-in-law hauled water from the well a few times every morning. That night she heated water on the stove for us, and we had a strip wash in the ruins of part of the house.

In the night, I woke up bursting for the toilet. Earlier in the day, Lipa had encouraged me to wake her up if I needed the toilet in the night. I waited until I saw her climbing out of bed and whispered, not wanting to disturb the others: "I need to go to the toilet too."

We quietly put on our coats and shoes and headed out into the crisp, silent night air. I glanced up at a glorious golden expanse of shimmering stars, twinkling like fireflies winking knowingly at us. And the cheery moon, nearly full and smiling at us in all its glory; the seas on the moon's surface were faintly visible from the inky black darkness of a world with no electric light anywhere for miles around.

"How wonderful, Lord. What a display of Your sovereignty! It's better than being in a planetarium," I thought.

There's nothing like looking at the night sky in the depths of the countryside far from civilisation to help you get things into perspective. You realise what a tiny person you are in a massive universe. And how incredible it is that the Lord knows each one of us intimately, even down to every minuscule cell in our bodies.

Still marvelling at the Lord's awesomeness, I followed Lipa as she headed up a small hill to the outhouse. The light from the stars and moon helped but you still had to really concentrate to avoid rocks, uneven ground, holes, and war wreckage.

I'd just used the toilet and was about to put my head through the curtain when the silence was abruptly shattered by a chorus of shots fired from behind me, seemingly just above the outhouse. From the other direction, a burst of gunfire was returned.

Suddenly an intense battle flared up all around, with tanks, guns, and who knows what else firing full-blast as the sky lit up in a myriad of colours.

For a moment I froze wondering what to do. Was it safer inside the outhouse? Its walls were extremely thin, barely providing any protection at all. But perhaps better than being outside, possibly visible to the gunmen.

I stuck my head out of the outhouse and immediately Lipa decided for us. She grabbed my hand and started running, keeping her head as low as possible. I followed suit, and we sprinted toward the house as fast as our legs could carry us. Somehow, miraculously, all the bullets missed us. And we didn't even twist our ankles!

When we were safely inside, Lipa explained that a Russian checkpoint stood just behind the hill. Sometimes during the night, Chechen rebels from the village would attack it, leading to gun battles over the outhouse.

There was never a dull moment in Chechnya. Not even in the outhouse!

The next day, after visiting a few more families, we started the long journey back to Grozny.

The following morning, I woke up to a lovely tranquil morning. No shooting, the birds were singing, and all seemed right with the world. I lay in bed for a while, enjoying the stillness and reading my Bible.

Our plan for that day was to search for any news of church friends in Minutka. This was the area where the intercity bus stopped, where I'd had my first glimpse of Grozny after the second war. It was an extremely damaged, desolate, and dangerous part of town.

When we arrived at Minutka, the extent of the devastation hit me again. I could hardly recognise anything. The driver dropped us off with a warning, "Be careful, girls – it's not advisable to walk around. There are still masses of unexploded landmines everywhere."

The other passenger spoke up. "Yes, be careful. When you see the red flags, it's warning of a minefield. One of my neighbours yesterday saw these red flags in her garden on returning home after the war and mistook them for tulips! The rebels mined everything in sight."

The driver urged us again before driving away. "Take care, girls. Walking round can disturb the masonry. There's been too many cases of buildings suddenly collapsing on people walking too near to them. Be careful."

Ahead was a checkpoint.

"Let's step off the road to avoid it," Larisa suggested. In front of us we noticed, just as the driver had said, a barbed-wire fence with red flags all the way along it.

"It's a good thing we saw the warning – just in time before unwittingly walking into a minefield," Larisa commented, drawing in a deep breath.

Suddenly I realised, to my horror, that we were on the wrong side of the barbed wire.

"Oh no, Larisa, we're standing in the middle of a minefield!" I exclaimed anxiously.

Deftly climbing over the barbed wire, we landed safety back down on the road. Larisa turned to one of the soldiers and pointed in the direction we were going, "Sorry to bother you, but we were wondering, is that part of Minutka still mined?"

"Sorry, ladies, we've no idea," they responded, shaking their heads, looking like they knew as little as we did.

"What shall we do?" Larisa asked me, imploringly.

"Well, we've come all this way and really want some news. Let's start by trying to find Masha's house."

We passed a bench with three ladies and a guard sitting on it. "Excuse me," Larisa asked, "Do you know, if there's a path there?"

The ladies nodded their heads, "Yes, it's possible to get through. People go back and forth. Just be careful of mines, *devochki* – girls."

"Place your foot in exactly the same spot I put mine," Larisa explained carefully. She'd become an expert at this. "Step by step. Okay?"

I watched her intently as she gingerly made her way through the rubble. With any wrong step I could lose a leg. As deftly as I could, I put my foot in the exact spot her foot had been seconds before.

I waited for an explosion. Nothing. I breathed a huge sigh of relief. Maybe we'd be okay.

I took another tentative step. No explosion. Another step, then another.

With every step I prayed, "Protect us, Lord".

I tried really hard not to think about spending the rest of my life with only one leg.

We slowly made our way to a recently well-trod path. Extremely relieved on arriving intact, we took a few deep breaths, then followed it to the end.

All our friends' houses had been obliterated, but in each place, we found a neighbour who told us that our church family were safe. They'd fled the fighting before their houses were destroyed. I was so thankful to the Lord for His kindness in sending people at just the right time and place to let us know everyone was safe.

On arrival home, we found poor Aunty Asya starving and desperate for a hot drink. We headed straight to Aishad's, another neighbour, to put the kettle on and heat up our potatoes. Lalita, Aishad's sister, slowly cracked the door open and smiled when she saw us: "Aishad's not here, but please do come in and use the stove."

"Tell me some more about God," she asked, her brown eyes filled with expectation. She was open to the Lord, but like many Chechens, scared of showing interest in front of others. But when alone with us, it was a completely different story. We shared the good news of Jesus' love with her.

"Please, can you pray for me – like you did last time? I really felt so peaceful after you prayed."

Experiencing the Lord's touch as we prayed, she began to cry. I took her into my arms and she sobbed and sobbed.

"Thank you so much, girls. You're so kind."

Not having gas at home forced us to get out and meet people.

A blessing in disguise. There was always something to be grateful for. Always.

Later on, a Russian friend asked us to come and pray with her teenage son. I explained the gospel to him and he was ready to surrender his life to Jesus. We prayed for him to be filled with the Holy Spirit as well. What a delight! It was exactly moments like this that reminded me of why I was here in the first place. Both in Chechnya but also on this earth. This was my purpose and destiny.

My heart was bursting with wonder and excitement as I lay down to sleep that night. I was just about to have my thirtieth birthday.

What an amazing life I had; In spite of all the hardships, dangers, and frustrations, at the end of the day, I wouldn't have wanted to be doing anything else.

I drifted off to sleep, marvelling at the honour of serving my Lord and so, so thankful.

For Application and Reflection

Do you go to sleep at night excited about your day and what you are doing with your life? If not, what could you change about your life so that you're truly doing what you were made for?

Chapter 41

HADIZHAT'S STORY

Never will I leave you; never will I forsake you.

HEBREWS 13:5

We still had no news about Hadizhat, our widowed friend from the refugee camp whose daughter had been healed of heart problems.

When I spoke to a friend, Pastor Valera who'd helped organise the Catch the Fire conference, he let me know exciting news: "Hadizhat's just called. She and the children are alive and well, thank the Lord."

I sobbed tears of relief and happiness on hearing this wonderful news about my precious friend.

When we finally met up, we cried as we embraced each other.

"Let me take a good look at you, my dear friend," I said, admiring Hadizhat's still stunning figure, tall and confident in a modest yet flattering green dress, which flowed elegantly over thin shoulders. Her piercing brown eyes, sparkling with delight at the joy of meeting up again, were tastefully accentuated by a perfectly matching green and brown silk headscarf.

Over a lovely cup of sweet black tea with a slice of fresh lemon, along with mouth-watering, just-out-of-the-oven and still warm *pryaniki* – a typical Russian spicy gingerbread filled with jam – Hadizhat told me her story:

"Bombers were roaring overhead and shells exploding all around us. It was the height of the second war, and I couldn't take any more. I decided we needed to leave, for the sake of the children.

I filled a bag with necessities and we joined the crowd. Hundreds were trying to leave. All desperate to flee the fighting. Grozny was totally on fire by then. Every time we heard the sounds of fighting or soldiers close by, we threw ourselves to the ground and prayed for the Almighty to have mercy."

Squeezing Hadizhat's hand across the table, I encouraged her: "*Ti molodets* – you're doing so well – considering the rough time you've had of it, my dear. I know the Lord is going to heal you of all this." She'd been through so much, including losing her husband and home five years earlier.

"*Spasibo* – thank you – He is. He really is. He's looking out for us. This time, praise Him, we were okay. We walked all day. We were absolutely exhausted. The children sobbing from hunger pangs, faces smeared with black grime, mud and sweat. We found a jam-packed bus and somehow managed to squeeze in. It was such a long, dangerous journey out of Chechnya. I thought we'd never get there. The Almighty alone knows how we made it safely through."

With a sigh of relief, I told her, "Praise the Lord – *slava Bogu* – we were so worried, and prayed so much for you."

"Yes, thank you for your prayers, they really made a difference," she remarked, her lovely brown eyes welling up with tears of gratitude. "So many others were not so fortunate. Some buses were bombed and shot at, others were blown up by landmines, or held for days at the border. People were kidnapped by soldiers."

"Anyway, where was I? Oh yes. On the bus. Finally in the early hours of the morning, we safely made it to a train station in Russia. I didn't know anyone there, so I'd no idea what to do. We ended up joining crowds of others. So many refugees, you wouldn't believe it. All dirty and freezing, sheltering in the station. We climbed over hundreds of people, all crammed in, as we tried to find a place to rest. It was so desperately overcrowded, but eventually we found a spot. It was such a tight squeeze there wasn't enough room for us to lie down, but we were so exhausted it didn't make any difference. At that point I could have slept standing up. We all fell asleep, sitting up, leaning against each other. We woke up to the news that bread was being handed out. And guess who was handing it out?"

I wondered. "A Christian mission of some sort, perhaps?"

"Yes, it was local believers. Of course, pandemonium broke out as people rushed to get the bread. We almost got crushed. People were so desperate. I was terrified they'd crush the children, and I clung on to them for dear life. Finally, after we were queuing for hours, a patient lady with kind eyes gave us a loaf of bread. She said, 'May God bless you and help you.'"

"And He did," I exclaimed. "Didn't He!" I was so pleased to hear God had sent believers to look after them. "That's just what we prayed for, for believers to help you."

Hadizhat continued. "And listen to what happened after that. The Almighty was really answering your prayers. The next night we slept in that same prized spot. The following day, officials came offering free train tickets to anywhere in Russia. They wanted to get rid of us refugees crowding the station. As you know, I have no relatives at all in Russia, and I decided to risk it and go for Moscow; it's the capital after all. I thought I'd try my luck there. After queuing for hours and filling in forms, I was given four tickets. That night we started the thirty-hour journey to the capital. The children were thrilled to be going to Moscow for the first time, and it was lovely to be able to stretch our legs and to have a bed to lie on. And to have the privacy of a proper toilet, even though it wasn't the cleanest; as you know, the ones on the train can be pretty dreadful. But the conductor did a good job of trying to keep it clean. And having a sink with running water, it was a relief to be able to wash away at least some of the grime and dirt."

"We enjoyed the ride there. As we approached Moscow, the sun was just peeking out over snow-covered fields, glistening beautifully, and all these quaint, sleepy villages. A real winter wonderland, making the children so excited. But we soon came down to earth as we saw the station, filthy and unwelcoming, and all those drunks and street people. I'd hoped someone would help us, but the few officials I could find were up to their eyes in it, and tired of hearing refugee stories. The winter wonderland was actually a freezing wasteland for us – Moscow winters make it too cold to stay outside for long."

"I tried desperately to find someone to help us and looked for the Immigration Office. We eventually found it, but after queuing for hours, were advised to come back the next day. We made our way back to the station, found a spot, and made our bed for the night. We huddled together for warmth, but woke up freezing with the gnawing ache of hunger pangs filling our bellies."

"So sorry to hear that. Talking of food, please, have another *pryanik*," I said, passing her the enticing plate of goodies. "And would you like more tea?"

"*Da, pozhalusta* – yes, please – just half a cup. That would be lovely."

"Sorry, I interrupted you," I said, pouring her some tea. "I'm eager to hear the rest of the story."

"Oh yes. Where was I? At the station, yes, we were at the station starving. And to make things worse, poor little Mogamed had developed a nasty cough. I eventually managed to find some bread for the children, and then, popped back into the office. Can you imagine, I spent ten frustrating, exhausting days trying to get some help, but it was no use. I was becoming extremely desperate, and I cried out to the Lord for help."

"One day a man came up to us. He looked Chechen, and he told us, 'I noticed you here at the station and wondered if I could help you. Where are you from?' When I named the village, he said excitedly, 'My mother was from the same village! You probably know her. Baba Aishat from Oktyabrskaya Street.'"

"Yes, I remember your mother well. How amazing!"

"'Please come back to my house, and my wife and I will help you get yourself back on your feet.' Of course, I was a bit frightened to go home with a strange man, but as I was desperate, and he was almost a relative, I decided to go with him."

"He lived a couple of hours from Moscow with his wife and young children. They didn't have much, but they shared what they had with us. We slept on the floor, but it was a real blessing to be safe and warm and to have a roof over our heads. After a couple of weeks, I phoned Valera, and he was so pleased to hear my voice. 'Hadizhat,' he said, 'we've been worried about you and praying for you. Are you okay?'

"I answered, 'Yes, we're fine, I just wanted to let you know the children and I are okay and we're staying near Moscow.'

"'Thank God, I'm thrilled to hear that. Where exactly are you staying?'

"'Actually it's a small village about two hours from Moscow called Dinskaya.'

"'Not Dinskaya!' he was astonished."

I interrupted excitedly: "You were in Dinskaya all that time? How amazing! His wife grew up there, didn't she?"

"Yes, she did, and most of her brothers and sisters are still living there."

"Yes, they are. Eight or nine of them, if I'm not mistaken."

"Yes, nine, I think."

"And her family are so lovely," I said, overjoyed. "I'm sure they were able to help you."

"Yes, they were. As soon as they phoned her family, they found that her sister lived in the street opposite to where we were staying. They helped us tremendously, found us a place to live, furnished it, registered us as refugees, organised treatment for Mogamed's bronchitis, and found me a job. Of all the places I could have ended up, I ended up in that village!"

"God is amazing, isn't He – in how He answered our prayers for you," I exclaimed, in awe, once again, of His goodness and faithfulness.

For Application and Reflection

Have you had enough to eat today? Thank God for His provision for you. Do you know any families who are struggling and in need of food? Can you be an answer to prayer and take them some food?

Chapter 42

IT'S FRIDAY – BUT SUNDAY'S COMING!

But we have this treasure in jars of clay to show that
this all-surpassing power is from God and not from us.
We are hard pressed on every side, but not crushed;
perplexed, but not in despair; persecuted, but not
abandoned; struck down, but not destroyed…
Therefore we do not lose heart.

2 CORINTHIANS 4:7-16

Depend on it. God's work done in God's way
will never lack God's supply. He is too wise a God
to frustrate His purposes for lack of funds,
and He can just as easily supply them ahead of time
as afterwards, and He much prefers doing so.

JAMES HUDSON TAYLOR,
MISSIONARY TO CHINA[1]

It was early 2000, and the plight of the hungry refugees in the tent camp was heavy on my heart.

I longed to see these precious people fed but it cost a whopping nine thousand dollars to provide a weekly food parcel for every family in the camp. The money we'd painstakingly raised in England, plus the money that David brought, meant we'd been able to feed the entire camp for one week. Yippee, one whole week! It was a great start but what about the following week when the children started crying again because their stomachs were aching for more food.

This sprawling camp of seven thousand people desperately needed food on a regular basis. And to raise such a large sum of money amongst my friends and supporters seemed impossible. We needed help on a much larger scale. We all cried out to God and He heard our cries and answered in a way which was beyond our wildest dreams.

The tremendous battle beforehand, however, almost caused us to lose heart on the way. But thank God we didn't, for as it turned out the answer was waiting, just around the next corner. All we needed to do was trust, find our strength in the Lord and wait for His intervention, and with His help, we managed to do just that.

The future King David was having a similar day in 1 Samuel 30. Talk about getting out of bed on the wrong side! He was already exhausted from years of escaping the murderous intentions of his old boss and father-in-law, King Saul. Now the Philistines, among whom he'd been living for the last year and a half, had just rejected him. Told him to get on his bike. Without any advanced warning.

But at least he still had his home and his wives. After a long exhausting journey, he was really looking forward to some lovely home comforts. Feet up by the fire, piping hot lentil soup, scrumptious homemade bread, and his wife massaging his aching shoulders.

As he got closer to home, he was surprised that no one ran to meet them. Then his heart missed a beat. Smoke. A lot of it. Overwhelming silence. All the women and children gone. Been taken captive. And their home, Ziklag, burned to the ground. The only thing left to their name was smouldering ruins.

David and his men crumpled into the midst of the sooty ash heap, weeping in anguish until they had no more tears left.

Then, as if it couldn't get any worse, David's men turned on him. The men he had lovingly and sacrificially taken in when they had nowhere to go. Men he believed in when no one else did and raised up to be outstanding warriors. His closest friends and colleagues. His best mates. They wanted to stone him.

Most normal people would have called it a day at that point. No one would have blamed him for throwing in the towel and walking away.

But no. David found his strength in the Lord. How did he do that?

Knowing David to be a man after God's own heart, I can imagine he picked himself up out of the ashes and walked far enough away from everyone to be by himself with his Abba. There he poured out his heart to Him, telling Him all his troubles. I'm sure he looked into His Lord's lovely face, shining like the sun in all its brilliance, and knew once again that he was loved. Completely and utterly. Deep down to the core. I expect he remembered all the good things His good Shepherd had done for him in the past and thanked Him for that, singing one of his psalms to Him. He would have taken up his harp, except that he probably couldn't do that since it had no doubt been stolen along with the rest of his possessions. But in the end, even that was not important.

Even though David had nothing else left, he still had his relationship with His God, the source of his strength. And that was all that mattered. He found the strength to go seek out the priest Abiathar and inquire of the Lord. Once he had a *rhema* word from the Lord that all would be well, he was able to go back and lead his disgruntled men to victory. They rescued the women and children and recovered everything the Amalekites had taken away. Nothing was lost. And not only that, God turned the whole situation around by blessing them with lots of plunder from the enemy's camp as a bonus. Wow, Lord! Isn't He amazing!!

In the midst of crying out to God for the refugee camp, we'd been invited to Cyprus to a gathering for those involved in missions in the Northern Caucasus. David Le Compte, Larisa, Dasha, and I were all attending. We had tickets from Mineraniye Vody airport, a five-hour drive from Vladikavkaz, on an early morning flight, so either we had to take an evening bus and sleep in the airport or take a taxi. As there were four of us, we decided to take a taxi, since sharing the cost between us all didn't cost much more than the price of four bus tickets.

The slumbering world around us was dreaming happily as we wearily threw ourselves out of bed to catch our taxi at 3:00 am.

It was a cold night, cloudy and starless. As we stepped out of the high-rise complex, playful snowflakes gently waltzed and swirled all around us as we sunk softly into the freshly fallen virgin snow lighting up the path.

I was relieved when I saw the taxi quickly drive up and thanked God that they weren't running on Ossetian time! But my heart sank when I saw two men step out of the car, one of them almost falling as he staggered to find his balance on the ice. He was completely plastered.

"Which one of you is our driver?" Dasha asked, surprised.

"I … I … I …" The inebriated man pointed at himself, slurring his words. "I … am your driver." He smiled, looking extremely pleased with himself, revealing a row of golden teeth. "And my friend is coming with us."

"We're not going on a five-hour drive on a dicey, slippery road with a driver who's under the influence," David insisted. "Plus we're not squeezing four of us into the back of that car for such a long drive."

David put his foot down. "Tell them we'll go with them only if they give us a sober driver for the journey."

Our local friends stood arguing with the two men for what seemed like a lifetime. Neighbours started stirring, turning on lights and glancing out of their windows.

After about fifteen exhausting minutes, we realised that if we waited around disputing for much longer, we would miss the plane.

Finally, the driver begrudgingly agreed to let the other man drive the car, but he insisted on coming with us. "It's m-m-my car, the documents are in m-my name, and he's not going anywhere in my car without m-m-me!"

We finally set off around 3.20 am.

The journey, not surprisingly, took longer than usual. In some places, freshly fallen snow hadn't as yet been cleared away. In other places, the road resembled a hazardous ice-skating rink.

And it wasn't the most comfortable journey I've ever been on either. After more than five hours lying scrunched up across the girls' laps, in a freezing car where the heater wasn't working properly, some parts of my body had gone numb.

During the journey we tried to have a normal conversation with the drivers, but they were fuming. It got worse when we started to talk to them about God. The more we talked, the angrier they got. The angrier they got, the wilder the driver became.

When we didn't think things could get any worse, our drunk 'friend' started ranting and raving: "P-e-e-e-o-p-p-le like you should be locked away. And they should throw away the key. You're a bunch of idiots."

Deep into the countryside, he started to threaten us, "You know, we could so easily slit your throats and throw your bodies into the snow. No one would ever know. E-e-v-v-e-e-r."

They both sniggered.

I was tempted to lose heart. Everything just seemed too much. How many times could we be in these awful situations? What if they threw us out of the car in the middle of nowhere in this weather? Or really did try to kill us?

I felt a bit like the future King David when he arrived in Ziklag. Life was just too hard. Every time you thought you'd taken a step forward, you found you've actually taken two steps back.

I'd completely forgotten that after every dark crucifixion Friday there's a Sunday coming just round the corner. And not just any Sunday, but Resurrection Sunday at that. And it's coming sooner than you can imagine. Yay, God!

In that dreadfully long journey wedged in like sardines, chilled to the bone, speeding precariously through the Russian winter countryside and unable to escape from the taunts and jeers, I desperately tried to take my eyes off the situation and focus on Jesus.

I'd just started to earnestly pray in tongues when Dasha's confident, authoritative voice broke into my thoughts: "You couldn't lay a finger on us, because our God is looking out for us."

Dasha's words were like the *rhema* word from God through Abiathar to David reassuring him all would be well and changed the atmosphere completely.

Suddenly the peace of God filled my heart. We started singing worship songs, and the more we sang, the more I could feel the strength of the Lord rising up in me. His glory enveloped the car. I felt as if Abba God was wrapping me up, like a newborn baby in a soft, warm blanket. I could feel that underneath me were His everlasting arms (Deuteronomy 33:27) and everything would be okay.

When we started singing, the driver turned the radio up louder. We just continued to sing our hearts out with a bit more volume. He, in turn, turned the radio up even louder, but we weren't bothered. Not one bit. We were having our own private audience with the King of kings and the Lord of all lords, who had put out the red carpet to welcome us into His presence. And we'd come running. It was almost irrelevant what was happening in the physical world, as we were already in heaven!

A little later, our intoxicated 'friend' pulled out a red police ID[2] and showed it to us. "I've got contacts. And I'm going to have you arrested when we get to the airport," he snarled.

At one checkpoint, we were pulled over.

"You were speeding," said the traffic policeman, peering into the car as biting snow flakes snuck surreptitiously through the window. "Do you know how fast you were driving?"

In a snap, the little red ID was flashed in front of the policeman's face.

"*Izvinite, pozhalusta* – I'm so sorry – I had no idea." Blushing, he waved us on. Our 'friend' obviously really was someone 'important' in the police. Maybe all along he'd been sent to keep an eye on us. But why on earth would he be so 'wasted' when he was on assignment?! Some things we will never know this side of eternity. And when we get to glory it will no longer be relevant, eh!

We breathed a sigh of relief when we saw the airport coming into view at last.

After dropping us off, both our driver and 'police escort' extended their hands to shake David's and then sped off into the horizon and out of our lives. Just like that. I couldn't believe it after everything that had transpired. But it was true. They were gone and we were safe. What a relief! "Thank You, Lord, for protecting us," I prayed.

But we hadn't got away with it so easily. The wind seemed to be picking up as we walked from the car park to the airport terminal. We checked in, sailed our way through passport control and customs and tried to make ourselves comfortable in the draughty airport lounge.

Soon we were told the flight was delayed because of the hazardous weather conditions. As the minutes turned into hours, we asked if we could be let out to get some food as the only thing on sale in the airport lounge were overpriced duty-free chocolates and alcohol. But no, as we'd already gone through customs and passport control and they were hoping the snowstorm would clear soon, the airline staff wouldn't let us back out.

As Russians always do in situations like that, we had lots of opportunities to get to know our fellow passengers and to share life stories. As more and more hours plodded by, David decided to treat us to a Toblerone washed down with a glass of Bailey's Irish Cream to quench our thirst! Oh the life of a missionary!! I must admit I felt very sick by the end of the day – not only was I not used to drinking alcohol, but too much sugar always makes me nauseous.

Eventually we were let out of the lounge and treated to a 'hotel' room – not the cleanest or warmest room I've ever slept in – but we were grateful for beds to lie down on to catch a few winks before being up at the crack of dawn the next day to go back to the airport.

Unfortunately the blizzard continued unabated all night and most of the following morning. At some point it was decided we should try to take off. As we sat in the plane watching the staff battling the elements and attempting to de-ice the rapidly re-icing plane, we prayed our hearts out. The plane slid along the runway as best it could and then took off at a ninety degrees angle and rattled like crazy, trying to hold its own against the barrage of an arctic snowstorm in all its might. Soon into the flight we were told we were going to make a detour into Sochi because, as we'd probably noticed, we were facing adverse weather conditions.

Yes, we *had* noticed, actually!!!

After a shaky landing, we skidded our way to the terminal building across Sochi's runway which had turned into a long slippery sheet of ice. After waiting a few more hours there for the weather to clear, the plane at last headed out for Cyprus.

We finally made a show at the conference – dishevelled, worn out and more-than-embarrassingly late – but *so* relieved to be alive and safely there. Speaking about the plight of the refugees in the camps touched the heart of one foreign delegate and on returning home, she shared the situation with a Christian Dutch broadcasting association called *EO*.

A few weeks later, *EO* sent a film crew to Russia to film Zhenya and team giving out aid in the camps. The resulting documentary was shown on TV in Holland, and *EO* raised two hundred thousand euros for the work in Chechnya.

Yes, you read that right, a massive two hundred thousand euros!!! Yay, God!!

Such mind-boggling provision over and above what I could ever have thought or imagined!

And so for the next three years, with that money, we were able to feed not only those seven thousand people in the refugee camp, but also around fifty needy Christian families living in and around

Chechnya. For most of them, this was their only constant supply of food during those difficult postwar years, as they tried to get themselves back on their feet.

Getting to that conference had been *so* worth it because the answer to our cries was waiting for us there. As is often the case, just before the breakthrough, it seemed that all hell had broken loose. This immense onslaught against us could so easily have caused us to give up on the way. But praise God, we didn't.

Let this be an encouragement to you. Don't give up. It's Friday, but Sunday's certainly coming.

If you just hold on, and strengthen yourself in the Lord, the answer will come. That's a given. It's only a matter of time.

Just as God pulled off a miracle of provision using a Dutch TV programme in answer to the cries of His children in Russia, He can pull off a miracle for you. What need do you have right now? Cry out to Him with a heart full of faith, and watch Him move mountains on your behalf. It's what He loves to do. With a passion.

For Application and Reflection

Are there situations in your life that seem hopeless? Are there areas where you have given up? Pour out your heart to Him about those things and give Him your disappointment. Strengthen yourself in the Lord and receive healing, fresh hope and vision.

Do you have any unmet needs right now? Let Him know what they are specifically and ask Him to give you supernatural faith to believe for the impossible.

Chapter 43

TREASURES HIDDEN IN THE DARKNESS

I will give you hidden treasures, riches stored in secret places,
so that you may know that I am the Lord.

ISAIAH 45:3

The Spirit of the Sovereign Lord...has anointed me...
to bind up the brokenhearted...to comfort all who mourn...
to bestow on them a crown of beauty instead of ashes,
the oil of joy instead of mourning...

ISAIAH 61:2-3

He has made everything beautiful in its time.

ECCLESIASTES 3:11

Numerous books have been written on the subject of suffering and God's will. And endless theological discussions conducted in sterile Bible school classrooms. However, life in a war zone brings you face to face with these questions in their grim reality.

In God's word, He warns us that trouble and persecution will come (Matthew 10:16-25). But He assures us that He'll be with us and He'll give us the strength to cope with whatever we have to go through (Philippians 4:13); no matter what. And He also promises He'll turn everything round for good (Romans 8:28), in spite of how desperate things seem at the time.

If you believe in a good, loving God, then heart-wrenching,

senseless tragedies that happen to you or your family can rock your beliefs to the core. The process of coming to terms with these things can be long and hard. Some people never make it through and are destroyed in the process. But there are treasures hidden in the darkness, waiting to be discovered, if only we have eyes to see.

I know beyond a shadow of a doubt that God is both good and Sovereign. He's a loving Father who weeps with His children when they're hurting. He hates it when horrendous things happen to us. The only reason He allows it is because He has given mankind free will as a gift. Once God has given a gift, He won't take it back (Romans 11:29).

Each person chooses how to live their life, and this in turn affects those around them. If a person chooses to be selfish and to disregard the needs of others, even though this is not God's will or plan, others will get hurt. But the converse is also true. If someone chooses to love and serve others, then their neighbours, family, and friends will be blessed as a result. So much of what happens in life depends on our choices and actions.

War is an extreme example of this. It brings out the worst and best in people. Monsters are created when those who choose evil do things that most people can't even imagine in their worst nightmares. But heroes are also made, as ordinary people put their lives on the line for others, doing things they never dreamed they were capable of, to save others' lives.

War changes your perspective on life. It clarifies your thinking, stripping away frivolities, superficialities, and niceties. Death is an ever-present reality. Eternity is closer than your next breath. Life, all too brief, is a precious gift to be valued and enjoyed now.

Your priorities change. Only important things matter, like making cherished memories with people you love. Community becomes vital to survive; family, neighbours, and friends become a lifeline to each other in ways they never thought possible.

Material things are no longer important; literally here today and gone tomorrow. You no longer have to prove anything to anybody.

The greatest treasure anyone can find in war is peace with God. War causes people to seek God in a way nothing else can. Even atheists pray in the trenches. You realise you're a tiny, tiny person in a massive universe, and you have no control over whether you live or die. This makes people search for their Maker and strive to make peace with Him.

Jesus talks about four different soils in the Parable of the Sower (Matthew 13:1-23). Living through a war ploughs up your soil; it can make you into good soil, ripe and ready to meet your heavenly Father.

If it wasn't for the war, the church in Chechnya might not have been birthed at all.

During my time in Chechnya, God and His angels worked overtime on my behalf, delivering me from danger over and over again. I never knew 100 percent if God would rescue me. I was pretty sure I wouldn't die yet, since I knew I had to fulfil the plans God had for me first. And there were things I knew I still had to do.

Then in the middle of my time in Chechnya, God promised me clearly that I would escape with my life. After that, I knew that was a given. Except a couple of times, when tormenting thoughts tried to frighten me that this was not the case.

When my life was threatened, I would often think, "This will make a great testimony later!" And it really did, as you can see from this book, full of such testimonies! But if I'd been killed, I would have gone straight to heaven, and the pain and suffering would have been over forever – another good option!

After friends were kidnapped, I worried that I too might get kidnapped. But I knew that even if that happened to me, not only would God give me the strength to walk through it, He would heal me completely, just as He'd done in the past. Thankfully in the end I never did get kidnapped. Or physically hurt in any way.

Something I won't understand fully until I'm promoted to glory, however, is why some friends were brutally raped, kidnapped, tortured, or murdered.

It seems that suffering is just a part of living in a fallen world where selfish people make selfish choices and people are hurt. And in war situations, the hurt can be especially severe.

God's plan from the beginning hadn't included pain and suffering. Far from it. In fact, He created us to walk with Him and enjoy life in a lush, verdant, tropical garden, a garden of delight. 'The Garden of Eden' literally means 'the Garden of Delight' in Hebrew! How amazing that we were created to walk with our Heavenly Father in His beautiful garden and enjoy His delights.

He also, however, gave us free will, because love has to be a choice. When so-called 'love' is forced on you, it's called 'abuse,' or in the worst case 'rape.' Our Father wanted a relationship with His children where they're free to love Him or free to walk away. Like in any healthy relationship.

Unfortunately, the first man and woman, Adam and Eve, chose to walk away from God, from His love, His peace, and paradise – unwittingly choosing death, violence, and suffering instead.

God had to throw Adam and Eve out of the garden of delight to stop them spoiling heaven.

With evil now present in humanity, sin and selfishness would soon lead to hatred, murder, and war. Heaven was free of these things, and God wanted to keep it that way.

Imagine Hitler knocking on your door. Would you let him in? No way! You wouldn't want a mass murderer messing with your family. Neither does God. He doesn't want Hitler coming into heaven and initiating a holocaust in His House. He closed the door firmly in sin's face. Forever. With only one way back in – through His Son, Jesus.

Jesus lived a perfect life. So He could die as a sacrifice in our place. If we believe in Him, turn from the wrong things we've done, and follow Him, He cleanses us from our sin and makes us pure enough to be back in relationship with Him, a holy God, and able to come back again into paradise.

Each of us has a choice: to follow God and live the way He

intended, or to walk away from Him and to live for ourselves. God's plan was for us to be in relationship with Him and live holy lives. Then no one would get hurt. Ever.

But unfortunately, we've chosen to walk away from Him, and as a consequence, innocent people are hurt. This breaks God's heart. But He's come up with a plan to restore us. If we allow Him to.

In the midst of the pain, if we have eyes to see, we may glimpse a light – dim at first – beckoning us forward. God wants to take us by the hand and lead us out of our suffering, to turn our sorrow into joy, our ashes into beauty. With His help, we can forgive, let go of the pain, and receive healing. As we emerge out from the other side of the dark tunnel into His glorious light, we discover treasures have been birthed in us: a strength and maturity we never knew was possible, a deep understanding of others in similar unspeakable situations, a determination to see people healed, and an authority to look others in the eyes and declare, "If God got me through this, He can get you through this too."

Now we know in part; only when we step through those pearly gates will we fully understand (1 Corinthians 13:12). Here our job is to trust Him, take Him by the hand, and allow Him to do His work. Knowing He will turn the pain around for our good (Romans 8:28). Believing He will restore us (1 Peter 5:10), making us more whole, free, and glorious than ever before. And being confident that He will truly make everything beautiful in its time (Ecclesiastes 3:11).

This has truly been my reality, time and time again.

For Reflection and Application

Are there painful things you've been through that you're still struggling with?

Do you agonise over why the Lord has allowed them to happen to you? Talk to Him about it and give Him your pain.

Are there any treasures, hidden in the darkness, that you've been able to discover out of any seemingly unredeemable experiences in your life?

Chapter 44

THE CALL

Go and make disciples of all nations, baptising them...
and teaching them to obey everything
I have commanded you.
And surely I am with you always.

MATTHEW 28:19-20

If a commission by an earthly king is considered an honour,
how can a commission by a Heavenly King be considered a sacrifice?

DAVID LIVINGSTONE[1]

Caught up in worship, together with two hundred students and staff at Holy Given School in Pemba, Mozambique, in 2006 we raised our voices in adoration to our Maker.

Suddenly the classroom and heat of the day disappeared, and I was caught up in a heavenly vision. Angels with delight on their faces, like children on Christmas morning, tickled with joy and anticipation, beckoned me to come up. At the top of the staircase, the Father was waiting for me. He lovingly showed me the house He'd carefully prepared for His children. We walked past room after room after room, as yet with no inhabitants.

With anguish in His voice, He uttered, "Paula, so many of My children don't know Me and don't know I'm their Father or that I've prepared a heavenly home for them." Continuing, He explained: "Many of My children have never heard about Me."

At this point, it seemed to me as if it was only me and the Father having a private conversation.

He suddenly urged me: "Paula, look over your shoulder."

As I turned around, to my utter amazement, I saw multitudes of men, women, and children standing behind me. Multitudes upon multitudes.

"What have they got to do with me?" I thought. I was wondering apprehensively what the Lord would say next.

"Paula, call them home," He encouraged me – with such love and longing in His eyes that it broke my heart.

I found myself weeping as I passionately cried out the name of a country. Astonished, I saw multitudes flocking home into the Father's house. I called out country after country. Hosts of lost sons and daughters found their way home.

The Father has already prepared a place; He's just waiting for us to call the lost in. And part of what the Father was and is asking me to do is to raise up workers to bring in the multitudes, to go and lay down their lives to love the poor, the lost, and the broken. It's time for His end-time army to be raised up to go to the nations and bring in the harvest. A host of laid-down lovers of Jesus – ordinary men, women, and children.

Those lost multitudes are all around us: our family, friends, neighbours, and fellow human beings. Some just across the street; others on the other side of the earth. Waiting for someone to come and call them. Desperate for physical needs to be met. Needing a listening ear. Longing to hear about Jesus' love. Each person yearns to know God's love and to hear of His salvation, even if they're not yet aware of it.

A few may be called to the ends of the earth, but each one of us is called to love the one in front of us, the family member sitting opposite us in the armchair, or a neighbour living across the street from us. Jesus' last command to His disciples on this earth was to 'Go' (Matthew 28:19), not to stay comfortably at home, or just camp out in our lovely churches, content to be saved and happy, surrounded by like-minded friends. No, it's to *go*.

This involves action. To go where the lost and broken are.

To roll up our sleeves, get our hands dirty, and show them the way forward.

And as we're obedient and go, we'll see God doing miracle after miracle, changing lives – providing, protecting, and healing.

He'll do more than we've ever imagined or dreamed.

His great commission hasn't changed. His command to us today is the same: Go and find the lost and bring them in. Go into all the world. And make disciples of all nations.

A myriad of reasons may seemingly disqualify you from obeying God's call. A difficult start in life, possibly similar to mine, may be hindering you. Unresolved issues in your life may be holding you back. Difficulties in your family relationships may be troubling you. The struggle to make ends meet can consume all your time and energy. Concerns about failing health may be plaguing you.

May my testimony encourage you. Just as God is able to use a weak, flawed, broken human being like me, He can use you too.

All the Lord needs is a willing heart. He will do the rest.

The Father is asking each of us: "Are you prepared to lay down your life today, so that the Father's house may be full?"

I don't know about you, but on that glorious day when our earthly pilgrimage is over, I want to hear those amazing words: "Well done, good and faithful servant" (Matthew 25:21). To be welcomed into heaven by smiling friends saying, "If it wasn't for you, I wouldn't be here now. Thank you for giving up your life that I might find life."

Hear the Father's invitation today: "Whom shall I send? And who will go for us?"(Isaiah 6:8).

So what is our response?

I pray that the cry of our hearts, together with Isaiah, will be a resounding, "Here am I! *Send me!*" (Isaiah 6:8).

For Reflection and Application

Are you aware of God calling you into something specific? If not, ask Him to show you what He has prepared for you. If you know you are called to something, ask the Lord to show you the next steps He wants you to take and for the courage to step out and be obedient.

A PSALM OF THANKSGIVING

We have this hope as an anchor for the soul, firm and secure.

HEBREWS 6:19

In the deepest night when all seems bleak
and I lack the strength to go on,
though enemies surround me and war breaks out against me,
even then will I be confident.

My Father, my superhero,
You always come to my rescue when I cry out to You.
You've always been there and You always will be.
You're closer than my very breath.
You'll never let me down.

Selah[1]

Surrounding me with Yourself,
You hide me under the shadow of your wings.
You prepare a three-course gourmet feast for me,
offering me mouth-watering goodies in full view of my enemies.
Your radiant countenance,
glorious like the sun in all its brilliance, shines upon me.
Therefore I can rest in Your arms and sleep in peace.

Selah

I marvel at the honour of serving You, the best boss in the world.
My heart bursts with gratitude for so many things:
For restoration, redemption and lives
forever changed by Your love,
thank You, O Lord my God, King of the Universe.

For Your sweet presence in the midst of suffocating darkness,
thank You, ever-present, gentle Holy Spirit.
For miracles abounding, provision
and a whole host of answered prayers,
thank You, Yahweh, the great I am.

For deliverance, healing and *rhema* words,
thank You, Wonderful Counsellor.
For faithful friends and sweet fellowship,
thank You, loving heavenly Father.

For Your peace that passes all understanding,
guarding my heart and mind,
a true anchor for the soul in the midst of war,
thank You, glorious Lord.

I will love you for all eternity.

Amen and Amen.

DO YOU KNOW JESUS PERSONALLY?

Look! I stand at the door and knock.
If you hear my voice and open the door, I will come in,
and we will share a meal together as friends.

REVELATION 3:20, NLT

So the young son set off for home. From a long distance
away, his father saw him coming, dressed as a beggar, and
great compassion swelled up in his heart for his son who
was returning home. So the father raced out to meet him.
He swept him up in his arms, hugged him dearly, and kissed
him over and over with tender love.

LUKE 15:20 TPT

Do you know God in the way the people in this book know Him? Are you a friend of Jesus?

As you've been reading this book, have you felt something stirring inside of you? A yearning, perhaps, for something more in life. A feeling of sadness or tears welling up. A sense of excitement or joy. An identification with someone's story and a longing to see similar miracles in your own life. Your heart pounding within you.

Jesus is standing at the door of your heart right now, knocking and patiently waiting. He's probably been knocking for a long time but as the Gentleman that He is, He won't come in unless invited.

He wants to get to know you and give you a new life that will last forever. Over time as you get to know each other, He desires to become the companion you've always longed for, who will walk alongside you no matter what you face in life.

Just like the Father in the parable of the Prodigal Son, your heavenly Father is patiently waiting for you to acknowledge you've made a mess of things and can't do life without Him anymore. As you take that first tentative step towards Him, He'll race out to meet you with outstretched arms. Sweeping you up tenderly into His embrace. Lavishing His love and forgiveness upon you. Healing you from the pain of the past. And giving you a new purpose and destiny.

He's got so much to teach you so you can *truly* live your best life. Sure there'll be lots of challenges on the way. But as you partner with Him to make this world a better place, your life will be filled with more excitement and fulfilment than you could ever imagine.

Why wait any longer? There's no better time than the present to open that door and begin a new life with Him. All you have to do is open your heart to Him and welcome Him in. You can do that in your own words or with similar words to these ones:

Jesus, I really want to know You personally, in the same way that the people in Paula's book know You. I open the door of my heart now and invite You to come into my life. I want to get to know You in reality. I've messed up in so many ways and I can't do life without You anymore. Teach me what it truly means to be Your friend and follower and how to live in a way that pleases You. And, lead me to those who can help me to grow in my new life with You. Thank you, Jesus. Amen.

I encourage you to start reading the Bible, asking the Holy Spirit to open your eyes to see the truth. Begin in the New Testament, with the Gospels. You'll be amazed by the life of Jesus and the astounding things He said and did. Then in the book of Acts you'll be envisioned as you see what the disciples of Jesus got up to.

Seek out modern-day disciples of Jesus who'll teach you how to be a true follower of Jesus today and help you take steps in your new faith including being baptised by full immersion in water and in the Holy Spirit.

As you hang out with Jesus and your new friends, your life will be transformed forever. Even though it's not always easy, being a follower of Jesus is the most exciting and fruitful life you could ever imagine and you'll see lots of miracles along the way. It's the life you were created for!

ENDNOTES

Introduction

[1] Used with permission

Chapter 1

[1] Mufti Said Mukhammad Abubakarov, Dagestan's respected Muslim leader, was killed in a car bombing, along with his brother and driver on 22 August 1998 in Makhachkala. Their car was blown up by a radio-controlled bomb after prayers at the main mosque in Makhachkala, the republic's capital.

[2] Throughout this book I have used the word *refugee* to refer to those displaced from their homes by the fighting. Most of the people we were working with would be technically referred to as IDPs – internally displaced persons – as they were still living in Russia, their official country of birth. On the ground, however, everyone called them refugees, and I will do the same.

Chapter 2

[1] Mount Elbrus is a whole 832m (2,730 ft) higher than Mont Blanc, the highest peak in the Alps.

[2] The 10/40 window refers to those regions located between the tenth and fortieth parallels north of the equator, which is the area of the world with the least access to the Christian message and Christian resources.

Chapter 3

[1] Public domain.

Chapter 5

[1] The writings of Mother Teresa of Calcutta © by the Mother Teresa Center, exclusive licensee throughout the world of the Missionaries of Charity for the works of Mother Teresa. Used with permission.

Chapter 6

[1] Public domain

Chapter 7

[1] Smith Wigglesworth (1859-1947) was a British evangelist and faith healer who was one of the pioneers of the Pentecostal revival that occurred at the beginning of the twentieth century. Thousands came to Christian faith at his meetings and hundreds were healed of serious diseases. He had a deep intimacy with his heavenly Father and an unquestioning faith in God's Word. He was often referred to as the 'Apostle of Faith'.

Chapter 8

[1] Public domain

[2] *Polochka* is a diminutive of my name. Russians love diminutives, affectionately using them for friends and family members. The endings *-ochka, -achka,* or *-echka* can be added to the root of girl's names: Pola / Polochka; Tatiana / Tanechka; Vera / Verachka. Boy's names can have *-ik, -chik,* or *-ochik* added: Igor / Igorochik; David / Davidik. At other times *-sha* is added to the root, as in Mikhail / Misha, Pavel / Pasha, Maria / Masha, Darya / Dasha.

Chapter 9

[1] Public domain

[2] YWAM – Youth with a Mission is an international missionary movement that seeks to encourage young people in their Christian walk through training, mercy ministries and evangelism. It operates in almost 200 countries and has tens of thousands of volunteer missionaries.

[3] 'People of peace,' based on Luke 10:6, are people open to the gospel and open to friendship with followers of Jesus; they also have an influence in their *oikos,* a Greek word meaning a household or family unit. The New Testament is full of examples of how the gospel spreads quickly when a person of peace meets Jesus. Cornelius in Acts 10 and the woman at the well in John 4 are good examples of people of peace.

[4] Many had lost their documents when their houses burned down or in the chaos of fleeing for their lives. The infrastructure of the country had fallen

apart, making it extremely difficult to get new papers. The rampant corruption also meant it could be very expensive. I remember, at one point, Larisa was quoted a price of $2,000 just to get her international passport renewed. We eventually managed to get it for only a few hundred at a different office.

Chapter 10

1. Public domain

2. The Ossetian-Ingush conflict, also called the East Prigorodny conflict, started in 1989 and by 1992 had developed into a brief ethnic war between local Ingush and Ossetian paramilitary forces.

3. Little huts called *khata* were cottages, typical in all southern Russian villages, made from log frames and a wattle-and-daub infill, and plastered over with a whitewash exterior and tin roofs.

4. The writings of Mother Teresa of Calcutta © by the Mother Teresa Center, exclusive licensee throughout the world of the Missionaries of Charity for the works of Mother Teresa. Used with permission.

Chapter 11

1. Chechens, like most of the other people groups of the Northern Caucasus, were not known for their time keeping and were often running late—sometimes hours late.

Chapter 13

1. Elliot, J & E (1978) *The Journals of Jim Elliot* p 174. Banker Publishing Group. Used with permission.

Chapter 15

1. Baker, H & Pradhan, S (2008) *Compelled by Love* Charisma Media, p. 35. Used with permission.

2. It was the worst premeditated attack in the history of the International Committee of the Red Cross, which was founded in 1863.

Chapter 16

1. Ten Boom, C (1974) *Tramp for the Lord* Old Tappan, NY: Fleming H Revell. Used with permission.

Chapter 17

1. Public domain

Chapter 18
[1] Prince, D. (2002) *Shaping History through Prayer and Fasting.* Whitaker House.

[2] *Meeteeng* is pronounced the same as the English word *meeting* but is a false friend in that it means something different than in English.

Chapter 21
[1] Wurmbrand R. (1967) *Tortured for Christ.* 2018 Edition, p.90. Orpington: Release International. Used with permission.

Chapter 22
[1] Remarque, E M (1929) *All Quiet on the Western Front.* Little, Brown and Company. London. Used with permission.

[2] A *samovar* nowadays is really only a glorified electric water heater. Traditionally part of Russian culture, they were once ornately decorated and heated with coal or charcoal.

Chapter 23
[1] *Injil* is the word Muslims use to mean the Gospels.

[2] At the time, worth about three years' wages.

[3] Orthodox priests are known as 'Father' just as Catholic ones are.

Chapter 24
[1] Public domain

[2] Apparently it was the fourth day of this *meeteeng,* where they were deciding whether to go to war.

[3] That evening on the news, I found out that a hundred and fifty armed Chechens had decided to go into Ossetia to rescue their two hostages and to take Ossetian hostages, but the Ingush wouldn't let them in and closed the border. A gun battle ensued. We arrived at the same border a few hours later.

Chapter 25
[1] The Avar people are the most populous people group living in Dagestan.

Chapter 26
[1] Baker, H & Pradhan, S (2008) *Compelled by Love* Charisma Media, 2008, p 143. Used with permission.

[2] Muslim men can have up to four wives simultaneously, according to Sharia law.

Chapter 27

[1] Unfortunately, Pastor Artur was tragically murdered by Islamic fundamentalists as he came out of a church meeting in July 2010.

Chapter 28

[1] Public Domain

Chapter 29

[1] The writings of Mother Teresa of Calcutta © by the Mother Teresa Center, exclusive licensee throughout the world of the Missionaries of Charity for the works of Mother Teresa. Used with permission.

[2] *Baba* is the diminutive for *babushka*, meaning 'grandmother.'

[3] From English into Russian, and vice versa.

Chapter 30

[1] An Alpha course is an 10-week evangelistic course introducing people to the Christian faith involving a weekly shared meal, a talk and a discussion. It started in 1977 in Holy Trinity Brompton, London, but is now being used in various denominations all over the world.

Chapter 32

[1] ICD-10 Diagnostic Criteria(1992) World Health Organization, Geneva.

[2] As cited in Haidt (2006) p 135.

[3] Joseph and Butler, 2010.

[4] Haidt, 2006 and Joseph & Linley, 2005.

[5] Tedeschi and Calhoun, 2004.

[6] Woodward and Joseph, 2003.

Chapter 33

[1] Scott, L (2010) *Lynda, From Accident and Trauma to Healing and Wholeness,* Sovereign World Ltd.

Chapter 34

[1] In Russia you could buy most medicines without a prescription.

Chapter 35

[1] Adam, D (1985) *The Edge of Glory,* p 34. SPCK Publishing. Used with permission.

Chapter 36

[1] Federal soldiers who were fighting on the side of the Russian government were not always ethnic Russians. Many Chechens, Ingush, and Ossetians were in the Russian army. This made things even more complicated when groups that had grievances against each other would fight, regardless of what uniforms they were wearing. I once saw federal soldiers, all speaking Chechen, having a gun battle with Chechen fighters in a dispute over a woman.

Chapter 39

[1] Public domain

[2] Public domain

[3] Grozny became known as the Caucasian Hiroshima. It burned so brightly that it was observable from space. When Google Earth went live, you could watch the city on fire, with smoke plumes drifting across Chechnya in the images. In 2003, the United Nations called Grozny the most destroyed city on Earth. Comparisons are now being made between the devastation in Grozny and that in Aleppo, Syria.

Chapter 40

[1] A fur hat made of *karakul* sheep skin; it has the general appearance of a cylinder with one open end, and is set upon the head in such a way as to have the brim touch the temples.

Chapter 42

[1] Public domain

[2] A red police ID is usually carried by important officials, particularly members of the FSB (formerly known as the KGB).

Chapter 44

[1] Public domain

Appendix 1

[1] 'Selah' is a Hebrew word found often in the Psalms which means a pause or a break. It gives you a chance to take time to ponder the verses you have just read or sang and let them sink in.

Recommended Reading

All books available from sovereignworld.com or Ellel.org

Lynda, From Accident & Trauma to Healing and Wholeness
Lynda Scott
Pages: 144
ISBN 978 1 85240 539 7

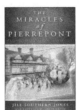

The Miracles of Pierrepont
Jill Southern with Kathleen McAnear-Smith
Pages:188
ISBN: 978 1 85240 740 7

Healing from the Consequences of Accident, Shock and Trauma
Peter Horrobin
Pages: 168
ISBN:978 1 85240 743 8

Healing through Deliverance
The Foundation and Practice of Deliverance Ministry
Peter Horrobin
Pages: 580
ISBN: 978 1 85240 866 4

Loved like never before
Discovering the Father Heart of God
Ken Symington
Pages: 160
ISBN: 978 1 85240 585 4

Soul Ties
The Unseen Bond in Relationships
David Cross
Pages: 128
ISBN: 978 1 85240 451 2

Forgiveness God's Master Key
Pray the Most Powerful Prayer on Earth
Peter Horrobin
Pages:112 pages
ISBN: 978 1 85240 502 1

Healing through Creativity
A Bridge from the Head to the Heart. How simple creativity can bring deep healing from our Creator
Fiona Horrobin
Pages: 352 full colour, HB
ISBN: 978 1 85240 837 4

ABOUT THE AUTHOR

Paula O'Keefe is the founder and international director of Living Waters Healing Communities. Born in Seattle, USA, to an Irish-American father and a Brazilian-British mother she grew up in England, meeting the Lord at a young age. In the early 1990s, as a recent graduate in Psychology and Russian and a newly qualified teacher, Paula moved to Southwestern Russia. Communism had just collapsed and doors were wide open for preaching the gospel.

The Lord soon led her to war-torn Chechnya to serve the destitute and traumatised. A few years later, while studying on the Ellel NETS 4 training school, Paula received healing from PTSD and childhood abuse. Returning to Russia she custom-built and set up a Trauma Counselling Centre which later blossomed into a healing community. She brought up four homeless children and her growing family now includes five grandchildren.

Paula has ministered in over twenty countries, taking teams to share the gospel amongst cannibals in Mozambique, in remote villages in the Himalayas, and to counsel orphans and war victims in Sri Lanka.

"Living Waters Healing Communities"

During her time in Russia, Paula set up a Trauma Counselling Centre which blossomed into Living Waters Healing Communities, presently operating in Russia and Spain, ministering to the poor and broken, the homeless and refugees.

If you'd like to contact Paula and her team, please send an email to warmiracles@protonmail.com

To financially support Paula and her ministry:
If based in the UK, through Karuna Action (previously Kingscare):
https://www.karunaaction.org/Spain

Karuna Action, 11 Wellington Street, Aldershot, GU11 1DX, UK
Phone: +44 (0)1252 333233
Email: office@karunaaction.org

If based in the USA, through Global Helpnet:
https://globalhelpnet.info/living-waters-ci/
Global Helpnet, 1424 S. Ocotillo Dr., Apache Junction,
AZ 85120, USA

Ellel Ministries
International

Our Vision
Ellel Ministries is a non-denominational Christian Mission Organization with a vision to resource and equip the Church by welcoming people, teaching them about the Kingdom of God and healing those in need (Luke 9:11).

Our Mission
Our mission is to fulfil the above vision throughout the world, as God opens the doors, in accordance with the Great Commission of Jesus and the calling of the Church to proclaim the Kingdom of God by preaching the good news, healing the broken-hearted and setting the captives free. We are, therefore, committed to evangelism, healing, deliverance, discipleship and training. The particular scriptures on which our mission is founded are Isaiah 61:1–7; Matthew 28:18–20; Luke 9:1–2; 9:11; Ephesians 4:12; 2 Timothy 2:2.

Our Basis of Faith
God is a Trinity. God the Father loves all people. God the Son, Jesus Christ, is Saviour and Healer, Lord and King. God the Holy Spirit indwells Christians and imparts the dynamic power by which they are enabled to continue Christ's ministry. The Bible is the divinely inspired authority in matters of faith, doctrine and conduct, and is the basis for teaching.

For details about the current worldwide activities of Ellel Ministries International please go to: www.ellel.org
Ellel Ministries International
Ellel Grange
Ellel
Lancaster, LA2 0HN
United Kingdom
Tel (+44) (0)1524 751 651

Sovereign World Ltd
Bringing together the Word & the Spirit

Please visit our online shop to browse our range of titles.
www.sovereignworld.com

Or write to us at:
info@sovereignworld.com

Sovereign world Ltd. Ellel Grange, Bay Horse,
Lancaster, LA2 0HN, United Kingdom

Most books are available in e-book format
and can be purchased online.

Would You Join With Us To Bless the Nations?
At the Sovereign World Trust, our mandate and passion is to send
books, like the one you've just read, to *faithful leaders who can
equip others* (2 Tim 2:2).

If you could donate a copy of this or other titles from Sovereign
World Ltd, you will be helping to supply much-needed resources
to Pastors and Leaders in many countries.

Contact us for more information on (+44)(0)1732 851150
or visit our website
www.sovereignworldtrust.org.uk

CPSIA information can be obtained
at www.ICGtesting.com
Printed in the USA
LVHW040734300322
714780LV00008B/836

9 781852 408343